Royal Festivals in the Late Predynastic Period and the First Dynasty

Alejandro Jiménez Serrano

BAR International Series 1076
2002

Published in 2016 by
BAR Publishing, Oxford

BAR International Series 1076

Royal Festivals in the Late Predynastic Period and the First Dynasty

ISBN 978 1 84171 455 4

BAR Publishing is the trading name of British Archaeological Reports (Oxford) Ltd. British Archaeological Reports was first incorporated in 1974 to publish the BAR Series, International and British. In 1992 Hadrian Books Ltd became part of the BAR group. This volume was originally published by Archaeopress in conjunction with British Archaeological Reports (Oxford) Ltd / Hadrian Books Ltd, the Series principal publisher, in 2002. This present volume is published by BAR Publishing, 2016.

Printed in England

BAR
PUBLISHING

BAR titles are available from:

BAR Publishing
122 Banbury Rd, Oxford, OX2 7BP, UK
EMAIL info@barpublishing.com
PHONE +44 (0)1865 310431
FAX +44 (0)1865 316916
www.barpublishing.com

To my parents

CONTENTS

Contents.. i

List of Figures.. iii

List of Tables.. v

Methodological note.. vi

Acknowledgements.. vii

Introduction.. 1

Chapter One: Historical Outline: The Unification Process and the First Dynasty
A.- The construction of a Nation: Main Hypotheses
about the Political Unification of Egypt.. 4
A.1) Introduction
A.2) The Unification process in Egypt
B) First Dynasty.. 10

Chapter Two: Festivals, Kings and Temples
A) The Definition of Festival.. 17
B) Royal Festivals in Ancient Egypt.. 18
C) The King in Ancient Egypt.. 19
D) Sources for the Study of Festivals in the Late Predynastic
and Early Dynastic periods.. 20
D.1) Contemporary sources
D.2) Later sources
D.3) The historicity of the sources
D.4) How to read the artistic evidence
E) The Concept of the Royal Temple in the late Predynastic
and Early Dynastic periods.. 26
E.1) Definition of Temple
E.2) The foundation of the temple: myth and ritual
E.3) The symbolic structure of temples
E.4) Some comments about the primitive shrines and enclosures
E.5) Monumental enclosures: Abydos, Saqqara, and Hierakonpolis
E.6) The city temple at Hierakonpolis (Nekhen)
E.7) The *pr-nw* in Buto

Chapter Three: Royal Festivals in the Late Predynastic period and the First Dynasty
A) The Coronation and the Ceremony of the "Appearance of the King"............ 38
- Conclusion
B) *Sed* Festival.. 42
B.1) Definition and genesis
B.2) Preliminary phases and localisation of the *sed* festival
B.3) Localisation of the *sed* festivals in the Late Predynastic
and Early Dynastic periods
B.4) Ceremonies of the *sed* festival
B.5) Elements of the *sed* festival
B.6) Material evidence of the *sed* festival in the Late
Predynastic and Early Dynastic periods
Appendix A: The *sed* festival in the Second Dynasty
Appendix B: The *sed* festival in Lower Nubia
at the end of the fourth millennium BC?
B.7) Conclusions
C) Festivals of Victory.. 79

C.1) The king harpooning a hippopotamus
C.2) Military victories
C.3) Conclusions
D) The Festival of Sokar.. 92
-Conclusions.. 97

Chapter Four: General Conclusions
1.- Royal festivals in Late Predynastic and Early Dynastic periods.................. 99
2.- Symbolic topography and royal festivals.. 100

Bibliography.. 103

Egyptian terms (in transliteration).. 115

LIST OF FIGURES

Figure 1: Kemp's hypothesis of the unification process,
from Kemp (1989: figs. 8 & 13)................................... 7
Figure 2: Wilkinson's theory for the political unification,
from Wilkinson (2000)... 9
Figure 3: Two labels found in tomb U-j at Umm el-Qaab,
from Dreyer (1998: Abb. 80, nos. 135 & 145)................... 21
Figure 4: Label bearing the name of Djer,
fom Helck (1987: 153).. 21
Figure 5: Labels of Djet (from Helck (1987: 155)) and Den
(from Petrie (1900: pl. XV, no. 16)................................ 22
Figure 6: Labels of Anedjib (from Kaplony (1963, 3: Abb. 845) and Qaa,
from Helck (1987: 164).. 22
Figure 7: The Palermo Stone (*recto*),
from Gardiner (1961; pl. III)... 25
Figure 8: The sites of Abydos with two more detailed enclosures,
after Trigger *et alii* (1983: fig. 1.6)................................ 32
Figure 9: Plan of Khasekhemui's enclosure at Hierakonpolis with earlier tombs,
After Adams (1987).. 33
Figure 10: Map of Saqqara,
after Kemp (1967).. 34
Figure 11: The city temple of Hierakonpolis (Nekhen),
from Adams (1974)... 37
Figure 12: Ceremonies of "Uniting Upper and Lower Egypt" and
"Circuit of the Wall" recorded in the Palermo Stone,
after Schäfer (1902: 15, line 2, no. 3)... 38
Figure 13: Ink inscriptions on pottery vessels found in the tomb of Horus Ka at Abydos,
after Petrie (1902: pls. I, no. 2 & III, no. 29) 39
Figure 14: The ceremonies of the "Appearance of the king of Upper and Lower Egypt"
and the "*Sed* festival" recorded on the Palermo Stone (certainly in the reign of Den),
after Schäfer (1902: 19, line 3, no. 3)... 41
Figure 15: Structural comparison between different enclosures,
After O'Connor (1992: Fig. 1)... 44
Figure 16: Netjerikhet complex at Saqqara,
from Kemp (1989: fig. 19)... 45
Figure 17: Relief panels from the complex of Netjerikhet,
from F. Friedman (1995: Fig. 2a-b).. 50
Figure 18: The king's mace-head from Hierakonpolis,
from Adams (1974a: pl. 1).. 51
Figure 19: The Narmer mace-head from Hierakonpolis
from Millet (1990/1991: Fig. 1)... 53
Figure 20: A provisional reconstruction of the HK29A complex by M. A. Hoffman,
from R. Friedman (1996: fig. 11a)... 55
Figure 21: Reconstruction and situation of the temples at Hierakonpolis,
Map from R. Friedman & B. Adams (eds.) (1992: map 1)....................... 56
Figure 22: The city temple of Hierakonpolis (Nekhen)
according to the depictions found at Abydos,
(a-c) from Dreyer (1998: Abb., nos. 127-129)
& (d) Petrie (1901: pl. III, no. 12)... 58
Figure 23: Horus Aha wooden label from Abydos,
From Petrie (1901: pl. X, no. 2)... 58
Figure 24: Fragmentary wooden label from Abydos,
From Petrie (1901: pl. XI, no.2)... 62
Figure 25: Two fragmentary ebony labels found in the tomb of Horus Aha at Abydos,
after Vikentiev (1949/1959: fig. 6).. 63
Figure 26: A reconstruction of the plan of the enclosure of Djer,
From O'Connor (1989: fig. 6)... 63

Figure 27: Ivory label of Djer from Abydos,
From Emery (1961: fig. 20)... 64
Figure 28: Seal-impression from Abydos with the name of Djer,
From Petrie (1901: pl. XV, no. 108).. 65
Figure 29: Reconstruction of a seal-impression,
From Kaplony (1964: Taf. 19, no. 1032, 2)... 66
Figure 30: Ivory label from Saqqara with the name of Djed
From Emery (1954: fig. 105)... 66
Figure 31: Fragment of vessel from Abydos
From Dreyer (1990: Abb. 8)... 67
Figure 32: Wooden label of Den from Abydos,
From Petrie (1900: pl. XV, no. 16).. 69
Figure 33: Wooden painted label of Den from Abydos
From Godron (1990: pl. III, no. 6)... 69
Figure 34: Seal impression from the tomb of Hemaka at Saqqara,
From Emery (1938: fig. 26)... 71
Figure 35: A fragment of label from the tomb of Den at Abydos,
From Petrie (1900: pl. XIV, no. 12)... 71
Figure 36: Fragment of label from Abydos with the name of Den,
Drawn by the author from the original picture
in Dreyer (1990: Taf. 26a)... 71
Figure 37: Fragmentary labels from Abydos,
Drawn by the author from the original pictures
in Dreyer *et alii* (1998: Taf. 12f-h) 71
Figure 38: Anonymous relief from Saqqara,
From Spencer (1980: pl. 9).. 73
Figure 39: Different inscriptions of Anedjib found in the underground galleries
of the Step Pyramid,
From Lacau & Lauer (1959: pl. III, nos. 1-7)... 73
Figure 40: Fragment of crystal bowl found in the tomb of Semerkhet at Abydos,
original picture from Petrie (1900: pl. VII, no. 6)... 74
Figure 41: Inscription of the "second occasion of the *sed* festival" of Qaa
From the original picture in Lacau & Lauer (1959: pl. 8, no. 41)......................... 74
Figure 42: Williams's reconstruction of the Siali seal-impressions,
From Williams (1986: fig. 58a).. 77
Figure 43: King Den harpooning a hippopotamus,
From Säve-Söderbergh (1953: fig. 7).. 82
Figure 44: Two fragments of labels found at Abydos
and probably depicting the same scene: the harpooning of the hippopotamus,
Left, from Petrie (1900: pl. XIV, no. 8). Right, drawn by the author
from an original picture in Dreyer *et alii* (1998: Abb. 12d)................................ 82
Figure 45: The "minor" relief at Gebel Sheikh Suleiman,
From Wilkinson (1999: fig. 5.3.1).. 82
Figure 46: The Narmer palette,
From Kemp (1989: fig. 12).. 83
Figure 47: Ivory label of Narmer,
from Dreyer *et alii* (1998: Abb. 29).. 85
Figure 48: Detail of the Narmer Palette of beheaded captives with and without penis,
From Davies & Friedman (1998: 22)... 87
Figure 49: Cylinder seal with Narmer smiting seven enemies,
From Kaplony (1963, 3: Taf. 5, no. 5)... 88
Figure 50: Aha wooden label from Abydos,
From Petrie (1901: pl. XI, no. 1)... 88
Figure 51: The "major" relief of Gebel Sheikh Suleiman,
From Murnane (1987)... 89
Figure 52: Djet label from Abydos,
From Dreyer *et alii* (1998: Taf. 12a).. 91
Figure 53: Den smiting the East,
From Spencer (1980: pl. 53).. 91

Figure 54: Four mentions of the festival of Sokar on the Palermo Stone,
From Schäfer (1902: 16, l. 2, no. 7, 19, l. 3, no. 6, 23, l. 4, no. 6 & 25, l. 4, no. 12) 93
Figure 55: Two reconstruction of the orignal label of Naqada:
(above) Garstang's reconstruction (1905: fig. 3);
(below) Helck's reconstruction (1987: 146) 96
Figure 56: Ivory comb of Djet,
From Emery (1961: fig. 146)... 97
Figure 57: Label of king Semerkhet found at Abydos
From Spencer (1980: pl. 54, no. 461)... 98

LIST OF TABLES

Table 1: Egyptian rulers of the Late Predynastic period and First Dynasty.................. 3
Table 2: Common elements seen on depictions of the *sed* festival
from the First Dynasty and the reign of Netjerikhet...................................... 75

METHODOLOGICAL NOTE

In this book, many ancient Egyptian transliterations have been used. European transliteration system has been followed, because as J. P. Allen[i] explains "it requires fewer special signs than the traditional system."[ii] J. Kahl's[iii] remarks and discussions about the transliteration system of Late Predynastic and Early Dynastic periods have also been followed, because this study is the latest and most complete which deals with the Egyptian language of those early periods.

Some French words or expressions together with some German words appear in this thesis and they appear in italics denoting their foreign origin.

---

[i] (2000: 13).
[ii] For the three systems of transliteration, see Allen (2000: 13-17).
[iii] (1994: 19-33).

ACKNOWLEDGEMENTS

This book is the result of my thesis (*Kingship and Festivals in the Late Predynastic and Early Dynastic Periods*) submitted to the Board of the University College London (Deparment of Egyptoloy), University of London, in application for the degree of *Master of Philososphy*.

I would like to begin this book by mentioning the people who assisted and supported me during my research.

First and foremost, my thanks to Professor Fekri A. Hassan, my first supervisor, and Miss Barbara Adams, my second supervisor, who taught me, and helped me to resolve the numerous questions that emerged during the conception of the thesis. Many thanks also to Dr. David Jeffreys, who became my first supervisor at the end of my research period, and also solved many problems derived from the end of the thesis.

Secondly, to Drs. John Baines and Jeffrey Spencer, who examined my thesis and made me many useful comments. Some of these comments have been presented in this book and are solely my responsibility.

Many thanks also to Miss Joanne Rowland and Mrs. Mary Joana Dunmall who kindly corrected the English of the thesis and suggested some additions, which are solely my responsibility.

To Dr. Josep Cervelló Autuori, Dr. John Tait, Dr. Marcelo Campagno, Dr. Toby A. H. Wilkinson, Dr. Reneé Friedman, Dr. Beatrix Midant-Reynes, Dr. José Ramón Pérez Accino, Dr. Edwin Van den Brink, Mr. Angus Graham, Mr. Ian Ralston, Mr. Joris F. L. Van Wetering and Mr. G. J. Tassie, with whom I had many discussions about the origins of the State, the topic of this book and many other aspects of Ancient Egypt.

To Miss Silvia Miguel Rodríguez, who supported me during the conception of this thesis and gave me all her affection.

To my friends from Jaén and London, Mr. Juan Manuel Anguita Ordóñez, Mr. Angel Carlos Belser Luque and his wife María del Cármen, Mr. Julio Burdman, Mr. Agustín Carranza, Mr. Rafael Curtoni, Mr. Antonio López Barragán, Mr. Fernando Martínez Hermoso, Mrs. Isabel Martínez Hermoso, Miss Cristina Martín Ollero, Dr. Tomás Mendizábal, Mr. Nicolas Nordquist, Mr. Ernesto Ruiz Rodríguez, Mr. Ferrán Salleras Vila y Mr. Georg Von Uckermann.

Especially, to my family, who gave me the opportunity to study at University College London; without their support and love this book would never have seen the light of day.

INTRODUCTION

"In fact, prehistorians call an item "ceremonial" when they have no idea how it was used", W. Davis (1992: 18).

The aim of this book is to make a study of the royal festivals in the Late Predynastic period and the First Dynasty. The chronological beginning of this book is the Naqada IId period, because this is when the Nile Valley -from Elephantine to the Delta- presents a similar material culture. I have also included a brief study of the royal festivals (mainly, the *sed* festival) in the contemporary Lower Nubia and the Second Dynasty.

The Late Predynastic and Early Dynastic periods are characterised by their chronological complexity, because different methods are used for dating. All of these methods continue to be used in the present, but some have been improved, although still presenting some problems related to their geographical situation.[1] One of the techniques that avoid this problem in part is Radiocarbon dating. The appearance of the Radiocarbon technique fifty years ago has permitted the chronological position of those early stages of human history to be more or less correctly dated. In this book, a new re-calibration[2] of some dates has been advanced.

There are many studies about festivals or about the role of kingship in Egypt, but no specific study about the topic presented here. For this reason, I believed that it was necessary to present a discussion about the two major subjects of this book: kingship and festivals.

The study of the role of kingship has a long tradition in anthropology and Egyptology,[3] therefore it is unnecessary to mention theories, interpretations, and views that in many cases are still under discussion. I have attempted to avoid the repetition of well-known controversies related to the role of the king in the ceremonies and the political evolution of the country. Certainly, the date of the unification of Egypt is still under discussion; however, as a historical introduction, it has been considered preferable to present the major theories about the unification that have dominated and still dominate Egyptology. The First Dynasty, however, is a different case; the succession of the kings is well known, together with some major events of their reigns, thus just a brief introduction of every reign and some of these major episodes have been presented.

Festivals have been analysed taking into account different aspects: meaning, equipment, transcendence, etc. The definition of festival has been dealt with from an anthropological point of view and later it has been discussed in the Ancient Egyptian context. This latter idea is presented here as a discussion of the significance that those ceremonies and rituals had for the ancient Egyptians as well as an enumeration of the sources that are used in this research, mainly archaeology and epigraphy. Although the historicity of the events represented in some of the monuments had been discussed until recent years, the debate was closed with the discovery of a label[4] that surely represents the same event as the Narmer palette. This discovery has proved that labels and other monuments have, amongst other purposes (magic, propaganda, etc.), that of differentiating years by means of historical events recorded for them. This is a key point in this book, because labels and other monuments are regarded as reliable, although the fact has been taken into account that they must be considered as part of the vision of the Egyptian élite.

In ancient Egypt, festivals were celebrated (completely or partially) in temples. These were pure and sacred places, where (some) humans could approach the deities. Thus, it is very important to be clear about the character that the temples possessed as single entities separated from the world. This special character is acquired in the mythical foundation, because they are located in the lands that first emerged. The religious transcendence of the temples in the early periods, which is dealt with here, is manifested in later

[1] Payne (1992: 192), after the re-analysis of the cemetery of Naqada, wrote "The differences between the Naqada and Armant sequences are relatively small, and they may only too easily be the result of gaps in our knowledge, particularly at Naqada. They may, however, reflect actual differences in the development of different sites as Kaiser (1957: 73) has suggested. It would be surprising if all Predynastic sites followed precisely the same development."

[2] All the details in Hassan & Jiménez-Serrano (unpublished).

[3] Frankfort (1948); Baines (1995); Cervelló Autuori (1996).

[4] Dreyer *et alii* (1998).

periods, for example when Hierakonpolis and Buto are still considered the primitive shrines of the kingship, or when the tomb of Djer is identified with that of the god Osiris at Abydos. In this respect, the enclosures at Abydos must be understood as temples, not only funerary temples (with the only aim of the maintenance of the royal cult after the death of the king), but also sacred places where the king carried out some of the royal ceremonies related to his divinity. The paradigmatic example is Netjerikhet's complex at Saqqara, which was used (while the king was alive) at least for the celebration of the *sed* festival of this king.[5]

The evidence of festivals of kings of the Late Predynastic and Early Dynastic periods is plentiful and is based primarily on evidence from labels and the Palermo Stone. From those sources, it is possible to reconstruct some royal ceremonies. As the sources generally only mention the festivals and do not give many details about them, it is necessary to look for later monuments, which represent similar events. Later examples offer scholars numerous comparisons,[6] which show the evolution of the royal concept of duality.

Most of the labels have been reinterpreted because their readings were mainly done by experts in archaeology,[7] and not experts in early Egyptian epigraphy. On other occasions, preconceived or fashionable ideas affected the readings: Narmer was the "Unifier" Menes, the Dynastic Race, etc. For that reason, most of the readings or interpretations of the monuments have been taken into consideration. To avoid an unintentional classification of the scholars, the readings and interpretations have been presented chronologically.

Two of the ceremonies are connected because they have similar features: the enthronement and the *sed* festival. In both cases, the king is enthroned (or re-enthroned), and receives the homage of the great personalities of the kingdom. They could be regarded as the zenith of the reign and must be understood as the paradigmatic feast of the kingship. In the Egyptian mind, the existence of Egypt is united with the monarchy, which guarantees the cosmic order (*maat*[8]).

The festivals called here "of victory" were the military expressions of the king, which show him as guarantor of the sacred order (*maat*). As has been mentioned in different studies about Ancient Egypt,[9] foreign peoples, who wanted to settle in the fertile lands of the Valley, surrounded Egypt.[10] That affected the Egyptian aim, which understood Egypt as the land of *maat*, a land blessed by the gods. Thus, Egypt was ruled by the goddess *maat* and the king was her son.

The festivals of Sokar have been studied in this book not only because there are many contemporary references, but also because Sokar is a god of Memphis and this city was the capital (?) of unified Egypt. As is well known, classical authors mention Meni (or Menes), the unification of Egypt, and the foundation of Memphis. This means that Memphis was a royal foundation, not a settlement evolved from prehistory (although this does not mean that different groups of population were not settled in the area later called Memphis). This aspect is very important, because kings could shape the deities that protect the city. At the same time, Sokar was the god of an area that had a very important meaning: Saqqara. At this place, high officials of the Early Dynastic period were buried, at least two large enclosures were built in the area for unknown reasons, and some kings of the Second and Third Dynasties were buried there. Another aspect is that the king had to maintain good relations with the gods, celebrating their cults and feasts. Thus, the festivals of Sokar might be understood as an example of the major ceremonies that the king celebrated to assure the protection of the gods over the king and Egypt.

Jaén, 28th of June, 2002.

---

[5] F. Friedman (1995).

[6] Logan (1999) has published an article in which some Early Dynastic monuments are compared with later monuments, mainly the Fifth Dynasty.

[7] For example, Petrie and Emery.

[8] As a goddess, Maat is attested from at least the First Dynasty, see Kahl (1994: 742), with references.

[9] E. g. Cervelló Autuori (1996), with references.

[10] See Belova (1998).

TABLE 1: CHRONOLOGY

Years BC[11]	**Phases after Hendrickx's revision**	**Rulers**[12]
3380(?)-3350 (3350-3295 BC)	Naqada IIIA2	Scorpion I Two (or three) unknown rulers
(3295-3175 BC)	Naqada IIIB Naqada IIIC1	Iry-Hor, Scorpion II, Horus Ka and Narmer
3175		Aha Djer Djet
3075	Naqada IIIC2	Den Anedjib Semerkhet
2940(?)-2910	Naqada IIID	Qaa

[11] Hassan & Jiménez Serrano (unpublished).
[12] For the succession of the Late Predynastic kings, see Jiménez Serrano (2000b: 43).

CHAPTER ONE
HISTORICAL OUTLINE: THE UNIFICATION AND THE FIRST DYNASTY

A. - THE CONSTRUCTION OF A NATION: MAIN HYPOTHESES ABOUT THE POLITICAL UNIFICATION OF EGYPT

A.1) Introduction

From the beginning of the Neolithic age in Egypt (at least in the 6th millennium BC), it is possible to differentiate two areas, Upper and Lower Egypt. In both regions, the productive economy was becoming more and more important. Although social differentiation can be observed in the last moments of the Naqada I, it was in the next phase (around 3600 B. C.) when these differences increased. At the same time, distinctive new products of Upper Egyptian civilisation appeared, which were seen by some scholars as evidence of the arrival of new people in the Nile Valley (see p. 5), who brought with them their own traditions. This does not mean that a great invasion took place; more probably there was a gradual and peaceful integration into the existing population.[13] In this period, three interrelated aspects[14] of the early Egyptian kingship appeared and evolved: aggression, conquest, and defence; large-scale architecture; and general royal ideology.

A.2) The Unification process in Egypt

- The mythic discourse

The unification was an important concept for ancient Egyptians. During the late Fifth Dynasty, a compilation of all records of events was written on one great *stela*, called the Palermo Stone (pp. 22-23, fig. 7). Even the fragmentary condition of the Palermo Stone permits one to imagine the conception that ancient Egyptians had of their past. The largest Palermo Stone fragment shows a row with Predynastic kings wearing the Red Crown (Lower Egypt), and, in the other rows, some years of the reigns of the kings of the First to Fifth Dynasties. Ancient Egyptians differentiated between kings who had recorded events in their reigns and those who are only attested by a name. In that period, they still had annals that recorded the preceding reigns, but in the later king lists (above all the Turin Papyrus of the 19th Dynasty), the Predynastic kings (?) were converted into a group of anonymous "spirits" and placed between the gods and the kings of the First Dynasty.[15] The first of these kings was Menes (Narmer),[16] who symbolised the person who unified Egypt and founded Memphis, as reflected in the later traditions of Manetho and the Greek and Roman writers.

From the beginnings of Egyptology, Egyptian unification was always a remote question. It was only known from the information that Herodotus of Halicarnassus included in his second book, called *Euterpe*. Herodotus recorded that the first Egyptian king was Mina.[17] In addition, Diodorus Siculus wrote about Menes (a derivation of Meni). But Menes appeared to have been just a mythical king, the founder of the royal succession.

- The origin of the Egyptian Monarchy: theories

1. - The first theories: the first excavations. Diffusionism, myth (Sethe´s reductionism) and Marxism

The ignorance surrounding ancient Egyptian Late Prehistory began to lift with the first excavations carried out at the end of the 19th century by Petrie. Other scholars who focused their research on this virgin ground followed Petrie. Some of the most important are: Quibell and Green, who discovered Narmer's palette and other Late Predynastic and Early Dynastic objects in Hierakonpolis,[18] and Garstang,[19] Amélineau,[20] De Morgan.[21] It was the first time that scholars saw real scenes that could represent the unification. After the discoveries at Hierakonpolis, Narmer was considered to be the king who unified Egypt. Egyptologists were able to reconstruct the first phases of Egyptian history with the excavations in Abydos[22], Saqqara[23] and other cemeteries.

---

[13] Spencer (1993: 34).
[14] Baines (1995: 106).
[15] It is doubtful whether there was any specific tradition about Predynastic kings after the Old Kingdom.
[16] Here, it is followed Cervelló Autuori's (in press) hypothesis.
[17] Herodotus II, 4.
[18] Quibell (1900); Quibell & Green (1902).
[19] (1905; 1907).
[20] (1899-1905).
[21] (1897).
[22] Petrie (1900; 1901; 1902; 1903); Peet (1914).
[23] Emery (1938; 1939; 1949; 1954; 1958)

Kurt Sethe suggested a mythological interpretation of the emergence of the Early Dynastic State.[24] From the Horus-Seth myth, he posited two prehistoric kingdoms in Upper and Lower Egypt, as symbolised in the mythological struggle between Horus (worshipped in Behdet, Lower Egypt) and Seth (Ombos [Naqada], Upper Egypt). The unification of Egypt is symbolised by the subsequent domination of Osiris, the god whom each dead king became and whose cult centre was originally at Busiris (in Lower Egypt). Breasted[25] argued for two Predynastic kingdoms of Upper and Lower Egypt and a united kingdom of Egypt before the First Dynasty. His argument was based on the list of kings in the top register of the Palermo Stone and the related fragment in the Cairo Museum. However, according to Henri Frankfort,[26] the dual monarchy had no historical foundation. If the geographical configuration suggested a division of the country into the Delta and the Nile Valley, there is no reason to believe that these were thought of as political entities any more than the equally obvious divisions of desert ("the Red Land") and arable soil ("the Black Land"). The Red Crown of Lower Egypt belonged originally, not to Lower Egypt as a whole, but to several Delta states, one with its capital in Buto and another in Sais. "The wider significance accorded to the symbols of Menes' homeland, on the one hand, and of Pe, on the other, are part of the stylisation of Egypt as a dual monarchy, an artificial but meaningful symmetry which holds in its spell even those modern authors who view his unification, not as piecemeal conquest in the manner of Piankhi the Ethiopian, but as the victory of an established Upper Egyptian state over an equally developed Lower Egyptian kingdom."[27]

At the same time and due to the context of colonialism, scholars developed a theory which did not accept the unification as an indigenous process, but as one result of the arrival of a "Dynastic Race".[28] This concept was based on the appearance of a new material culture in the beginning of the First Dynasty and apparently a much greater skull-capacity in the north than in the south.[29] According to Derry[30], a massively built, mesocephalic people entered Egypt at about the start of the First Dynasty, probably from Asia, since they can be identified with the armenoid physical type found in Upper Egypt. By the end of the First Dynasty, they had penetrated as far south as Abydos and were gradually merging with the indigenous population. He expressed such ideas as "the pyramid builders were a different race from the people whose descendants they had hitherto been supposed to be"; "the Dynastic people were far removed from any Negroid element"; (the Dynastic race) "not only had broader skulls but the height of these skulls, while exceeding that in the Predynastic Race, is still less than the breadth. This implies a greater cranial capacity and of course a larger brain in the invading people."[31]

In the 1950s, Murray[32] stated that the superior weapons of the Gerzean peoples suggested a conquest of the earlier Amratians. According to her, the invasion of the dynastic people was preceded by the acceptance of new ideas long before the actual conquest. She affirmed[33] about the Semainean period that it "has hitherto been neglected by the archaeologist owing to its being regarded as merely showing the decadence of the Gerzean culture. It is true that much of that culture survived, but there is evidence to show that the Semainean had its own characteristics as distinct from those of the earlier or later periods. It is, however, considerably more complex than the cultures which preceded it, and as such it offers to the archaeologist more problems for solution than any other of the Predynastic cultures".

According to Emery,[34] the dynastic race was a reality and he confessed that he thought that the invaders were "Africanised" before penetrating into Egypt proper. In the 1960s, he still continued to express this theory in his book *Archaic Egypt.*[35]

From the same theoretical background (Diffusionism), but showing less racism, the "Eastern Invaders" theory was supported by the reliefs found by Winkler[36] in the Eastern Desert, in

[24] (1930: 70-82).
[25] (1931: 712; 724).
[26] (1948).
[27] Frankfort (1948: 20).
[28] Petrie (1939: 3, 7, 77); especially, Engelbach (1943), Derry (1956) and Emery (1961: 39-40). For an analysis of this theory and a critique, see Arnett (1982: 53-64).

[29] Derry's conferences at University College London in 1914, Vandier (1952: vol. I, tom. I, 11-13).
[30] (1956).
[31] Derry (1956: 81 & 84).
[32] Murray (1956: 94).
[33] Murray (1956: 96).
[34] Emery (1952: 12)
[35] Emery (1961).
[36] Winkler (1938). Similarly, some years later, Baumgartel (1955; 1960).

which boats very similar to Mesopotamian craft were carved. According to him, there was an invasion via the Wadi Hammamat of these people that resulted in the birth of the civilisation.

All those theories (mainly, the "Dynastic Race" theory) concluded when Berry, Berry and Ucko[37] showed that the Predynastic population of Lower Egypt was ancestral to Derry's Dynastic Race and that he was interpreting a basically geographical difference as an appearance of new settlers into the Nile Valley. Hassan and Matson,[38] and Holmes[39] also denied this possibility after the analysis of the pottery and the lithic artefacts respectively.

Gordon Childe[40] was one of those men that thought beyond their age. For this reason, and obviously due to his political ideology (Marxism), he developed a new theory for the origin of the Egyptian State. According to him, the rise of Egyptian civilisation is based on agricultural surpluses produced by Gerzean farmers, with a concomitant increase in wealth and inequality in the distribution of surpluses. This was not a process of peaceful expansion, but one that involved warfare for the acquisition of cattle, booty and land.

2. - Recent years: interdisciplinary excavations; reanalyses, unpublished excavations, environment, Anthropology and Archaeology in the Delta

At the end of the 1960s, after the Nubian campaign, new excavation campaigns began first in Hierakonpolis,[41] later in the rest of Egypt, especially the Nile Delta[42] and Abydos[43]. These new archaeological methods (mainly a consequence of interdisciplinarity) have changed our view of the Egyptian unification process. It is known that the Egyptian unification process was very long (from the middle or even early Predynastic period) and involved many factors, not only indigenous traits but also those with a foreign origin. This process culminated in the establishment of a national administration presided over by a single ruler claiming divine authority. Nowadays, it seems clear that:

- Late Predynastic Egypt was divided into two different ceramic traditions:[44] Naqada[45] (Upper Egypt) and Buto-Maadi[46] (Lower Egypt).
- Maadi settlement was abandoned in Naqada IIC period and new settlements (with a material culture from Upper Egypt) appeared in the Eastern Nile Delta (for example, Minshat Abu Omar[47]). The Maadi material culture continued in peripheral areas, such as the small cemetery at es-Saff.[48] "The arrival in the area of the Naqada Culture seems to have led swiftly to demise of the local ceramic traditions."[49]
- Upper Egyptian pottery appeared in Buto in the Naqada IID1 period.[50]
- A unified Egyptian state was most likely not the result of a single battle, but the culmination of alliances, as well as fragmentation and reunification, over a period of at least 250 years.

With these facts, scholars have tried to rebuild the unification process, but there are many hypotheses for the unification of Egypt. Here, some of them are presented:

---

37 (1967). For a modern analysis of the cranial material of the First Dynasty, see Keita (1992), who also denies the invasion and emphasised the continuity of the population.
38 (1984).
39 (1987).
40 (1969: 81)
41 Hoffman *et alii* (1982).
42 Van den Brink (1988; 1992).
43 Since 1979, see *Mitteilungen des Deutschen Archaölogischen Instituts Abteilung Kairo.*

44 Köhler (1996: 219).
45 Petrie (1921: pl. I-LI).
46 For Maadi, see Rizkana & Seeher (1987; 1988; 1989; 1990); for Buto, see von der Way (1992a; 1997a), Köhler (1998a); partially summarised in Midant-Reynes (1992: 197-206).
47 This settlement might assume the role of Maadi in the trade with Canaan, Jiménez Serrano (1996). Thus, this settlement appeared in Naqada IIC, Kroeper and Wildung (1985), Kroeper (1992), the same period in which Maadi was abandoned. About the trade between Maadi and Canaan, see Pérez Largacha (1993b). About the material culture, Kroeper (1985; 1986-1987).
48 Habachi & Kaiser (1985).
49 Wilkinson (1996a: 6).
50 Von der Way (1992a). However, it seems difficult to confirm the existence of a unified Egyptian state only because Egypt presented the same pottery. In this regard, Spencer (1993: 48) holds that the process of the unification of Egypt took place in two stages: the spread of a uniform material culture throughout the country on the one hand, and the establishment of unified political control on the other.

Werner Kaiser[51] was the first scholar who suggested that the conquest of the Delta by the Upper Egyptians took place considerably earlier than the First Dynasty. He estimated that the unification of Egypt may have taken place 100 to 150 years prior to king Narmer.

From this idea and using different approaches, many scholars have proposed distinct developments of Upper Egypt. One of the key points in this discussion is the number and identification of the proto-states from which emerged one single Upper Egyptian State. Fekri Hassan[52] was the first to suggest the existence of two major political units. According to him, at the end of the Late Predynastic period (3300 BC), a dramatic reduction in Nile flood levels served as a catalyst, promoting the fusion of two major political units in Upper Egypt, Hierakonpolis (Elephantine, Edfu, and El-Kab nomes) and Naqada (Karnak, Coptos and Dendera nomes).[53] Further expansion northward to control the rich granaries of Lower Egypt and the trade routes to the Near East led to a gravitation of power from the south to the north via Abydos to Memphis.

Almost at the same time, Kemp[54] proposed a model of state formation in Egypt (Figure 1), which many authors have followed. He proposed the existence of three proto-states in Upper Egypt (at Abydos/This, Naqada and Hierakonpolis) with a unified kingdom achieved by military expansion northward of an Upper Egyptian state centred on Hierakonpolis. However, Kemp[55] has recently changed the number of proto-states, from three to two, Hierakonpolis and Naqada, considering Abydos as a site in which, for an unknown reason, the rulers of Hierakonpolis were buried from the Naqada III period.[56]

Fig. 1: Kemp's hypothesis of the unification process.

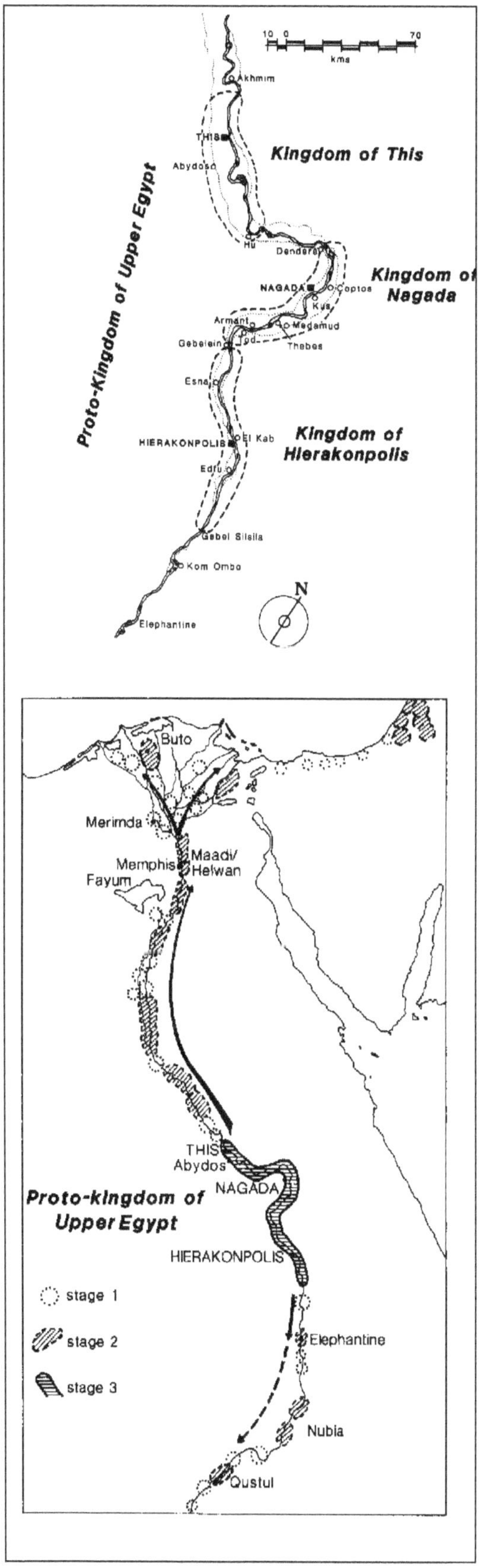

---

[51] (1964); Kaiser & Dreyer (1982).
[52] (1988:165-166).
[53] All the nomes that completed each proto-state in Hassan (1993a: 554).
[54] (1989: 34; 41-43; 45).
[55] (1995: 685).
[56] In Naqada II, the chiefs of Abydos were buried at Cemetery U.

Toby Wilkinson[57] has most recently proposed a theory for the political unification (Figure 2). According to him, as early as the Naqada I period, powerful centres had developed at Thinis-Abydos, Naqada and Hierakonpolis. During the Naqada II period, together with those centres appeared others (Abadiya and Gebelein (?)) with powerful local rulers. However, it was Thinis-Abydos, Naqada and Hierakonpolis and their rulers who led the state formation. At some point early in the Naqada III period, Thinis-Abydos probably incorporated the predynastic kingdom of Naqada. According to this author, it is possible that the rulers of this new kingdom were those represented with the double crown in the supposed fragment of the Palermo Stone in Cairo. At that time, This-Abydos would have some influence over Lower Egypt (tomb U-j),[58] and at the same time several rulers continued co-existing in other regions of Egypt (Hierakonpolis, Buto, Helwan and Tarkhan-Fayum). One of them, Hierakonpolis, began military action against Lower Nubia. Certainly it was the rulers of This-Abydos who ultimately triumphed over all Egypt, although there is a possibility that This-Abydos and Hierakonpolis co-existed as different entities. In this context, the colonies in southern Canaan were established and a coercive policy was adopted against Lower Nubia.

Most scholars have assumed Kemp's theory as the basis for their discussions on different aspects that could lead to or affect the unification process, for example Pérez Largacha,[59] Baines,[60] and Cervelló Autuori.[61]

Kathryn Bard[62] suggested a different model, working from Carneiro's Circumscription Theory.[63] According to her, conflict arose in later Predynastic times as economic competition within the narrow valley increased, and the resolution of these conflicts (by alliances, warfare and/or the establishment of new communities) was through the formation of larger polities, and eventually the unification of Egypt under one centralised government.

A different vision of the unification has been suggested by Köhler.[64] According to her, the relationship between Upper and Lower Egypt has been more and more intensive since the Neolithic period. During the Chalcolithic period, there were analogous developments in Upper Egypt (Naqada culture) and Lower Egypt (Buto/Maadi), thus "At this time both regions have nearly the same utilitarian pottery and lithics."[65] For the last stage in Lower Egypt, Köhler affirms that the changes were due to an increasing cultural and ethnic Naqadan influence and the use of the Naqadan material culture. She maintains that Egyptian material culture was common long before the unification of the political system of Egypt. According to her, both parts of Egypt came together by trade and cultural exchange, which made trading posts or conquests unnecessary. Finally, she wonders if there ever existed an ethnic territorial expansion during the Late Predynastic Naqada expansion.

---

[57] (1999: 49-52); (2000a).

[58] Wilkinson follows Dreyer's interpretation of some labels, in which Dreyer (1998: 139, 142) identified the temple *Djebaut* from Buto, and Bubastis. However, about the temple of *Djebaut* see pp. 53-57 and Figures 21-22 in this book.

[59] (1993a: 79-94, 295-298). Pérez Largacha suggests that the unification of all the Upper Egypt proto-states (Kemp's "proto-kingdoms") occurred in the Naqada IIC period after an independent social development. At this moment, Maadi was abandoned and Upper Egyptian material culture appeared in the Delta. In the Naqada IId1 period, Buto was assimilated culturally and peacefully. Thus, Egypt was under the same culture and government in the Naqada III period, as the international commercial relations (Palestine and Mesopotamia) would show. The main reason for the unification (the Delta and Upper Egypt) is that the Upper Egyptian élites wanted to control trade directly with Canaan and Mesopotamia: rare objects (that increase the status of its owner), new ideas, etc. This idea was hypothesised by Hoffman (1979: 336-340), although without evidence. Trigger (1984: 103) affirmed that "The desire to eliminate intermediaries and control long distance trade along the Nile river also may have produced the increasing competition and conflict among these rulers that ultimately resulted in the political unification of the Nile Valley north of Aswan."

[60] (1995: 102-103). Baines (personal communication) composed a similar theory before Kemp's appeared.

[61] (1996: 189, 197, 219); his interpretation has a sociological, religious-historical, and symbolistic (neo-symbolistic) character. He considers that the Upper Egyptian ruler added to his cosmic potency the political-military power (the fetish kingship) in Naqada II, all of these being under the concept of *maat*. He defends, following Frankfort, the idea that the Delta never had a unified kingdom and it was a concept created by the priests of Ptah, appearing as State symmetry (dual country, dual monarchy, dual heraldic, and dual administration), which represented the perfect unity (*smꜣ tꜣwj*).

[62] (1994: 116-117)

[63] More details about the Circumscription Theory in Bard & Carneiro (1989).

[64] (1996: 219-220; with more details, Köhler (1995: 85-89).

[65] This fact does not mean that all pottery types were used at the same time in every region of Egypt. Obviously, there were some common types in every period, but there were also regional differences.

Fig. 2: Wilkinson's theory for the political unification

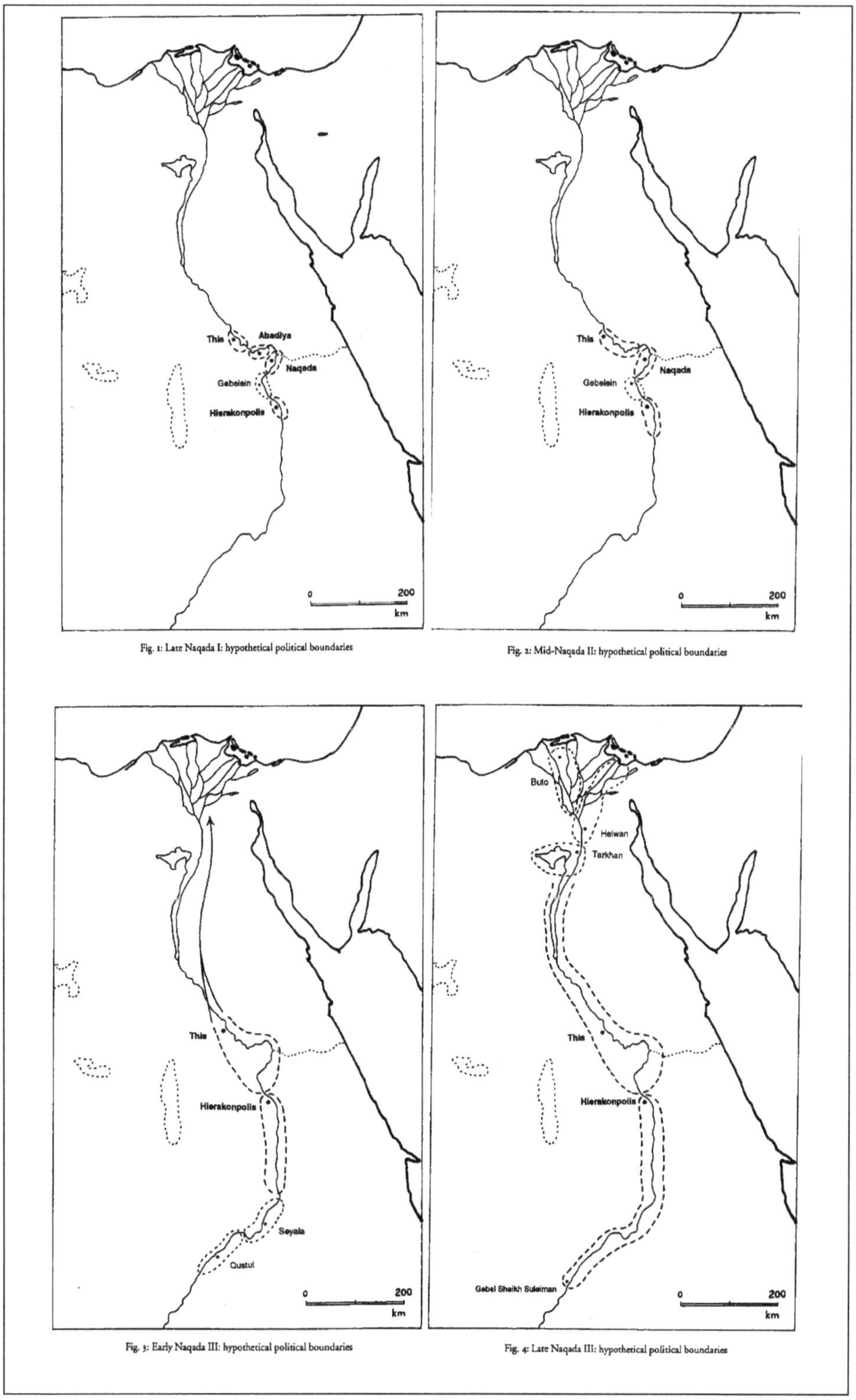

Fig. 1: Late Naqada I: hypothetical political boundaries

Fig. 2: Mid-Naqada II: hypothetical political boundaries

Fig. 3: Early Naqada III: hypothetical political boundaries

Fig. 4: Late Naqada III: hypothetical political boundaries

Recently, I have expossed my own view about the last stages of the unification process, concretly, in my PhD thesis, in which I analysed all the signs and symbols that might repressent the power or even predynastic kings.[66] I have based my study on the three elements that conform a "classical" *serekh*: the falcon, the name, and the palace-façade. According to my interpretation of the data, it is possible to note that, at the beginning of the Naqada IIIA period, there were two different areas that represented the power with different elements: in Lower Egypt, since Naqada IIc, the power is represented with a palace-façade. Since Naqada IIIA, representations of power in the Thinite region are characterised by a hieroglyphic sign that represents an animal (for example, Scorpion I). In this period, the falcon (surely, Horus of Nekhen) begins to be associated to the name of the king, which might indicate a close relationship between Abydos and Hierakonpolis. In the next two phases (Naqada IIIB and C1), Upper Egyptian kings clearly directed their efforts to assimilate the Memphite region and Lower Egypt. There, they found a different way to represent a king, the palace-façade. Then, the Upper Egyptian kings (Scorpion II and Ka) associated this new element to their names (together with the falcon) and constructed what we know as "classical" *serekhs*. This does not mean that every region continued representing the king with their traditional ways during the first kings of the First Dynasty: in Lower Egypt with a palaca-façade and in Upper Egypt with a hieroglyph sometimes surmounted by a falcon.

[66] Jiménez Serrano (2000a); see also *id.* (2001b) & *id.* (2002a).

B) FIRST DYNASTY

The sequence of kings for the First Dynasty was established through the work of Flinders Petrie[67] on the excavation and the re-excavation of the royal tombs at Abydos, after a pseudo-archaeological investigation carried out by Amélineau.[68] This sequence has been confirmed recently by a discovery which resulted from a meticulous examination of the same site by the German Archaeological Institute in Cairo. In recent years, the sequence of the kings of the First Dynasty has been confirmed thanks to several seal-impressions found at Abydos. The first one was a clay seal-impression with inscriptions giving the names of the kings of the First Dynasty in chronological order: Narmer, Horus Aha, Djer, Djet, Den and with the addition of the name of Queen (*mwt nzwt* "Queen Mother") Mer-Neith, and Khentamentiu, the principal god of Abydos.[69] The order of the last kings of the First Dynasty was Anedjib, Semerkhet and Qaa, and this is known thanks to an important fragment with the *nebty* names of Den and his successors.[70] The succession has been confirmed by the publication of more seal-impressions;[71] they belonged to the same seal and bear the names of all the kings of the First Dynasty, from Narmer to Qaa.

It is noticeable that the earliest king mentioned is always Narmer, although the existence of many others before him is known (for example, Horus Ka).[72] Wilkinson[73] explains this fact by saying "Narmer seems to have been regarded as a founder figure, at least in the context of the royal burial ground at Abydos. In this context, it may also be significant that the earliest inscribed stone vessel from the hoard of thousands buried under the Step Pyramid at Saqqara dates from the reign of Narmer."

[67] (1900; 1901).
[68] (1899-1905).
[69] Dreyer (1987); Dreyer *et alii* (1996: 72, Abb. 26).
[70] Three stone vessels found at Step Pyramid at Saqqara, Lacau & Lauer (1959: 9-12, pl. 4, nos. 19-21). Emery (1961: 73).
[71] Dreyer *et alii* (1996: 72, Abb. 26, Taf. 14 b-c).
[72] Against the existence of Horus Ka and Iry Hor, see Adams & Cialowicz (1997: 60), who read Horus Ka as "*Ka (soul) of the king*" and Iry Hor as "*Mouth of the king*". For a possible list of three kings before Narmer, see Jiménez Serrano (2000b: 42, fig. 5), with reference.
[73] (1999: 68).

- Narmer

Petrie[74] was the first to read the name of Narmer; later some authors have tried to read it a different way; for example, Weill[75] thought that the Horus name of this king was Nar (or Naru), while the royal name would be Mer. His argument is based on the appearance of some seal impressions[76] in which the sign Nar (*nꜥr*) is the only one that can be found inside the *serekh*, with the other sign (*mr*) being outside. Petrie[77] also found a vase with the signs Nar and Mer separated, but he concluded that Nar was the Horus name and Mer was the personal name. Weill's suggestion is very possible, but for reasons based on the academic tradition, here this king's name appears as Narmer. This name means "the Cleaving Catfish"[78] or "the raging catfish (nꜥr-fish)".[79]

From the palette found at Hierakonpolis[80] and a recent label unearthed at Abydos[81] depicting the same scene, it seems possible that Narmer had to fight in the Delta (see pp. 83-87, Figures 46-48). In addition, one expedition was sent to the Eastern Desert as the inscription from Wadi el-Qash[82] shows. Narmer celebrated at least onc *sed* festival at Hierakonpolis (see pp. 52-57).

Narmer was buried in a tomb at Abydos. Two chambers known as B17 and B18 formed the royal burial.[83] Petrie[84] found many depictions that show Asiatics taking offerings to Narmer (?), as well as captives of undefined ethnic origin. It is impossible to know if these scenes represent real events. However, the relationship between Southern Canaan and Egypt in the times of Narmer is well attested by numerous *serekhs* discovered in the former region.[85] The kind of presence that Egypt had in Southern Canaan (if any) is still under discussion, as the following words show: "Modern Scholarship is divided in its interpretation of the *raison d'être* for the Egyptian presence in Canaan at this time. The Syro-Palestinian archaeologists, for the most part, see it primarily as an imperialistic presence, established by military force and maintained by military control ... The Egyptologists, however, and a few Syro-Palestinian archaeologists have viewed the evidence as reflecting a purely commercial relationship, with no overtones of political domination..."[86]

- Aha

His name means "Horus the fighter"[87], but he also assumed as his *Nebti*[88] name the word *mn* (Established?[89]), as is known from a small ivory label discovered in the tomb of Queen Neithhotep at Naqada (pp. 95-97, Figure 55). The ascription of this tomb was based on the occurrence of two wooden labels in the tomb, and

[74] (1900).
[75] (1907: 33-34). For another reading of Narmer's name, see Vikentiev (1931: 67-71). Wilkinson (2000c: 26) mentions another reading suggested by John Ray in an unpublished paper. This new reading would be *ḥr-sꜣb*. It must be noted Wilkinson's (2000c: 24-26) reflections about the royal name at the beginning of the First Dynasty and earlier. According to him, the royal name is associated to animals with a strong component of domination and control (catfish, scorpion, ...).
[76] Petrie (1901: pl. XIII, nos. 91, 92).
[77] (1914: 10 & pl. VI, no. 3).
[78] Goldwasser (1992: 68); Godron (1949: 220) proposed the reading *mr(j)-nꜥr(j)*, which would mean 'Beloved of *Nꜥr(j)*'.
[79] Redford (1986: 130, n. 10), with many references. As this author has pointed out, the names of the kings of the First Dynasty indicate bellicosity, rather than the personification of benevolence and fertility.
[80] Quibell (1900).
[81] Dreyer *et alii* (1998: 138-141, Abb. 29).
[82] Original picture, in Winkler (1938: pl. XI, no. 1). A drawing, in Emery (1961: fig. 6).

[83] Petrie (1901); Kaiser & Dreyer (1982: 220-221, 227, 229, 235-241, Taf. 56c). In this regard, see some interesting reflexions made by Wilkinson (2000c: 32).
[84] (1901: pl. IV, nos. 4, 6, 9, 11, 12, 13, 14 & 17).
[85] Tel 'Erani, Yeivin (1960); Arad, Amiran (1974); Nahal Tillah, Levy *et alii* (1995: 29-30). *Serekhs* partially compiled by van den Brink (1996).
[86] Schulman (1992: 409).
[87] Wilkinson (2000c: 26); Redford (1986: 130, n.10) translates it "Horus fights".
[88] The two principal goddesses of el-Kab and *Dp* formed the *nebti* name; these were the vulture goddess  *nḫbt* Nekhbet and the cobra-goddess  *wꜣḏt*, Wadjet. These cities were in close vicinity of the early capitals of Hierakonpolis and Buto.
[89] Spencer (1993: 63) prefers "to endure, to be permanent" and he adds "...used in later times as a designation for the founder of the state, whose true identity had been forgotten."

About the role of this sign and even its reading there has been a long controversy, see pp. 95-96.

it is possible that she was Horus Aha's mother.[90] According to Wilkinson,[91] "it is not unlikely that Narmer – a member of the Thinite royal family – would have taken as his wife a member (perhaps the heiress?) of the ancient Naqada ruling family, to cement an important political alliance between two of the key centres of Upper Egyptian authority."

Aha undertook a campaign against the Nubians (A Group), according to a label found in his tomb (p. 88, Figure 50).[92] Those campaigns implied the beginning of the decline of the indigenous culture in Lower Nubia.[93]

Aha's funerary complex was at Abydos and consisted of 3 separate brick-lined pits (B10, B15, & B19) with a surface of 394 square meters[94]. Beside them, there was a group of small subsidiary tombs (B16). There, many human bones were collected, and although very disturbed it was possible to determine that most belonged to males of about 20 years of age, none being older than 25, suggesting to scholars[95] that they must have been killed when the king was buried.[96] The bones of seven young lions, which had been kept in captivity, were found near the long eastern chamber, and show that the king wanted to enjoy hunting in the afterlife.

As in the tomb of Narmer, many ivory-tablets (fragments of boxes?, pieces of furniture?) with depictions of Asiatics (?) doing homage or being captured were found by Petrie[97].

The final year and a half of Aha's reign are probably recorded on the Palermo Stone, if the following boxes of the Palermo Stone have been attributed correctly to Djer. About possible boxes of Aha, they only mention the biennial royal tour of inspection (*šmsw ḥr*) and the creation of a figure of the god Anubis.[98] Recently, I have published a translation of the Palermo Stone into Spanish.[99] Although Wilkinson[100] has also published another one in English, I prefer to quote mine, because I have found some discrepancies with Wilkinson's. Thus, my translation for the reign of Aha is as follows:

X+1: Año de los Seguidores de Horus. Consagración de la estatua(?) de Sed (Upuaut).
X+2: Año del mes sexto, día séptimo.

- Djer

According to Wilkinson,[101] Djer's name meant 'Horus the Strong'. His wife could be Herneith, as it is possible to conclude after the examination of tomb 3507 at Saqqara.[102] Her tomb could have received the name of *ḥw·t mr(y) Jnpw* "House of the beloved of Anubis". There, the title of the queen *smꜣ·wt nb·wj* was found 'She who is united with the Two Lords' (see Horus Aha), "the foremost (*ḫntj·t*) wife of Djer"[103].

This king was buried in tomb O at Abydos, which was much later considered the cenotaph of the god Osiris.[104]

Emery[105] affirmed that Djer's reign was a period of prosperity as shown by the expansion in the production of arts and crafts, examples of which may be seen in the jewellery recovered from the king's tomb at Abydos. There were discovered lapis lazuli beads[106] in his tomb at Abydos. From the black market of Thebes, The Royal Ontario Museum obtained a flint knife with the *serekh* of this king on the golden handle with the inscribed signs: *pr.w nṯr.*[107] Metalwork (copper tools, vessels and weapons) from tomb 3471 at Saqqara[108] is among the finest levels of the First Dynasty.

---

[90] Spencer (1993: 61).
[91] (1999: 70).
[92] Petrie (1901: pls. III & XI-1).
[93] Nordström (1972: 27).
[94] O'Connor (1987: 28). His tomb was excavated by Petrie (1901) and the *DAIK*: Kaiser & Dreyer (1982: 213-220, 226-228, 235-241, Abb. 1-2), Dreyer (1990: 62-67).
[95] Dreyer (1990: 81-89).
[96] It is necessary to take into account the average life expectancy in this age, David Jeffreys (personal communication).
[97] (1901: pls. IIIA, no. 2 -homage-, IV, nos. 3 -homage?-, 5 & 15 -homage-, 20 -captured-).
[98] Edwards (1971: 22).
[99] Jiménez Serrano (2002c).
[100] (2000b).
[101] (1999: 202).
[102] Emery (1958: 73; 1961: 60).
[103] Emery (1958: 93-94). However, see note 153.
[104] O'Connor (1989: 61-81, figs. 6-19).
[105] (1961: 61).
[106] From a bracelet, Spencer (1980: 78, no. 572B), the form is a *serekh*.
[107] Needler (1956: 41-44, pl. III). Reading from Kahl (1994: 624).
[108] Emery (1949).

On a fragmentary piece of ebony label, there is a representation of an enclosure with three bound captives.[109] This scene could be related to a ceremony of the *sed* festival, in which the sacrifice of captives was part of the ritual (see p. 62, figure 25). In tomb 3471 at Saqqara, a grey schist palette was found bearing a scene in which the king (wearing the *nemes* headdress) is sacrificing a prostrate enemy (according to Emery[110]) before the forequarters of a lion. In front of the lion, Emery interpreted two hearts.

In Djer's tomb of Abydos, many potsherds of Canaanite origin have been found[111] and a stone bowl and a piece of an ivory wand bear the name of Mer-Neith.[112]

From the Palermo Stone, I have translated:[113]

X+3: Año del mes cuarto, día decimotercero. (Ceremonias de) la Unión de las Dos Tierras, (y de la) circunvalación del muro.

Seis codos.

X+4: Año de los Seguidores de Horus. Festival Desher.

X+5: Año de la consagración de la estatua (?) de los gemelos reales.

Cuatro codos y un palmo.

X+6: Año de los Seguidores de Horus. Ofrenda y sacrificio a la estatua del rey.

Cinco codos, cinco palmos y un dedo.

X+7: Año de la circunvalación alrededor del (recinto) Semer Necheru (en el) Festival de Socares.

Cinco codos, cinco palmos y un dedo.

X+8: Año de los Seguidores de Horus. Consagración de la estatua(?) de Iat.

Cinco codos y un palmo.

X+9: Año de la aparición del rey del Alto Egipto. Consagración de la estatua de Min.

Cinco codos.

X+10: Año de los Seguidores de Horus.

Consagración de una estatua de Upuaut.

Seis codos y un palmo.

X+11: Año de la primera vez del festival de Dyet.

Cuatro codos y un cuarto de codo.

X+12: Año...

Djet (Wadji, Edjo/Adjo[114])

His name meant "Cobra-like"[115] and his *nebti* name was Iterty[116]. During his reign, there was an expedition (mining?, control of the nomads?) to the Eastern Desert (Bir Abbad, in Wadi Abbad), as it is possible to conclude from a *graffito* at this site on the way to the Red Sea.[117] But his policy did not stop there, because Schulman[118] has identified his *serekh* in a seal impression from 'En Besor, and pottery vessels from Canaan were found at Saqqara[119], Tarkhan[120] and Abydos[121].

The reign of Djet was short, as is possible to conclude from two pieces of evidence: Queen Mer-Neith was regent during the first years (?) of the reign of Den,[122] the son of Djet, and a high official called Amka began his long career in the reign of Djer, which culminated in Den's reign.

- Den (other readings: Udimu, Dewen, Wedymuw)[123]

His name meant "The Cutter"[124] and, according to Edwards[125], during his reign, the double-crown (*sḫmtj* "the Two Powerful Ones")

[109] Petrie (1901: pl. VA, no. 13).
[110] (1949: 60).
[111] Petrie (1900: 6, pls. VIII, nos. 2, 3, & 13); Porat & Adams (1996); Serpico & White (1996).
[112] According to Petrie (1901: 22, pl. V, no. 6; 23, pl. V, no. 21), these pieces may have strayed over from the tomb of that queen or could represent a later offering undertaken during the regency of this queen. Another possibility is that the Merneith material from Djer could have been moved there during Amélineau's work (comparable shifts are known for many objects).
[113] Jiménez Serrano (2002c).

[114] About another reading of the name of this king, Sainte Fare Garnot (1958).
[115] Redford (1986: 130, n. 10).
[116] Gardiner (1958: 38); Emery (1961: 69), which would be very close to the fourth king in the Abydos king list, called Ita, Edwards (1971: 24).
[117] Clère (1938: 85-87).
[118] (1980: 31-32).
[119] Emery (1954: 75).
[120] Petrie, Wainwright & Gardiner (1913: 16, pls. XVI, no. 1, XIX, no. 24).
[121] Petrie (1925: pl. IV, nos. 9-10).
[122] About Mer-Neith, see Wilkinson (1999: 74-75).
[123] About the different readings of the name of this king, see Godron (1990: 11-17), with references. Here Godron's thesis is accepted, *idem* (pp. 14-17), which shows that his Horus name was *dn* or *dwn*.
[124] Redford (1986: 130, n.10).
[125] (1971: 26).

made its first appearance and the title *nzwt-bjtj* ('He who belongs to the sedge and the bee'), which used to be translated as 'King of Upper and Lower Egypt', though in origin it may have referred in particular to the towns of Herakleopolis and Sais. At the same time, the double crown is attested for the first time during his reign, marking a development in royal ideology[126].

His *nzwt-bjtj* name was , read Semti (or *zmjtj*) or *ḫȝstj*.[127] The origin of this name could be in a victory of this king over the Bedouins.[128] According to Godron,[129] the reign of Horus Den lasted between 33 and 65 years (more probably between 35 and 40 years), but this argument is based on calculations of the number of his *sed* festivals (considering that the first one was celebrated in the 30th year of his reign) on the Cairo fragment. Certainly, his reign seems to have been long. According to Wilkinson,[130] the increase in the number of officials tombs not only reflects the length of Den's reign, but also those changes that were carried out in the structure of the administration.

He was buried in tomb T at Abydos. The floor of the burial chamber of his tomb at Abydos was built with red granite blocks from Aswan (300 km to the south),[131] which means a new step in the development of the royal tomb.

Although many fragments of vases of Canaanite type were classified with the provenance of Semerkhet's tombs at Abydos, Spencer[132] holds that they may be attributed to the tomb of Den, because they bear Petrie's excavation mark T. His name is read by Schulman[133] in 'En Besor (Canaan). According to Fischer,[134] the Mesopotamian influence finished after his reign.

The Ebers medical papyrus (1500 years after Den) records a prescription, which was reputed to belong to his reign, and Chapter 64 of the Book of the Dead was attributed to his days[135]. In the tomb of Hemaka at Saqqara, the oldest papyrus was found.[136]

In the third row of the Palermo Stone, some of the years of his reign have been recognised. They constitute the major source of information of all this reign:[137]

...[Me]r(t)-[Neit]
X+1 : Año del levantamiento del templo...
Tres codos, un palmo y un dedo.
X+2: Año del golpe a los *iuntiu*.
Cuatro codos y un cuarto de codo.
X+3: Año de la aparición del rey del Alto Egipto y de la aparición del rey del Bajo Egipto. (Primer) festival *sed*.
Ocho codos y tres dedos.
X+4: Año (siguiente a la) inundación de las tierras cultivables (lit. *arurai*), del oeste, del Bajo Egipto, del este, de toda la gente.
Cuatro codos y dos palmos.
X+5: Año de la segunda vez del festival de Dyet.
Dos codos y dos palmos.
X+6: Año de la circunvalación del recinto Sut-Necheru. Festival de Socares. Cinco codos, un palmo y dos dedos.

---

[126] Wilkinson (1999: 75).
[127] Emery (1961: 73) defended Semti. Before, Sethe (1905: 23-24) related this name with the name of Hesepti in the Turin Papyrus and in the label of Abydos, and with Usaphais in Manetho's *Aegyptiaca*; for this problem of interpretation, see Newberry & Wainwright (1914: 148). Weill (1907: 26-28) questioned whether these signs could be a royal title, because it is possible to see it in other monuments of the time of Anedjib and Semerkhet. According to him, this title could be read "King of the Desert" or "King of the Two Deserts". Sethe (1905: 23) also offered another reading, "the Foreigner". For a complete study and discussion, see Godron (1990: 17-21). See also Kahl (1994: 600-602).
[128] Godron (1990: 180).
[129] (1990: 106, 195).
[130] (1999: 76).
[131] Needler (1984: 32).
[132] (1980: 47-48, no. 330, n. 1).
[133] (1976: 25-26) the reading of this *serekh* is not very clear; according to Schulman (1980: 24, 33), there is no doubt in seal impression no. 26; see also (1992: 399-401, 409, no. 50).
[134] (1989: n. 13).
[135] Emery (1961: 80).
[136] Emery (1938).
[137] In this row, there are no names of kings, so Sethe (1905: 48) attributed it to Anedjib, but Newberry & Wainwright (1914: 149) compared this row to the monuments of Den (labels) and they concluded that it must be attributed to Den.
For a complete discussion, see Godron (1990: 105-137), with references.
For the translation, see Jiménez Serrano (2002c).

X+7: Año en el que el sacerdote de Seshat extiende la cuerda. [Construcción de(?)] la gran puerta (del recinto) Sut-Necheru.

Cuatro codos y dos palmos.

X+8: Año de la inauguración del monumento Sut-Necheru. Caza del hipopótamo.

Dos codos.

X+9: Año de la estancia en Heracleópolis, templo de Herishef.

Cinco codos.

X+10: Año en el que el rey viajó (al norte) a Semen y a Urka.

Cuatro codos y un cuarto de codo.

X+11: Año de la consagración de la estatua de Sed.

Seis codos, un palmo y dos dedos.

X+12: Año de la aparición del rey del Bajo Egipto. Primera carrera del toro Apis.

Dos codos y un cuarto de codo.

X+13: Año de la consagración de la(s) estatua(s) de Seshat y Mafdet.

Tres codos, cinco palmos y dos dedos.

X+14: Año [de la aparición del] rey (del Alto Egipto)...

Consagración(?)...

Scholars assume that queen Mer-Neith sheltered those years of Den's reign, under his minority. Thus, it is difficult to support Helck (see above) who places the *sed* festival in the 30th year of reign (see p. 42).

- Anedjib

Apart from the celebration of the *sed* festival during his reign, little more is known of his reign. It is known that his *nzwt-bjtj* name was *Mr-pj-bjꜣ*, but he usually combined with it a new title composed of two falcons on perches (*nbwj*, "The Two Lords"), which identified the king with Horus and Seth, symbolising Lower and Upper Egypt respectively.[138]

Perhaps the most noteworthy of his reign was the use of architecture in the construction of a tomb in Saqqara. Tomb S3038[139] - surely built for a high official in the administration[140] – is the oldest precedent of pyramidal architecture in Egypt. It is impossible to know if the symbolism expressed with the pyramidal shape of this tomb is the same of later royal tombs, but without a doubt it is considered as a great architectural innovation.

- Semerkhet

His Horus name was translated by Wilkinson[141] as "Companion of the Corporation" and his *nebti* name (*smsw*) as "the Elder".[142] His Horus name was confused until the 1950s with that of the Third Dynasty king Sekhemkhet, who was represented in a relief in Wadi Maghara at Sinai. The unfinished step pyramid of Sekhemkhet (and his existence) was discovered in the 1950s by Zakaria Goneim at Saqqara.[143]

Some vases with the name of Semerkhet suffered the *damnatio memoriae.*[144] Emery[145] tried to explain this fact by the problems that appeared at the end of the Dynasty, in which some kings were more strongly supported by Lower Egypt (in this case Anedjib) or by Upper Egypt (Semerkhet). Perhaps, in this context might be placed the fragment of a stone vessel with the sign 𓇓 -"king"-erased[146] (but without *serekh*). But the stone vessels from the Step Pyramid bearing the sequence of four royal kings and last seal-impressions discovered at Abydos are contrary to such an interpretation.[147]

[138] Edwards (1971: 27). The transliteration of his name in Kahl (1994: 743).

[139] Emery (1949: 82-94).

[140] Due to the size, location (Saqqara, the high status Memphis cemetery).

[141] (1999: 202); Wilkinson relates this name to the relationship between Horus and the other principal deities of the pantheon. Griffith, in Petrie (1900: 39), preferred "Close friend of the Affections".

[142] Gardiner (1943: 75-76); Weill (1908: 447) preferred Samsu; Grdseloff (1944: 284-288) read *jry-nṯr*; Kaplony (1963, 1: 1123) and Kahl (1994: 431) read *jry*; Ogdon (1984: 17-18) transcribed *sm.*

About the meaning of "Corporation" see Hornung (1999: 205), who explains this concept as an undefined plurality formed by all gods.

[143] (1957).

[144] See Petrie (1900) and Lacau & Lauer (1959; 1961).

[145] (1961: 80-81). For Edwards (1971: 28), it is strange that his *sed* festival, which appeared on fragments of vases from Abydos, was not mentioned on the Cairo Stone, unless it was included in one of the two year-frames of this reign, which is now illegible.

[146] Petrie (1900: pl. VIII, no. 6). It was followed by the name of the *sed* festival, Griffith, in Petrie (1900: 39).

[147] Wilkinson (1999: 79).

Schulman[148] has read his *serekh* on a seal-impression from 'En Besor, and ten or eleven imported Canaanite vessels were found in Semerkhet's tomb.[149]

- Qaa

.

His name meant "With uplifted arm (i. e. ready to strike)"[150] and until recently scholars thought that his *nebti* name was Sen,[151] but the recent excavations at Abydos[152] have provided his true *nebti* name *sḥtp(-nbtj)* "the One who Pacifies (the Two Ladies)." Like Den, Anedjib, and Semerkhet, he used the epithet *sḫm-ḥr-jb*[153]. He may have had a long reign according to Wilkinson[154]. This author bases his argument on a fragmentary bowl from Saqqara, which mentions the king's second *sed*-festival[155] (Figure 41), also the different building phases of his tomb at Abydos, which must have been separated by a significant period of time,[156] and the great number of mastabas that were built at Saqqara in his reign.

There are many inscribed stone vessels (from Abydos[157] and Saqqara[158]) with an inscription bearing the names Semti, Merpabia, Irynetjer and Qaa, the *nebti* names of the last four kings of the First Dynasty. On two of these vessels, the name Merpabia was erased and replaced by the name of Irynetjer[159].

Some jar-sealings show the name of Semerkhet erased,[160] while Anedjib's name was allowed to stand, which suggested to Edwards[161] that Qaa regarded his predecessor with the same disfavour as Semerkhet had.

---

148 (1980: 30-31), he can also interpret the fact that the royal name was accompanied by the title "district administrator" (*ꜥḏ-mr*) of Horus Semerkhet.

A contemporary grave at Abusir contained a typical Canaanite painted handled flask. Kantor (1965: 5F).

149 Petrie (1901: pl. LIV); Kantor (1965: fig. 5B, 5E).

150 Redford (1986: 130, n. 10).

151 For Edwards (1971: 28), Sen is probably not a name but is the verb "to embrace", so with the *nebtj* title the meaning would be "The Two Ladies embrace (the Horus Qaa)."

152 Dreyer *et alii* (1996: 74, pl. 14e).

153 Petrie (1900: pl. XXIX, no. 78); tomb 3500 at Saqqara, Emery (1958: 109).

154 (1999: 80-81).

155 Lacau & Lauer (1959: 12, pl. 8, no. 41).

156 Dreyer *et alii* (1996: 57-71).

157 Naville (1914: 35, pls. VIII & XIV, no. 1). This vessel was made of crystal.

158 Lacau & Lauer (1959: pl. 4).

159 Amélineau (1895-1896, I: 95-96, pl. XLII); Spencer (1980: 42, no. 271).

160 Petrie (1900: 26).

161 (1971: 29); he also supported this suggestion, arguing that a relic of Semerkhet's unpopularity may be detected in his omission from the 19th Dynasty Saqqara List, in which it is possible to see Anedjib and Qaa, but not Semerkhet.

CHAPTER TWO
FESTIVALS, KINGS AND TEMPLES

A) THE DEFINITION OF FESTIVAL

The study of festivals has a long tradition in the contemporary world. As Cannadine[162] argues, two major disciplines have focused their research on them: Sociology and Anthropology. The questions and the visions of each one have been different and present open discussions, which have enriched the general knowledge about those social events. Due to these different approaches, the definition of the term festival[163] can be very complicated and always depends on the culture and the information that has survived.

For the purpose of this study, it is enough to understand the festivals as extraordinary events, which might be celebrated with a determined periodicity (yearly, monthly, etc.).[164] In these events, rituals play a very important role.[165] The periodicity is not a determinant characteristic, because many festivals could be celebrated due to a special momentum, as will be seen.

Basically, the main object of the religious ritual is to use the cosmos for achieving men's desires.[166] According to Lane,[167] "The two properties of ritual which enable it to act in this way are:

(1) the iconicity of ritual, that is the capacity to present things in direct sensual form rather than in statements about things, and
(2) the capacity for objectification, that is the endowment with authority of shared meaning, through presentation in forms external to the subjective experience of the individual".

Festivals have always been part of human social behaviour and as Hocart[168] pointed out "no man can perform the ritual for himself". Thus, it is necessary to have the presence of people, who can play an active or passive role in the ceremony. There are many elements that take part in the rituals, but the common ones are the word and the sacrifice.[169] There are many common features in rituals: encoded by the performers, formality (decorum), invariance, and performance (written instructions, postures, etc.).[170]

In most cases, festivals are related to the king.[171] As Hocart[172] stated, the function of the king is not only to govern, but also to be the repository of the gods. In antiquity, the king is connected to the State.

The population size of a State is not crucial to the existence of those events, because royal festivals are attested in small and large states.[173] Royal festivals were unique occasions, on which the king showed his importance as a superior entity to the common people. However, the whole society might participate actively in the festivals,[174] because there was a common benefit as a result of the ceremonial. But it must be remembered that ancient societies were "less rich, less egalitarian, less literate and less sophisticated than are those of the contemporary West".[175] Thus the benefit of those ceremonies is differently conceived depending on the social position.

Two major consequences of most festivals are iconographic representations and architectural remains. The representations could have different functions, from magic to propaganda, depending on the context in which they are found. The architecture has its own meaning.[176] Certainly, architecture could have connotations of propaganda (i. e. size), but it can also be understood as a mirror of a different reality: heaven or paradise, for example. Thus, these two major consequences must be considered as a different dimension of the festivals, but participant entities of this universe.

---

162 (1987).
163 Similarly to festival, the definition of ritual is an open debate; in this regard, see Lane (1981: 11), who defines it as "a stylized, repetitive social activity which, through the use of symbolism, expresses and defines social relations". Recently, Rappaport (1999: 24) defined it as "the performance of more or less invariant sequences of formal acts and utterances not entirely encoded by the performers".
164 More definitions in Handelman (1990: 10-11), with references. This author (p. 12) defines it as an event organised as a sequence of practices.
165 Handelman (1990: 11).
166 Hocart (1970: 202).
167 (1981: 17).
168 (1970: 190). Also, *idem* (p. 196).
169 Hocart (1970:192-193).
170 Rappaport (1999).
171 Hocart (1970: 86).
172 (1970: 99).
173 Cannadine (1987: 13).
174 Cannadine (1987: 13).
175 Cannadine (1987: 14).
176 Rappaport (1999: 258).

B) ROYAL FESTIVALS IN ANCIENT EGYPT[177]

As Cervelló Autuori[178] has stated, the three main "moments" of the ceremony of kingship are the succession (death and funeral of the predecessor and the enthroning of the new king), the annual confirmation (symbolic death and re-birth of the same king) and the periodical rejuvenation.

Royal festivals are present in Egypt during the whole of ancient Egyptian history. The necessity of the celebration of festivals could be synthesised in Quirke's[179] words: "The conception of the universe as a fragile entity that was perpetually threatened with oblivion gave to the Egyptian cult of the gods an urgency and an extension beyond the bounds of what the Christian and Islamic traditions hold proper to worship". One of the duties of the king was the maintenance of this sacred order, which was called *maat*. The festivals were the ceremonies in which the king invoked all the forces to keep the mentioned sacred order (*maat*) on the earth.

The concept of *maat*[180] is very complex to understand, mainly because there is no equivalent concept in our Western minds. *Maat* could be translated as "truth", "order", and "justice". At the same time, it has connotations of religion, wisdom, morals and law. Thus, *maat* participated in the principal dimensions of the Egyptian universe: the sacred, the cosmos, the State, the society and the individual.[181] It was personified as a goddess and was closely related to the monarchy. As Hornung[182] noted, *maat* came down to earth from heaven after the Creation and, through different rituals, *maat* was returned to the gods.

The existence of *maat* is intimately related to the existence of the Egyptian State (none of these concepts is independent of the other). Moreover, the existence of *maat* is indispensable for the life of the world. At least since the Middle Kingdom, the texts offer the following vision: the god Ra has established the king on the throne of Egypt and his main function is the maintenance of *maat*.[183] The derived conclusion of this argument is that if *maat* rules over the world, mankind is judged (universal justice) and the gods are satisfied.[184]

Maat is that which remains at the end, but it is not a utopia, it "is a point of orientation or a standard of measurement; it is the "ought" against which the "is" of life is ruthlessly and repeatedly measured and almost found lacking".[185]

The ancient Egyptian word for festival is ḥb (). The word is followed by a so-called determinative, which consists of a primitive hut standing on a dish. Both are conventional hieroglyphic signs. The latter sign represents an alabaster dish, which was used for purification ceremonies (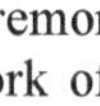). The former represents the frame-work of a rude hut, made of rushes or reeds and supported by a pole in the middle (). About this construction, Bleeker[186] commented: "It is the simplest type of the tabernacle, which, as W. B. KRISTENSEN showed, occurs in the cult of the gods and the dead in all sorts of different forms representing a primitive temple of the god of vegetation".

Bleeker[187] assumed in principle that a festival honoured each Egyptian god. According to Fairman,[188] ceremonies for the royal ancestors formed part of the daily ritual in all temples, and they were celebrated immediately after the conclusion of the daily ritual before the chief god. Furthermore, ceremonies for the ancestors were part of many, if not all, of the great annual festivals.

The current work will deal with four types of festivals.[189] One type was directed to one god (for example, Sokar) and another was celebrated for the king and kingship. In both of them, the king played the main role, but the second type was also a confirmation of his royal position.[190] The other two festivals (The festival of the

[177] Apart from the royal festivals, it is necessary to mention the existence of private feasts, which have begun to be studied recently, see Spalinger (1996).
[178] (1996: 166).
[179] (1992: 70).
[180] A good introduction, in Hornung (1992: 131-145), with references.
[181] Assmann (1989: 12-16).
[182] (1999: 197-199).
[183] In accordance with Hornung (1999: 194), gods fought against the chaos in heaven, and the king did the same on earth.
[184] Assmann (1989: 115-119).
[185] Hornung (1992: 143).
[186] (1967: 27).
[187] (1967: 29).
[188] (1958: 103).
[189] For other different types of festivals, see Bleeker (1967: 24, 35).
[190] Quirke (1992: 90).

enthronement and the *sed* festival) share many common elements.[191]

All festivals became part of the calendar, which in origin had a distinctly religious function; thus many ancient calendars are mainly calendars of festivals.[192]

The dramatic intensity of the festivals and other religious manifestations has been seen as a sort of performances very close to the theatre.[193] In this book, the existence or absence of the theatre has not been discussed; here, it is held that in ancient Egyptian festivals possessed a dramatic character, which played a role that was close to the performance: gods, king, priests, musicians,[194] and, in some rituals, the populace.

C) THE KING IN ANCIENT EGYPT

The role of the king in ancient Egypt is very complicated and needs deep analysis and discussion. There are many specific studies[195] about this figure, but our intention is to present some aspects of the king that are basic in the global picture of this book.

Many scholars (among others, J. Leclant, H. Frankfort, Cervelló Autouri) have connected the anthropology of African peoples to the Egyptian society, focusing on Egyptian kingship. According to Cervelló Autuori, [196] the Egyptian kingship is related to the "African Divine Kingship." He claims that the African Divine Kingship may be divided into two kinds: the Fetish Kingship and the Complex Kingship. In the Fetish Kingship, the ruler would be the receptacle of the cosmic power. In Egypt, the king until the end of the Gerzean period would be a proto-Osiris. In anthropological terms, the figure of proto-Osiris is regarded as a nutritious plant and as a victim for sacrifice, which would ensure fertility and abundance. At the same time, the king would be the intermediary between the gods and society, which would ensure the cosmic order (*maat*). On the other hand, the Complex Kingship is united with the elements of predatory violence (military force): the king is a political leader and a warrior, who has inherited the cosmic power from the preceding cycle (Fetish Kingship). At the end of the Predynastic period, the king is identified with Horus.

In this respect, Frankfort[197] suggested that in early Predynastic times each village was autonomous and had a headman whose power rested on his reputation as a "rainmaker king" (in the case of Egypt, a "floodmaker"), who was presumably able to control the Nile flood. There is no doubt that the king became both a real and a symbolic focal point for the process of national unification and for the process of civilisation.[198] As Campagno explains "There is a wide debate about the problem of the pharaoh's divinity. To simplify, opinions polarise to two positions. On the one hand, it is stated that the king himself was a god, that his essence and that of the gods was the same. On the other hand, it is argued that the divine status was not an attribute of the king but of the kingship: so, if the king was seen as a god, it is only because of his function. In either the social effect of prostration before the pharaoh had to be the same. However, considering the Egyptian belief in the consubstantiality of all entities of the Universe ..., it seems difficult to envisage that Egyptians would distinguish rigorously between the pharaoh's person and his charge".[199]

As Pérez Largacha[200] has stated, the function of the king is to ensure the maintenance of the cosmic order: the Nile floods had to arrive annually and in sufficient quantity, and harvests had to be abundant. The king had to combat the forces of chaos that surrounded Egypt and tried to disestablish the order (*maat*) created by the gods. Sometimes, these forces of chaos arose in the interior of the state (rebellions) and their resolution could be interpreted as victories by the king. At the same time, a religious and political ideology appeared to justify some actions of the king in the unification process.

Another role of the king was the direction of ceremonies and rituals; those could be addressed to gods or to themselves. In the first place, the king was the true High Priest of all

[191] Cervelló Autuori (1996: 166).
[192] Bleeker (1967: 23), with references.
[193] For an introduction to the discussion, see Bleeker (1967: 40-43), with references.
[194] Gauthier (1931: 121).
[195] For example, Frankfort (1948); Posener (1960).
[196] (1996-174-178, 189-208).

[197] (1948: 33-35); such rainmakers have been found in recent times among African tribes, such as Dinka, Ngonde and Jukun, and, in some tribes, they were slain once their magical powers were believed to have begun to wane. Egyptologists saw a manifestation of similar ideas in the *sed* festival of the historic period, Cervelló Autuori (1996).
[198] Hoffman (1979: 267).
[199] Campagno (1998: 238, n. 7).
[200] Pérez Largacha (1993a: 144-145); also Campagno (1998: 239).

Egyptian gods and he had to direct the most important ceremonies, although for the daily cult priests replaced the king. The king was the true intermediary between the gods and mankind[201]. In many of the phases of the festivals, the gods or the king are perfumed with incense, which is reserved only for the divine entities.[202]

D) SOURCES FOR THE STUDY OF FESTIVALS IN THE LATE PREDYNASTIC AND EARLY DYNASTIC PERIODS

As Bleeker[203] has noted, the lack of complete (and contemporary) evidence or visual sequence of most festivals conditions the interpretation of all the sources, especially iconography and epigraphy.[204] According to this scholar, isolated pieces of evidence can be considered of real value, because they are repeated continuously in historic times. Thus, in this work, I compare the iconographic elements that are attested in both early and later times.

It is possible to divide the sources for the festivals of the Late Predynastic and Early Dynastic periods in two large groups:

D.1) Contemporary sources

Archaeology is one of the most important disciplines that help scholars to reconstruct this difficult period, because it provides a great deal of information, not only from the point of view of historical events (destruction, foundations, etc.) but also in the environment, which directly affects human beings and their behaviour, as well as their perception of the world. One of the problems, encountered by modern scholars who attempt to study this period, is that a large amount of information was lost forever during the very first excavations that were carried out with dubious techniques even for those days, for example the "*affaire* Amélineau",[205] and the uncompleted publications of many excavators (in most cases, in others there was only a brief publication): Quibell (Hierakonpolis),[206] or Garstang,[207] for example. In other cases (as with Petrie or German scholars in general), the publication and analysis was done in a satisfactory way. During the middle of the 20th century, the international community reconsidered many theories and conceptions previously established.[208] Since the end of the 1960s and mainly since the 1980s excavations have begun again, not only in cemeteries (as it was at the beginning), but also in settlements, increasing our vision of daily life.

The other main source is the **epigraphy** which, since the exhaustive work done by Kaplony,[209] hardly anyone[210] has questioned, mainly due to the emphasis on necessary work: re-excavation, publication of unpublished materials, and possibilities of new excavations in Egypt in recent years. This important fact has revealed that some materials had not been analysed since Kaplony or even earlier, at the beginning of the 20th century. The epigraphic record can be divided depending on the object where the inscription appears:

-The labels (sometimes also called tablets)

These small rectangular pieces made of wood (ebony) or ivory (also bone) are an excellent source of information. The main reason for this is that most of them used to have inscriptions that, in the best cases, inform about events and other aspects (royal administration, for example), including the kind of offerings, their quantity and quality. Describing the event of the year and the content, they were attached with a string to the object. As Egyptians did not have a chronological system such as ours, they had to name the years with an important event that occurred in this period of time: a religious festival or military campaign, for example.[211] Ancient Egyptians only recorded those events which the court considered significant and which presented the institution of kingship in the best light, which means that they

---

201 Bleeker (1967: 91).
202 Gauthier (1931: 119).
203 (1967: 28-29).
204 As rituals had a magic character, their diffusion was very restricted, possibly only on papyri, avoiding the walls of temples. About the power of magic, see Hornung (1999: 192-196).
205 Hoffman (1979: 267-275).
206 Adams (1974a/b).
207 Needler (1984); Adams (1995).
208 With some noticeable exceptions: Frankfort (1948); Kantor (1942; 1965); Baumgartel (1955; 1960).
209 (1963,1-3).
210 With the notable exception of G. Dreyer, who has studied new inscriptions found at Umm el-Qaab in different papers from 1982, and Kahl (1994).
211 Millet (1990: 59) suggests that the primary purpose of the scenes on these monuments was not to celebrate historical or other events in themselves, but simply to name the year in which the gift was made and offered to the god (presumably at the New Year's Festival).

are not objective.[212] Most surviving examples are from large tombs (mainly at Abydos or Saqqara): royal tombs or from the burials of the king's relatives.

According to Redford,[213] the labels were the archetypes for the purposes of clerical notation. He comments that for the early reigns at least, commemoration and identification can be seen in tension in the purposes of the recorder. But the archivist's instincts soon took hold, and it became desirable to record all the events deemed important in administration, though this made a mockery of the prima facie need to name a year for the purposes of identification only.

A new evolution of labels might be suggested from their writing complexity and internal division:

-First phase (From Scorpion I to Ka?) (Figure 3): [214] the most ancient labels found in Egypt were discovered in tomb U-j (Scorpion I)[215]. They consist of small pieces of ivory/bone or wood with numbers, religious buildings depicted, or signs, most of them with unknown meaning. The name of the king does not appear, except in two cases (and there he is always alone).

Fig. 3: Two labels found in tomb U-j at Umm el-Qaab. (Left) The name of king Scorpion I. (Right) One label read by Dreyer (1998) "Hills of the Light". Not to scale.

-Second phase (Narmer) (Figure 47): the labels dated in the reign of Narmer are very simple but more evolved. On the surface of them, the royal *serekh* appears with some objects that make reference to the content. In one case,[216] the image depicted makes reference to an event, and it is divided into two horizontal registers.

-Third phase (Hor Aha and Djer) (Figure 4): the labels are more complicated; they are divided into at least three horizontal registers (maximum four). The number of hieroglyphs is not very large; the scenes represented have much more importance. In the first one, the title of the king and objects related to the monarchy are depicted. In the register/s, the most important event of the year is represented.

Fig. 4: Label bearing the name of Djer. Not to scale.

-Fourth phase (Djet and Den) (Figure 5): although there are a small number of labels with the name of Djet, and these are not so evolved as those dated to the reign of Den, it is possible to detect some changes: vertical (mixed with horizontal registers) disposition of the registers, the appearance of the sign *rnpt* 'year' on the right side of the label. During the reign of Den, the labels are divided in two parts; the right side, with the year sign, is sub-divided into horizontal registers (maximum four), in which are depicted and narrated the most important events of the year. On the left side, the royal *serekh* stands out together with the name of high functionaries. In the lower part of this side the offerings are mentioned.

[212] Wilkinson (1999: 62).
[213] (1986: 86-87).
[214] There is no label dated to the reigns of Iry Hor, Scorpion II or Ka.
[215] Dreyer (1992c).
[216] Dreyer *et alii* (1998: Abb. 29).

Fig. 5: Labels of Djet (above) and Den (below). Not to scale.

-Fifth phase (Anedjib[217] and Qaa[218]) (Figure 6): the labels are designed with vertical registers. All these labels are full of hieroglyphs without the representation of any scene. On the right side, behind the year sign used to appear a mention of the ritual (?) Following of Horus; in the second the *nebti* name of the king sometimes with the royal *serekh*; and in the third one, the offerings.

-Varia proto-dynastica

In this group, different royal monuments are grouped: palettes and mace-heads,[219] seal-impressions,[220] the stone vessels from the Step Pyramid,[221] and stone architectural elements from the royal buildings.[222] They were monuments contemporary with the kings, and present the same problem as the labels: they are not objective, although they are very important because they present the iconography of early kingship[223].

Fig. 6: Labels of Anedjib (above) and Qaa (below). Not to scale.

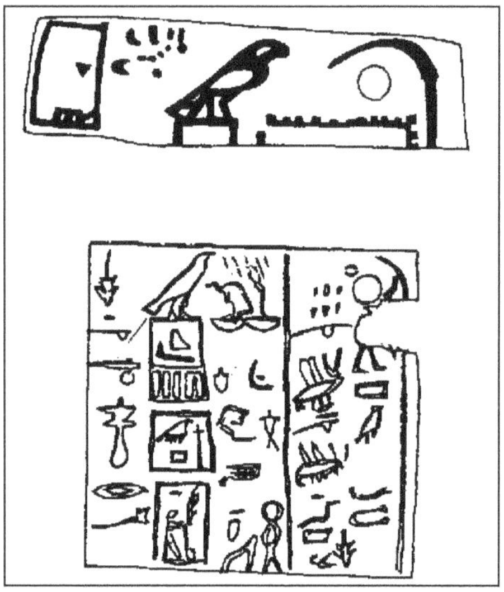

The developing conventions of the palettes and mace-heads in the Late Predynastic period are a mixture of the representational, the compositional and the iconographic aspects. Although the style of the object is Egyptian, it is far from the "classical" style of the end of the Early Dynastic period.[224]

Many of the most important palettes and mace-heads were probably dedicated during the Late Predynastic period in the principal temple at Hierakonpolis,[225] due to the close relationship between the god Horus (worshipped at Hierakonpolis) and the Egyptian kingship.

-The Annals (the Palermo Stone) (Figure 7)

The Annals found on the Palermo Stone originally represented the kings and events from

[217] Only a small fragment of label has been discovered dated in the reign of Anedjib, see Petrie (1901: pl. XLII, no. 41), and it follows the same organisation of those from the reign of Semerkhet and Qaa.

[218] Recently, a large number of additional labels (notably from the reign of Qaa) has been discovered at Umm el-Qaab. These are alluded to in the preliminary reports, although not published.

[219] Quibell (1900); Quibell & Green (1902).

[220] Emery (1961); Kaplony (1963; 1964); Dreyer (1987); Dreyer *et alii* (1996); Roth (1991: 145-195).

[221] Lacau & Lauer (1959; 1961).

[222] Weeks (1971-72).

[223] Wilkinson (1999: 62).

[224] Baines (1997: 221).

[225] Dreyer (1986: 37-46). According to Baines (1997: 221), "the highest forms of representational art with the most portentous content were concentrated in temples".

the period from before the First Dynasty to the Fifth. The first information known about this chronicle was in 1877, when the Palermo Museum received from a particular collection a great fragment which represented five rows in which it was possible to read the names of kings that wore the White Crown in the first register. In the other registers, some events of different kings appear depicted.[226] At the beginning of the 20th century, a similarly sized fragment was acquired by the Egyptian Museum in Cairo; this is called the Cairo Fragment.[227] From that time, further fragments have been bought on the antiquities market.[228] There have been different suggestions for the reconstruction of the original,[229] but all assume that the Annals began with the reign of Aha, a supposition that is not based on any evidence.

Recently, O'Mara[230] has proved convincingly that the fragment conserved in the Cairo Museum "is a clumsy modern hoax from the year 1910". After this new investigation, the unique fragment of the annals that is used in this book is the Palermo Stone, although it must be taken into account that there are some other small fragments that might be original.[231]

D.2) Later sources

During the Old Kingdom and the following periods of Pharaonic history, festivals continued to be celebrated by kings. References are numerous,[232] but the main information is provided by reliefs from different places and periods: the sun temple of Neuserre,[233] Amenhotep III's *sed* festival at Soleb,[234] Akhenaten's *sed* festival at Karnak,[235] the festival of Sokar at Medinet Habu (Ramesses III),[236] and Osorkon II's *sed* festival at the temple of Bubastis.[237]

D.3) The historicity of the sources

Newberry and Wainwright[238] made the first successful attempt to relate the archaeological remains (mainly from Abydos) to the Palermo Stone. They compared objects dated to the reign of Den with some of the years attributed to him in the Palermo Stone. Since then, more discoveries have confirmed the historicity of those sources. Recently, Dreyer and others[239] have discovered a label, which depicts a motif that appears on the Narmer palette. From this discovery they consider that labels and palettes represent historic events.

According to Hornung,[240] "The records of historical events have three components: the events themselves, which furnish both the framework of the action and a series of individual details; a political aim that determines particular accents; and an underlying sense of history that provides a fundamental pattern for rendering the events. With this pattern, all those involved play set roles much as they would in a religious drama". All those features might be observed in the monuments that are going to be discussed in this book.

D.4) How to read the artistic evidence

Whitney Davis[241] holds that images probably «reflect the real reorganization of the social relations and cultural activities of the Neolithic economy according to the new rules of the emerging state», but also that these images depict reality symbolically and metaphorically. In this regard, the iconography of these images is a product of its time. Due to this, scholars risk mistaking the real meaning of the depiction. At the same time, it must not be forgotten that the images are a mirror of an ideology that is developing, and this ideology is a necessary product supported by a new social class, involved in a process of

[226] Schäfer (1902).
[227] Daressy (1916).
[228] Gauthier (1914); Cenival (1965).
[229] Daressy (1916); Borchardt (1917); Ricci (1917); Kaiser (1961); Helck (1974); O'Mara (1979); Barta (1981). About the small fragment deposited in the Petrie Museum, see Petrie (1916).
[230] (1999: 82). The authenticity of small fragments of the "Annals" have not been studied by O'Mara. I agree that the points O'Mara makes in his article appear to have some substance, but without an examination of the original there is no means of deciding the matter.
[231] See the most recent readings of all the fragments of the Annals in Wilkinson (2000b).
[232] References in Schott (1950: 114-118); Bleeker (1967: 27-31), with references; Gohary (1992: 6-39), with references.
[233] Von Bissing & Kees (1923); Kaiser, mentioned by Gohary (1992: n. 145).
[234] Gohary (1992: 11-18), with references.
[235] Gohary (1992).
[236] Mentioned by Bleeker (1967: 81-90), with references and figures.
[237] Naville (1892).
[238] (1914).
[239] (1998: 138-141). Millet (1990: 53) defends the historicity of those sources. Wignall (1998: 102) also considers that labels are depictions of historic rituals.
[240] (1992: 152-154).
[241] (1992: 13-14).

expansion which culminates (partially) with the unification of Egypt.

The question which emerges is who had access to these images and who could understand them? Most of the representations discussed here were found in places where surely the common people had no access (for example, temples)[242] or even where (theoretically) nobody had access (for example, the royal tombs at Abydos).[243] To answer the question it is necessary to define the function of the images. There have been many proposals about the function, which have been synthesised by Davis[244] in three major ideas: ceremonial, magical and propaganda. Following Davis,[245] the function of propaganda is rejected in most of the cases that will be discussed.[246] It has to be taken into consideration that Late Predynastic and Early Dynastic representations had a function that was ceremonial or magical (or both together at the same time), depending on the context in which they were originally placed or used. From those premises it is possible to conclude with the words of Erik Hornung,[247] who affirms that "By recording words and acts in tombs and temples, they gave them permanence and increased their effectiveness".

The objects that have been partially discussed in this book were made to commemorate special events or ceremonies but none of them were used in those ceremonies, thus they are a subjective result and not a tool. In this regard, they do not take part in the event, but it was in this way that all the acceptable scenes were recorded masking the reality.[248] But this is due to many factors, from the economy of space to the conception of the scene or the craftsman's skills. The image-maker is a social entity, who employs a mode of representation, and participates in the contemporary artistic conventions.

The method of interpretation used here is based on the argument expressed by W. Davis,[249] who considers that late prehistoric palettes have narrative[250] or symbolic ends. Obviously, this formula is followed not only in the analysis of the palettes, but also in the rest of contemporary monuments. In this analysis of the labels, mace-heads, reliefs, and palettes, the cognitive point of view is taken into account, which means that every object is "a cluster of different linguistic components, comprising a semiotic system, in which a constant point of balance and tension is maintained through the triadic support of picture, emblem, and phonetic sign."[251] At the same time, it does not forget, in most cases, that monuments mixed iconographic motifs with inscriptions. For this reason, it has had to present the concept of decorum, which was defined by Baines[252] as something that circumscribes "the subject and the context of the representation, like the nature of the inscriptions that can accompany the image", in other words, unwritten laws about the composition.

242 See Davis (1992: 17) for a discussion.
243 The royal tombs at Abydos were in an isolated place far away from the fertile fields. There is no evidence that supports the idea of the maintenance of the royal cult in the cemetery of Umm el-Qaab. However, it seems more plausible that these functions were carried out in the temples (enclosures), close to the city.
244 (1992: 18-22), with references.
245 (1992: 19).
246 With the exception of the royal gifts. But they can be considered prizes for fidelity or any special service, and not as a way of spreading the royal ideology, although it is implicit in them.
247 (1992: 156).
248 Whitney Davis (1992: 37-42).
249 (1992: 38).
250 As W. Davis (1992: 234) noted "My interpretation of late prehistoric Egyptian image making assumes that many of the images are pictorial narratives".
251 Goldwasser (1992: 69).
252 (1990: 7).

Fig. 7: The Palermo Stone (recto).

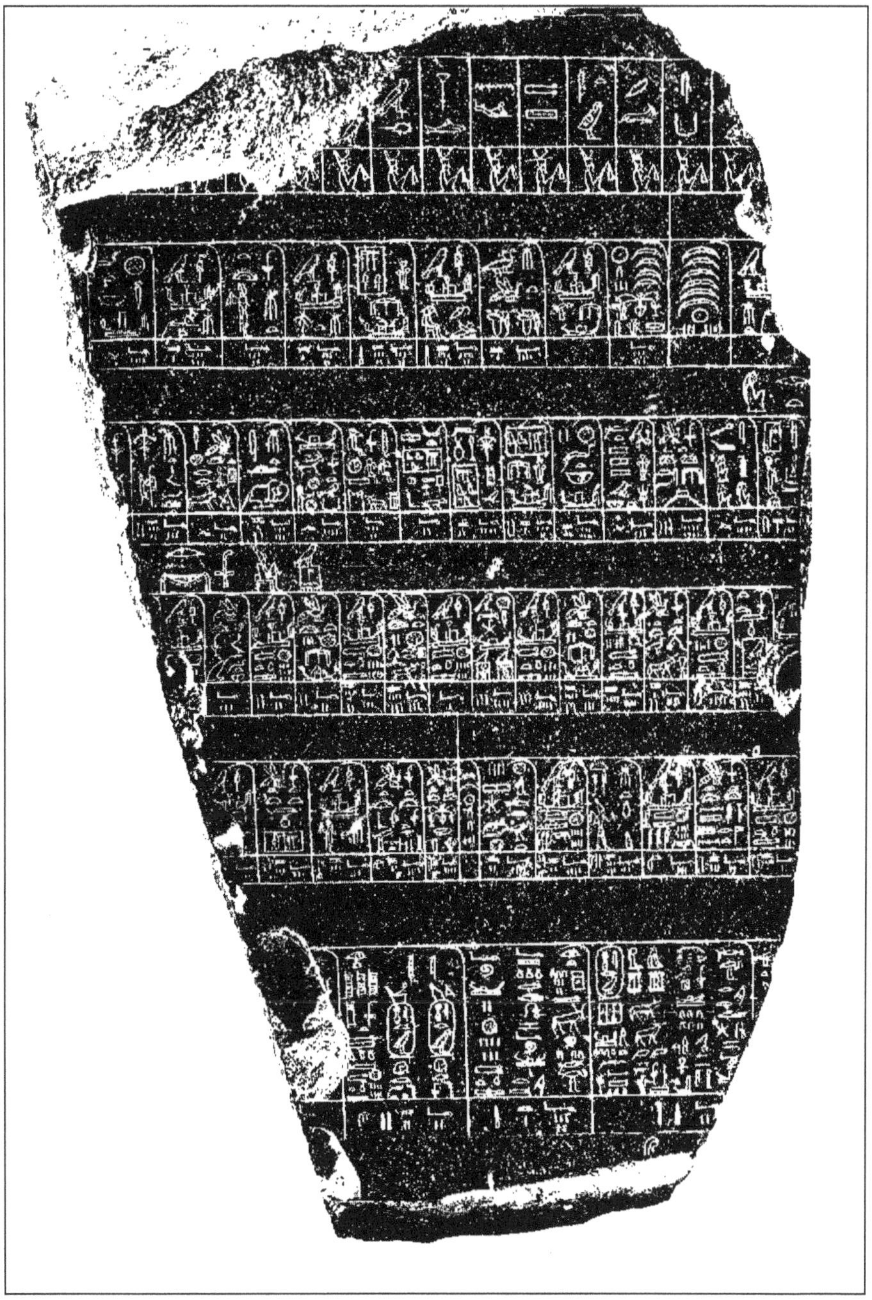

E) THE CONCEPT OF THE ROYAL TEMPLE IN THE LATE PREDYNASTIC AND EARLY DYNASTIC PERIODS

Although some Late Predynastic and Early Dynastic local temples have been discovered in Egypt,[253] their size cannot be compared with those temples built for the kings. However, they have in common the purpose and many other characteristics. They were places in which ceremonies were celebrated for the glory of gods or deified kings. Due to this, the temples of the gods and the kings in essence share the same principles.

E.1) Definition of temple

In general terms, temples are understood as buildings and complexes addressed primarily to the gods. But, the first Egyptian temples were also conceptualised as houses of gods, which gradually transformed their significance. These buildings were also included in political action and political rhetoric, because all of them were built for the celebration of festivals, and some of them were even the receptacle of the royal festivals. In addition, Egyptian temples were also a cosmos, in the sense of "the world of man, and can thus be said to portray both the place where god lives and the place where man lives".[254]

Finnestad[255] has pointed out another aspect of the temples: "The temple is not only the place where the god creator appears and in which he lives, but also the form of the living god". This means (following Finnestad) that the temple is an icon of the god, in other words, it embodies the divine presence.[256] Below, it will be possible to discuss this assertion, because gods are represented by their temples in many depictions of Late Predynastic and Early Dynastic periods.

In ancient Egyptian, there were two terms for temples: *r-pr* and *ḥwt-nṯr*. Only the latter is attested in the Early Dynastic period.[257] There were also three names for the state temples: *ḥwt*, *pr*, and *wbꜣ*.

ḥwt (𓉗 temple, funerary chapel; administrative district; estate)[258] was used as an abbreviation for *ḥwt-nṯr* (temple),[259] and it was a productive foundation, supplying offerings for funerary cults and their administration. It was under the control of officials appointed by the king.

Pr (𓉐 house; household, palace, temple)[260] was different from the *ḥwt*, because the staff employed were responsible not only for the physical and spiritual upkeep of the cult-centre, but also for the welfare of subsidiary cults, the care of sacred animals, and the administration and economic control of all the land and property owned by the temple.

Unlike *pr*, *wbꜣ* was the temenos and all the land sacred to the god and did not have administrative connotations.[261]

Of all these kinds of temples, only the *ḥwt* is attested from the Early Dynastic period.[262] The shape of the hieroglyph *ḥwt* has the same design as some of the funerary temples at Abydos.[263] However, rectangular houses are attested since the Early Gerzean period in Upper Egypt[264] as well as the hieroglyph *pr* in the Early Dynastic.[265]

Patricia Spencer[266] establishes the difference between the god's temple (*ḥwt-nṯr*) and the state temples (*ḥwt*). According to her, "Since the cult-centre of the king was called a *ḥwt*, it will have been a logical step to indicate that a temple was devoted to the cult of a god rather than a king by the addition of *nṯr* to the basic stem".

Finnestad[267] points out the epithets that identify the temple of Edfu (which was taken by him as a paradigm). According to her, the temple is known as *tꜣwj* (The Two Lands) and the *ꜣḫt* (The Horizon). The former is a result of the developed concept of Egypt as a duality, which, as will be seen below (pp. 38-41), it is not possible to connect with the period that is dealt with in this book. The latter connotes the limits of the country, although, in origin, it may refer to the limits of the cosmos (see below). As Finnestad[268] confirms "the

[253] For an introduction, see Kemp (1989: chapter 2), with references.
[254] Finnestad (1985: 8).
[255] (1985: 121).
[256] Finnestad (1985: 124-126).
[257] P. Spencer (1984: 42), with references.
[258] Faulkner (1962: 165). With more details in Moreno García (1999).
[259] Faulkner (1962: 166).
[260] Faulkner (1962: 89).
[261] P. Spencer (1984: 27).
[262] Less common is *pr*, P. Spencer (1984: 14).
[263] P. Spencer (1984: 22), with references.
[264] Hoffman (1980).
[265] Kahl (1994: 624-626).
[266] (1984: 43).
[267] (1985: 8-10).
[268] (1985: 9).

name The Horizon has the additional connotation of a place of transition from chaos to cosmos".

E.2) The foundation of the temple: myth and ritual

a) Mythical origin of temples

The mythological origin of the temples could be summarised from the Edfu cosmological records (Ptolemaic period).[269] But, as Reymond[270] noted, the Egyptian cosmogony did not contain a single theory concerning the site of the first constructed enclosure of the god and his temple. Thus, the Edfu cosmological records are only the explanation that was conceived by the priests of the Edfu temple. However, "It is the only known source that enables us to illustrate the stages that preceded the foundation of the first constructed enclosures".[271]

The Edfu cosmological records mention a number of lands that appeared around the edges of the original island[272] in the beginning of the world. These lands emerged gradually out of the primeval waters. Each of them was regarded as representing a definite terrestrial unit, which was called *pʿy*, "shore". Those were the primeval domains of the god (in the case of Edfu, the falcon) and were founded by the *šwbtjw*, the creators of the Earth. Thus, *pʿy*-lands were subsidiary to the domain of the Creator in the first phase of their existence. Moreover, the *pʿy*-land represented the primary extent of the god in which his first cult place was to be founded thereafter and which became the centre of the subsequent development of the sacred area.[273] In the case of Edfu, the falcon was established on the grounds of the former domain of the *ka*, and then, other lands appeared, which are denominated by Reymond[274] the secondary *pʿy* lands. They were subsidiary to the already existing sacred domains of the falcon and there might have been relics of other sacred domains from an earlier world, which needed to be restored. The purpose of those lands would be the resting place of an Earth-God (*jr-jẖt*, "maker of substances"), who was in decay. *Jr-jẖt* is interpreted by Reymond[275] as an Ancestor and his resting place would be the *bw*, "place".[276] Since this *bw* is described as the *bw tpj*, "The First Place" or "The Place of the First One", Reymond[277] explained it as the land of an early settlement of a divine power which was an Earth-God, who after having been destroyed, became the foundation of a new sacred domain.

The emergence of the *pʿy*-lands marks the final phase of the creation of the world of the gods, but it is also the starting point of the physical world of mankind.[278]

The *bw* – where the Ancestor's dwelling was - was the site of the first enclosure (*sbtj*) made by the Builder Gods, shortly after the *pʿy* land was created and the gods conquered the area of the Ancestor and the battlefield was purified.[279] The *pʿy* land was given the name of the Falcon and then the *ḏd* pillar (𓊽) was enshrined in the *bw*.[280] The enclosure was protected with magic by the god Tanen, who created protective symbols for that purpose.[281] Afterwards, the mansion of the god in the *pʿy* land was founded. The foundation of the temple was therefore a new phase of creation. The following scene is very obscure and Reymond interpreted it as a procession performed by the creators in which the Lord of the *pʿy* land was conducted to his place within the enclosure. Then, the god entered his house in the company of the creators of the Earth.[282]

Reymond[283] held that, at this moment of the myth, it is neither possible to see the earliest

---

269 It was studied mainly by Reymond (1969) and, more recently, Finnestad (1985).

270 (1969: 205).

271 Reymond (1969: 208). However, Finnestad's (1985: 18) affirmation must be taken into account: "She [Reymond] supposes that the book was of general application and not a special work with restricted reference to Edfu temple".

272 The place where the Creator appeared.

273 Reymond (1969: 171-173).

274 (1969: 188-197) with a complete discussion.

275 (1969: 193-194).

276 Reymond (1969: 198, n. 1) interpreted the *bw* as "a technical term and describes any original place, a place of creation or the site in which a sacred domain was to be founded". *bw* is the term used in later Egyptian, whereas *st* was the normal earlier term.

277 (1969: 194).

278 Reymond (1969: 173).

279 The enclosure was delimited by a procession of gods (*šwbtjw*), and there was fumigation for the magical protection of the sacred place. However, there is information about some episodes of the ritual foundation of a temple, see Montet (1964).

280 The Djed pillar served as a symbol of rebirth and resurrection. In the rituals of enthronement, the erection of this pillar meant the concluding rite for the king's predecessor, Frankfort (1948: 128).

281 The soldiers of Tanen are said to have appeared on the scene, and they then performed the duty of protecting the god, Reymond (1969: 206).

282 Reymond (1969: 198-205).

283 (1969: 214).

enclosure of the falcon nor the private residence of the *ka*, and the temple must be imagined as resembling in detail the developed *ḥwt-nṯr*. They would be simpler structures.

b) The artistic evidence of temple foundation

There is no artistic or epigraphic evidence dated to the Late Predynastic or Early Dynastic periods that shows an understandable sequence of temple foundation. Only the Palermo Stone suggests that the foundation of a new religious building comprised a sequence of events. Three different ceremonies are recorded (in each consecutive year) for the temple of *swt-nṯrw*, "Thrones of the Gods". The first ceremony is called *ḥꜣ*, in which the temple is planned. In this ceremony it is possible that the king performed a ritual circuit of the building.[284] The Palermo Stone also mentions the ceremony of *pḏ-šs*, "stretching the cord", which represented the formal laying out of the temple and accompanied the sanctification of the land on which the temple was going to be built. The last ceremony mentioned is *wpt-š*, "opening the (sacred) lake".[285] There is also another foundation scene dated to the Second Dynasty, but unfortunately does not show more details that those carved on the Palermo Stone.[286]

Apart from those references to the ceremonies, perhaps related to the construction of a small temple,[287] there are no more clues for reconstructing a foundational procedure in this period. Due to this lack, it is necessary to use later examples (New Kingdom) to reconstruct the rituals that may have been in practice at earlier times. Montet[288] published a formal compilation of all the scenes related to temple foundation. According to him, the rituals would follow this sequence:[289]

1. - The king goes out of the palace preceded by two standard bearers and Inmutef.
2. - The king, Hathor, and Horus. This scene completes the first one.
3. - The king and one goddess, Seshat. The king is holding a long mace and a stick, and, together with the goddess (who holds the same tools), is performing the ritual "Stretching of the Cord". In fact, the king is marking the boundaries of the temple and delimits and arranges the internal distribution of the buildings.
4. - The king holds a hoe and smooths the ground.
5. - The king holds an ordinary mould for making bricks. This scene could refer to the thousands of bricks that are going to be necessary for the construction of the temple.
6. - The king empties a basket of sand.
7. - The king presents Horus with a dish with some labels of different materials (gold, faience, etc.). They are going to constitute the foundation deposit of the temple. In this way, the king takes possession of the ground.
8. - The king and Horus. The king is placing a stone with square angles.
9. - The king throws grains, which form an oval that surrounds a small building (naos). The inscriptions relate this action to a purification ritual.

As it is possible to see above, the main protagonist of the foundation of the temple is the king. He is the master builder who directs the foundation and the construction. However, our complete ignorance about who ordered the building of the city-temples permits only the suggestion that the New Kingdom scenes studied above are related to the foundation of the royal enclosures of the First Dynasty. For the moment, it is impossible to know if in the foundation of the Late Predynastic city-temples the king played an important role.

E.3) The symbolic structure of temples

In pharaonic Egypt, the architecture and decoration of the temple represented the landscape of the earth before it was cultivated by mankind: columns as plants or the pylons as the hills of the desert, for example.[290] However, in the Late Predynastic period, city-temples are different: *pr-*

[284] F. D. Friedman (1995: 14).
[285] For these ceremonies in the Palermo Stone, see in the recto: 3rd row, years x+6 to x+8.
[286] Engelbach (1934).
[287] Wilkinson (1999: 305).
[288] Montet (1964).
[289] Montet (1964: 75-100).

[290] Finnestad (1985: 10). She also holds that Egyptian temples had two main characteristics of chaos: water and darkness (p. 11-12).

wr at Hierakonpolis had an animal shape,[291] the Elephantine shrine was almost a cave, etc. This difference could be explained as a result of a process of local evolution.

According to Baines,[292] the most characteristic aspects of the Egyptian temple presented to the world were exclusion and protection. They were guarantors of order (*maat*). At the same time, the temples were a symbol in their architectural and environmental aspects. But, they were as well the sacred area (inside) versus the secular area (outside).

Baines[293] has remarked that the particular emblems on the enclosures of the Predynastic shrines or temples have few parallels among Early Dynastic representations.

At the beginning, most of the temples would have been made in light materials (wooden posts and reed matting). During the two first dynasties, these temples had new constructions made in stone or other materials (brick), but they suffered destruction or they were reused at a later time.[294] Thus, the representations of some temples are very important, not only because they inform about their own existence, but also to help archaeologists in their interpretations in future excavations.

Basically, Late Predynastic and Early Dynastic temples may be divided into two parts:

- The **enclosure**, in which some (public?) rituals would be carried out. It could contain emblems of the divinity and some ritual objects. According to Baines,[295] the function of an enclosure is to exclude, but also define the sacred area.[296] Thus, it is possible to understand symbolically, the enclosure as the boundary between the sacred area and the secular area.[297] For Finnestad,[298] the walls of the enclosure had not only a symbolic purpose as transition from chaos (outside) to cosmos (inside), but also a functional reason: to protect the sacred area from floods and the progression of the desert.

- The **shrine**, preceded in some cases by post-poles with pieces of cloth.[299] In this small, mostly single-roomed interior space, the statue of the god would be looked after, and there, some private and secret rituals would be practised. One of the most important rituals was the (food) offering act. According to Finnestad,[300] the gods received their sustenance in the temples.

Rituals took place not just in the shrine building but also in the enclosure. Baines'[301] explanation for the origin of the hieroglyphic sign of a god on a pole with a pennant ( ) was that entrance to the temples would be restricted to only members of the élite, thus the reference point of the temple would be the pole(s).

Until recently, knowledge about primitive temples was limited to inscriptions, pictorial representations, and mentions in religious texts (mainly the Pyramid Texts). Thanks to representations, scholars know that the most important temples in Early Egypt were: *pr-wr*,  [302] (in Upper Egypt), and *pr-nw*,  [303] and *pr-nsr*,  [304] (both from Lower Egypt). The situation of this knowledge has changed in the last few years, not only due to new archaeological discoveries, but also with the re-analysis of the material found in the first excavations. Thus, the appearance of the Coptos *colossi* implied the

[291] Jiménez Serrano (2002a).
[292] (1997: 218-219, 225).
[293] (1991: 37).
[294] Vandier (1952: 555).
[295] (1991: 37).
[296] Baines (1991: 38) suggests that the enclosures might have two different functions in origin: practical (windbreaks or keeping out animals) and symbolic.
[297] Baines (1997: 225).
[298] (1985: 14-16).

[299] According to Baines (1990: 28), the function of these cloths would be the attention that they would receive when being blown by the wind. For a monographic study of the poles, see Baines (1991). For the discussion of the relationship between the pole and the word *nṯr*, see Hornung (1999: 33-35).
[300] (1985:120).
[301] (1991: 38).
[302] R. Friedman (1996: fig. 13). About a discussion of all the aspects of this temple, Weill (1961, 1: 88- 99).
[303] On the Narmer mace-head, for example.
[304] *pr-nw* was the shrine at Dep and *pr-nsr* was the shrine at Pe. Both villages formed a city known later as Buto. For both temples, Weill (1961, 1: 83-88).

existence of permanent monumental structures that housed them,[305] and the recent discoveries of religious structures at Hierakonpolis[306] and Buto[307] have thrown much light on the obscure aspects of the Late Predynastic and Early Dynastic temples.

However, before any deeper analysis, it is necessary to comment on two different theories about the character of Egyptian temples that have appeared recently.[308] Barry Kemp[309] proposes that the royal funerary monuments in the Early Dynastic period and in the Old Kingdom were designed in a "Formal" style (specifically, he calls it "Early Formal"), contemporary provincial temples were designed in a "Preformal" mode, and these were not replaced until the Middle Kingdom. Examples of this "early monumental architecture" are the royal funerary enclosures of Early Dynastic Abydos and the royal pyramid complex in the Old Kingdom.

There are only two examples of Preformal temples: Elephantine and Medamud. They are smaller than Early Dynastic temples from Abydos, and for their construction a minimum of stone elements was used. In addition, they have elements that are "strange" in Egyptian temple architecture. The plan of these temples is more spontaneous, unlike the pre-planned temples of the Formal tradition. This situation continued because the élites "were concentrated on pyramid building and court cemetery construction",[310] in other words, the state was not interested in the elimination of two co-existent cultures during the Old Kingdom.

However, David O'Connor[311] argues that Kemp's theory was presented as an evolutionary process. He denies the existence of two co-existent cultures during the Old Kingdom. According to him, some provincial temples and complexes were, in contemporary terms, as large-scale and formal as in the Early Dynastic period; and they were the result of initiatives of the élites. He considers that there is a high probability that the main early Old Kingdom temples at four sites (Medamud, Elephantine, Hierakonpolis and Abydos) have not yet been located and excavated. O'Connor suggests that Old Kingdom provincial temples were probably relatively large in scale and complex in plan. He relates the enclosure and mound of the Hierakonpolis temple and Abydos (?) to the Abydos royal funerary enclosures and to Netjerikhet's (Third Dynasty) enclosure at Saqqara. The monumental scale was the characteristic of the temples of Hierakonpolis and Abydos (?). The rest of the temples that Kemp analysed (Elephantine and Medamud) are considered as peripheral shrines, without the real importance (in Early Dynastic times) that Kemp has suggested.

Contrary to O'Connor's theory, Roth[312] states that "O'Connor's interpretation does not, however, explain the small shrine at the north east corner of the great court in the Djoser [Netjerikhet] pyramid complex. It is nearly identical to the two Abydos chapels in both plan and orientation, but is unlikely to be a ka-chapel, since it is already located in a mortuary monument". In addition, Seidlmayer[313] finds O'Connor's theory difficult to sustain, since extensive excavation on the island of Elephantine has markedly failed to produce any evidence for another temple of the Early Dynastic period or Old Kingdom besides the local shrine of Satet.

In this book, Kemp's theory is mainly followed, because it is possible to detect peripheral architecture, which contrasts with the royal architecture (mainly represented by the enclosures of the First Dynasty). Both groups are not opposite concepts, but contemporary architecture. Their main difference is the origin. On the one hand, peripheral architecture is the result of different religious evolution, which has its genesis in each god or goddess. On the other hand, the royal architecture is the result of a conceptualisation developed at the same time that the attributions of kingship are becoming more and more complex (see below).

E.4) Some comments about the primitive shrines and enclosures

As has already been established, the unification of Egypt was a long process in which different parts of the Delta came under Upper Egyptian control. The theory supported here is that the unification process caused the assimilation of many Lower Egyptian concepts into Upper Egyptian culture. One of those would be the architecture. It is tempting to see that the construction or improvement of temples was made for a special occasion. In addition, the magnificence of the temple would be restricted by

[305] Williams (1988: 47); Kemp, Boyce & Harrell (2000).
[306] R. Friedman (1996).
[307] Von der Way (1992a: 7).
[308] Kemp (1989); O'Connor (1992).
[309] (1989: 55, 65-83).
[310] Kemp (1989: 83).
[311] (1992: 83).
[312] (1993: 39, n. 19).
[313] (1996: 116-117).

the resources that the king might have at that moment and in that area. Moreover, the "fashion" of building and, above all, the religious concepts must be considered.

The different style of temples might be explained as a heterogeneous process in which, together with the traditional temples built before the end of the unification (Elephantine, for example), with a more spontaneous style of architecture, the monarchy encouraged construction of a particular type of temple all over Egypt. This fact may have religious or political reasons (for example, encouraging national religious integration). The existence of earlier temples was not contradictory to the new architectural policy, because most ancient temples had a strong religious value. Thus, the appearance of the two types of temples in the same monument is very common. The paradigmatic examples with the presence of different types of temples can be found carved on the Narmer mace-head and the wooden labels of Horus Aha from Abydos.

This system can be also shown in another case. In Abydos, the kings had mixed two elements: the traditional primitive burial system with the funerary enclosures, at least from the beginning of the First Dynasty (Djer).

E.5) Monumental enclosures: Abydos (Figures 8 & 15), Saqqara (Figure 10), and Hierakonpolis (Figures 9 & 11)

In this chapter, it is necessary to distinguish between sacred areas in general and royal enclosures (*Talbezirke*). Royal enclosures are understood as those that were built for royal ceremonies and the royal cult. Concerning sacred areas, there are many examples of them as well as temples from the Late Predynastic period.

The origins of the royal enclosures are obscure. According to Patricia Spencer[314] "Since the form of the hieroglyph [𓉗, *ḥwt*] was already well-established by the start of the dynastic period, it would be logical to assume that similar enclosures had existed in the pre-dynastic period".

Later royal enclosures were built at Abydos[315] and Saqqara.[316] Many scholars have interpreted the enclosures located at Abydos differently: as surrounding the Upper Egyptian residence of the king,[317] or as magazines for the temple of Osiris.[318] Here, the royal enclosures will be considered as part of the funerary complex that was formed by the tomb (located at Umm el-Qaab), and the ceremonial area (royal enclosure).[319] Thus, the enclosures were cult-places for the dead kings.[320] At the same time, they could be used for the celebration of the *sed* festivals, like Netjerikhet's complex.

With the discovery of the royal tombs at Abydos, there is much epigraphic evidence, which indicates that there were many religious foundations (temples) in Early Dynastic Egypt.[321] The names of those buildings were inside the hieroglyph 𓉗 *ḥwt*, which was sometimes depicted as a single rectangle.[322] In the 1920s, Petrie excavated a group of graves, which he called "Tombs of the Courtiers". [323] These consist of three groups of small brick-lined graves, for the most part constructed in continuous trenches, and so arranged as to enclose large rectangular areas. From the contents of these graves, two of the groups were assigned to the reigns of Djer, Djet and Mer-neith (Figure 8, right). Concerning their function there were many hypotheses[324]. Kemp[325] pointed out that Peet[326] excavated some parts of that area before and he discovered the remains of mud brick (Mer-neith's enclosure), which were destroyed by time. Ten years later, Petrie re-excavated this area. According to Kemp[327], the tombs that encircle a rectangular area were really surrounding panelled brick enclosures of the reign of Djer and Djet. The explanation that he offers for the lack of mud bricks in these enclosures is an intense denudation accelerated by deliberate destruction. Kemp[328] also relates the enclosures of the Second Dynasty (also called forts) to the so-called "Western Mastaba."

Concerning the "forts" or royal enclosures, Kemp[329] says that their fortress-like character is striking and, in the funerary context provided by the subsidiary burials, leads him to suggest that they served as dwelling-places for the kings' spirits.

314 (1984: 23).
315 Close to the later temple of Osiris, see Trigger *et alii* (1983: fig. 1.6).
316 Beside the Step pyramid, see Baines & Málek (1980: 144).
317 Emery (1939: 116).
318 Lauer (1969: 83).
319 Kemp (1966; 1967).
320 P. Spencer (1984: 22).
321 In general, Kaplony (1963; 1964).
322 P. Spencer (1984: 24).
323 (1925).
324 See Kemp (1966: 13-14), with references.
325 (1966: 14-15).
326 (1914: 30-34).
327 (1966: 15).
328 (1966: 16).
329 (1966: 16).

Fig. 8: The sites of Abydos with two more detailed enclosures (right).

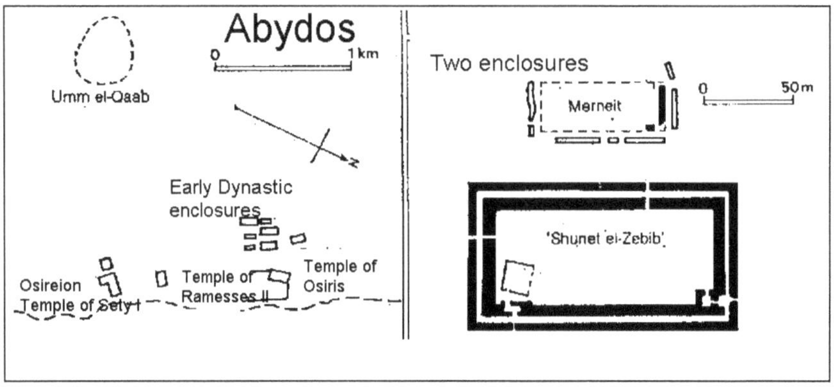

Kemp[330] suggested a hypothesis about the appearance of these enclosures and the construction of the tombs. He believed that it was very strange that, until the reign of Djer, all the royal tombs have two or more separate chambers, whereas, after this king the plan of the tombs was articulated in a central chamber with subsidiary ones. Coincidentally, in Djer's reign the first enclosures ("Tombs of the Courtiers") appear on the plateau.

Although archaeology could not find any trace of Qaa's enclosure, epigraphy has attested its existence: *sm nbtj qˁ ḥwt* "The *sem*-priest of the temple of the King of Upper and Lower Egypt, Qa'a".[331]

By the end of the First Dynasty the expression *ḥwt-k3* had also come into use as a term for the funerary temple. The earliest example that has been found is dated in the reign of Hotepsekhemui, first king of the Second Dynasty.[332]

In the late 19th century, De Morgan drew the outlines of a great rectangle placed to the west of the Netjerikhet pyramid complex. Aerial pictures taken almost thirty years later confirmed these outlines. In these pictures, two rectangles appeared, one known today as Gisr el-Mudir and another near the tomb of Ptahhotep.

Swelim[333] was the first who suggested that those enclosures could be earlier than Netjerikhet. Stadelmann[334] argued that these enclosures could have the same purpose as those from Abydos, but only for some kings of the Second Dynasty: Hotepsekhemui, Ninetjer and Khasekhemui. At the same time, Kaiser[335] attributed them to the Third Dynasty, and, later, O'Connor[336] dated them to the Second Dynasty.

In 1947, Abd el-Salam Hussein excavated the one known thereafter as Gisr el-Mudir, but the conclusions of this excavation are only known from the comments made by Swelim.[337] According to him, the pottery belongs to the Third Dynasty.

In the last few years, geo-electrical surveys[338] and sondages[339] have been carried out, and have revealed the existence of fragmentary stones. This enclosure is probably unfinished.[340]

Surely related to the Gisr el-Mudir,[341] but on a smaller scale, is the so-called "Fort of Hierakonpolis", which was built by Khasekhemui. According to Alexanian,[342] this building had two special functions, the celebration and

---

330 (1966: 21-22).
331 P. Spencer (1984: 23).
332 P. Spencer (1984: 23).
333 (1983: 29, 33-35, 224); (1991).
334 (1985: 306).
335 (1985: 54).
336 (1989: 83).
337 (1983: 33).
338 Mathieson & Tavares (1993: 29-30).
339 Mathieson *et alii* (1997: 53).
340 David Jeffreys (personal communication).
341 Pottery beer-jars found in the fill of the south-west corner of the enclosure have been provisionally dated to the end of the Second Dynasty or beginning of the Third Dynasty, Bettles *et alii* (1995: 3-4).
342 (1998).

commemoration of the royal cult. Swelim[343] related this enclosure to the Shunet el-Zebib:

- Both enclosures are located to the west of the temple of the city (Khentamentiu at Abydos and Horus at Hierakonpolis).

- Their structural details are very similar: both buildings are double-walled and the entrance has the same orientation.

"Peribsen Fort" (also called "Middle Fort") was investigated by Ayrton and his colleagues.[344] In this enclosure, they found seals with the name of Peribsen and one with the name of Khasekhemui, and dated the building to Peribsen's reign. Khasekhemui's name was discovered there because this king celebrated Peribsen's funerary ceremonies.

In the enclosures of Peribsen and Khasekhemui, the same plan and style of ornamentation was followed: even in the details of the south-east corner of each fort, where an entrance led into a small court and thence to the interior. As in Khasekhemui's fort, inside there would be magazines with a special purpose[345] and buildings of a religious or symbolic nature[346].

Garstang[347] and Lansing[348] excavated the so-called "fort" of Hierakonpolis. In recent years, Renée Friedman[349] has resumed the excavations in this fort. Thanks to all these investigations (but mainly to recent analysis) it is well known that this fort was built with mud-bricks, had niches and was plastered in white. Its interior had "a sumptuous edifice at least 15 meters long and 10 meters wide, entered though a richly ornate doorway and featuring at least two columns supported by granite column bases".[350] According to R. Friedman,[351] this building was a palace that could be built (together with the enclosure) for the commemoration of the king's *sed* festival or perhaps even the reunification, when Khasekhem changed his name to Khasekhemuy.

Fig. 9: Plan of Khasekhemui's enclosure at Hierakonpolis with earlier tombs.

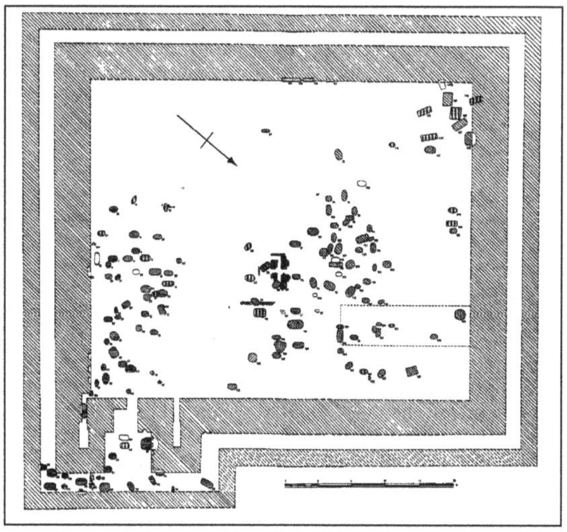

E.6) The city temple at Hierakonpolis (Nekhen) (Figure 11)

The city area was excavated by Quibell and Green,[352] and by Garstang;[353] due to inadequate investigation (Quibell and Green only published a catalogue with a brief summary),[354] the available information about many factors has been lost. Fairservis[355] dated the occupation of the city area to Naqada II period, related to the sites at the nearby wadi.[356] The form of the Early Dynastic temple (or temples) has not survived, because it was replaced in the Middle Kingdom (?) by a mud brick building which covered the earlier temple mound. The earliest temple (or series of temples) was "probably constructed of mud brick and must have been quite small", while the mound supporting it gives the temple "a character alien to our expectations of Egyptian temple architecture."[357]

343 (1983: 31).
344 (1904: 4).
345 Kaplony (1963, I: 166).
346 Kemp (1966: 16) adds "prototypes of those which occur inside the Step Pyramid enclosure".
347 Adams (1987).
348 (1935).
349 (1999).
350 R. Friedman (1999: 11).
351 (1999: 11).

352 (1900; 1902).
353 (1907).
354 (1900; 1902). After the publication of photographs and drawings of the important ceremonial artefacts, which Quibell had found in the temple, Green tried to reconstruct the original stratigraphy.
355 (1983a: 10).
356 Hoffman *et alii* (1986).
357 Kemp (1989: 77).

Fig. 10: Saqqara. (1) Tombs of Early Dynastic period. (2) Small tombs of the First Dynasty. (3) Royal Tombs of the Second Dynasty. (4) Netjerikhet's step pyramid. (5) Sekhemkhet's step pyramid. (6) Gisr el-Mudir. (7) Second enclosure near the tomb of Ptahhotep.

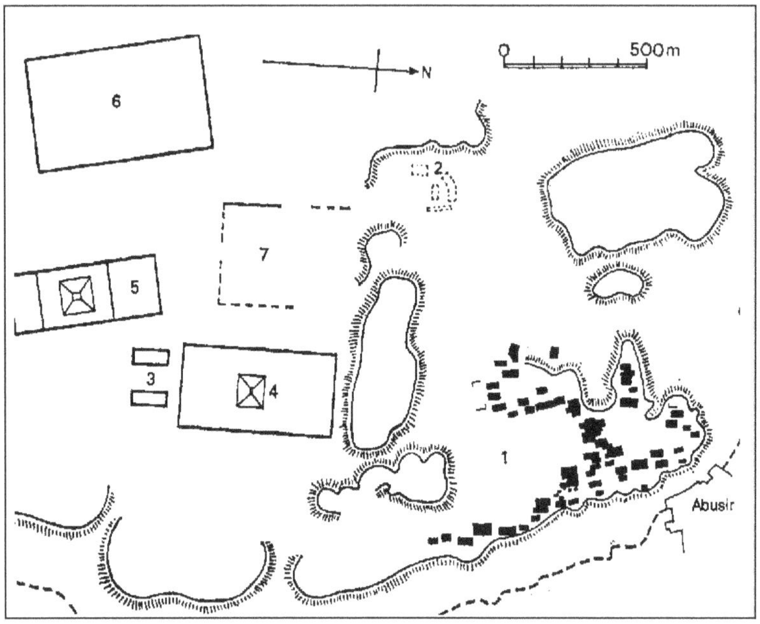

The interior of the temple is practically impossible to reconstruct.[358] Scholars only have the information provided by Quibell and Green.[359] They found an extant stone structure, which was circular. This structure could be seen in the centre of the temple plan as an incomplete oval. The circular revetment was composed of rough blocks of sandstone laid in horizontal courses, and battered at an angle of 45°, and it enclosed a filling of desert sand. Beside it was found a number of other features, including a number of possible limestone pillars (the largest fragment was 40 cm wide and had been broken off at a height of 1.25 m). This structure has been dated to the Early Dynastic Period[360] and symbolised the primeval mound,[361] upon which the falcon Horus had first alighted, and served as the foundation for a temple. The Main Deposit was a mass of objects that were found near the stele of Pepi II (Sixth Dynasty). The character of these objects was votive and they consisted of stone mace-heads, stone vessels, stones, pottery and faience figures of men and animals (baboon, bull's heads, falcons and scorpions), faience models of vessels on stands and shrines, faience beads, glazed quartz plaques, animal jawbones, full size and model pots, gold foil and crumpled copper plates, a limestone and breccia model bed, fine flint knives (some of which are very large), three ceremonial, decorated pear-shaped mace-heads of an unknown king, Scorpion II and Narmer, the decorated "two dogs palette", a mass of ivory figures, cylinders, decorated fragments and wands (two of them with the inscriptions of Narmer and Den), and a statuette of Khasekhemui. Two life-size statues of limestone were found 2 meters apart near the Main Deposit. Each of them portray a semi-kneeling man with a short, square-bottomed wig and false beard wearing a belt with a tassel in front. The meaning of them seems clear: the supreme power of the divinity (embodied in the king) over the foreign peoples. Behind these statues to the south-east, Quibell found a diorite door socket with a human face projecting from its front with a limestone doorjamb still standing on it. Just behind there was a group of small objects: a limestone ape, a fragment of faience, a coarse-ware vase containing spiral faience beads, a disc-shaped bead of obsidian, etc.[362]

At the end of the 1960s, a niched mud-brick wall with a gateway was discovered 40 m to the south of the mound in the Early Dynastic

[358] Some attempts in Dreyer (1986); Williams (1988); Adams (1999).

[359] (1900, 1902). The important works of Adams (1974a/b; 1995; 1999) are fundamental for the comprehension of the remains.

[360] Hoffman (1976: 36; 1979: 131).

[361] Many authors, for example, Wilkinson (1999: 309).

[362] Adams (1995: 56-62). Similar objects have been found at Elephantine in the same disposition, Dreyer (1986).

enclosure. It was dated to the beginning of the First Dynasty "only a generation or two after the construction of the Protodynastic temple precinct and not more than a century after the close of the prehistoric epoch."[363]

O'Connor[364] has reinterpreted the early monumental architecture at Nekhen, dating the large rectangular enclosure in the town to the First Dynasty by its similarities with the funerary enclosures at Abydos. He believes that the circular revetment supporting the temple mound pre-dates the enclosure wall by a considerable period of time. O'Connor[365] interprets the enclosure as a royal cult complex and the Early Dynastic palace gateway (discovered by Fairservis in Hierakonpolis[366]) as the entrance to a second (hypothetical), adjacent enclosure, which had its own mound, evidenced by traces of sand found during the course of excavations.

From O'Connor's interpretation, Barbara Adams[367] has compared the distribution of some objects and elements of the structure of the temple, as they were found by Quibell and Green, with the Step Pyramid enclosure. According to her, "early stone walls, pavements, pillars, and Main Deposit and statuary groups east and west of the central revetment are part of an early temple complex at Nekhen". In other words, the disposition of many elements in the temple of Hierakonpolis is coincident with the structure of the *wsḫt* court and the early mastaba in Netjerikhet's complex. Adams also attempted this comparison with Locality HK29A, but as she confirmed "much of this analogy is fanciful, but the comparisons are worth noting from the point of view of the longevity of architectural styles in religious and funerary architecture."[368]

It would be possible to reconstruct the city temple of Hierakonpolis from the images in some monuments from the reigns of Narmer and Aha. As recent investigations have shown, the temple in Locality HK26A was used at the beginning of the First Dynasty (Friedman suggested Aha/Djer, see above), thus it might affirm (for other reasons see the chapter in which Narmer's monument is discussed) that the depictions of a similar temple that only appear on Narmer's (mace-head) and Aha's (label) monuments represent the city temple of Hierakonpolis.

The temple can be divided into two areas: the enclosure and the shrine. On the Narmer mace-head, some objects appear in the enclosure: a pot(?) over a triangle and a post. The type of the shrine is characteristic of that of Lower Egypt. This is not a contradiction because the interchange of concepts in Egypt is attested in the Late Predynastic period.[369] Moreover, the construction of the temple could have taken place during the reign of Narmer or shortly before. If this interpretation is right and the building that appears depicted in the Hunter's palette[370] represented the temple of Hierakonpolis, the main door of the shrine would be on the right. Over the façade of the shrine there is a bird, which was interpreted by Weill[371] as *bꜥḥ*, but it would be preferable to see a jabiru *bꜣ*, "soul".[372]

E.7) The *pr-nw* in Buto

The *pr-nw* (in Buto) was simpler than the *pr-wr.*[373] The temple depicted on the Narmer mace-head is the *pr-nw* type, a low structure with a curved roof.

In recent years, a German expedition has found two buildings in two different layers in Buto. The more ancient (Layer IV), dating from the end of Dynasty 0 to the beginning of the First Dynasty (Narmer and Horus Aha), is a rectangular building. It shows in the interior two icons of bulls, impressed [by finger] in the wet clay.[374] After a disruption with vast pits filled with pottery shards, appears layer V (Second/early Third Dynasty), in which there was a rather large building with many small rooms or corridors. The building had a roof of wood, which was destroyed

---

363 Hoffman (1976: 37, 39, fig. 4).
364 (1992).
365 (1992: 87).
366 Although Weeks (1971-1972) interpreted it as a palace.
367 (1999).
368 Adams (1999: 27).

369 Jiménez Serrano (2002a).
370 For a new drawing, see Baines (1995: fig. 3.5).
371 (1961, 2: 4-5).
372 The representation of this animal is very common not only in the Predynastic objects but in those discovered at Hierakonpolis; for example, Quibell (1900: pls. XII, no. 1, XIII, XIV, XV, especially 15, etc.).
A deeper study of the representation of this bird in Jiménez Serrano (2002b).
373 Vandier (1952: 559).
374 Compare to the following fragment -1266 (utt. 534)- in the Pyramid Texts, which may make reference to this stage of the building: "... The hall of this is purer than the firmament, the door which is on it is two opposing bulls (?), and its lock is two evil eyes", Faulkner (1969: 201).

by fire. For many reasons, von der Way[375] maintains that these buildings could be "in connection with a cult or with a certain consecrated character of the king".

The connection between this building (and the bulls) and the *pr nw* has not been proved. However, it is possible to relate the depiction of the bulls to another temple that was situated at Buto, in which a bull was worshipped, *pr ḏbʿwt*[376] (see also, pp. 53-57).

****

It would be possible to continue describing more Early Dynastic temples and shrines discovered in Egypt (such as Elephantine),[377] but they are closer to the cult of local gods than to the royal cycle. In other words, there is no evidence of royal ceremonies in those temples or shrines.

---

375 (1992a: 7).
376 Montet (1957, 1: 92).
377 As introduction, see Kemp (1989: 65-74), with references.

Fig. 11: The city temple of (Hierakonpolis) Nekhen.

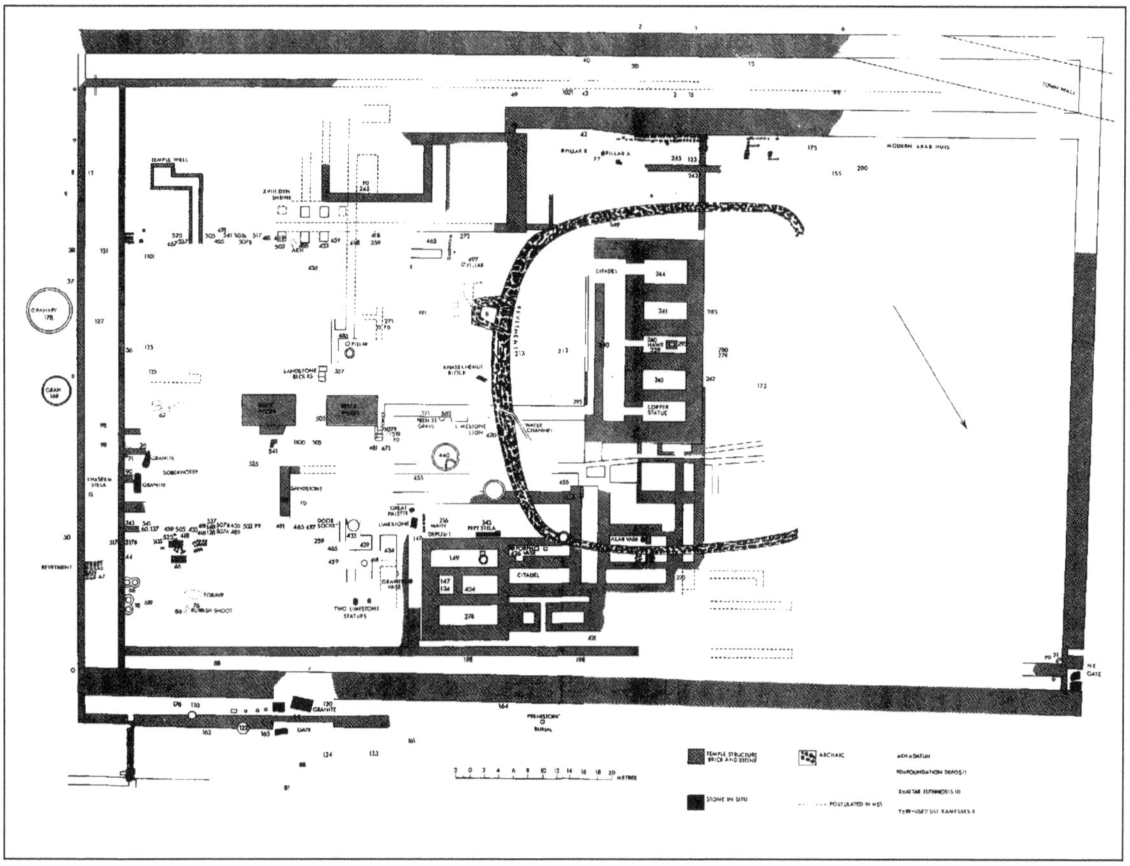

CHAPTER THREE ROYAL FESTIVALS IN THE LATE PREDYNASTIC PERIOD AND THE FIRST DYNASTY

A) THE ENTHRONEMENT AND THE CEREMONY OF THE "APPEARANCE OF THE KING"

In the enthronement, the king acquires two dimensions of his future power: cosmic and political.[378] Although the king is predestined to the throne before his birth, he acquires the divine aspect through the ceremonies of the enthronement. In these ceremonies, the king assumes the role of Creator and assures the power of action of the gods.[379]

In Ancient Egypt, the death of a king was a time of great cosmic danger, because the forces of chaos could seize the opportunity to establish the opposite of *maat* in the whole country. Those forces of chaos could be seen in many ways: plagues, disastrous floods, administrative corruption, etc.[380] That situation was mostly avoided in the Middle and New Kingdoms with co-regencies at the end of a king's reign, but co-regencies were much the exception. However, there is no data which confirms the existence of co-regencies in the Late Predynastic and Early Dynastic Periods, or even in the Old Kingdom. If the co-regency was not used during those centuries, it is easy to imagine that usurpation and intrigues might be very common. Due to this apparent danger, the enthronement of a new king was an occasion of celebration in the whole country, because with this ceremony that menace disappeared.

There are no contemporary monuments that show the rituals performed in the enthronement ceremony. From some sources, it is possible to trace some ceremonies with every new reign. In the Palermo Stone, every first year of a new reign begins with the ceremony of "Uniting Upper and Lower Egypt" (*zmꜣ tꜣwj*) and "the circuit of the wall" (*pẖr ḥꜣ jnb*).[381] However, here it is assumed that the unification of the Two Lands was a concept created later (mid-First Dynasty). Moreover, in recent years, all scholars have denied the theory of the unification as a result of a single event (see pp. 6-ff). Late Predynastic Egyptians could not celebrate a ceremony that had no sense until the unification of the whole country. Thus, the original significance of the ceremony of "Uniting Upper and Lower Egypt" must be different.

Fig. 12: Ceremonies of "Uniting Upper and Lower Egypt" and "Circuit of the Wall" recorded in the Palermo Stone. Not to scale.

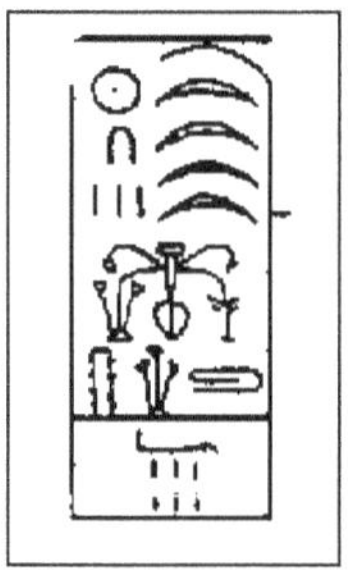

In the Old Kingdom, most of the concepts of kingship were established, but it is known that they derived from ideological constructs made during the Early Dynastic period and the Third Dynasty.[382] It was a long process in which many concepts were associated for political and ideological reasons. In Ancient Egypt, with the exception of the ogdoads, most of those concepts had a dual aspect,[383] whose genesis is heterogeneous. Here, some of them are mentioned:

- Political: the two crowns, the *nzwt-bjtj*.
- Religious: Horus and Seth (*nbwy*), *nbtj*, order and chaos.
- Natural: floods and low waters, day and night, valley and desert, man and woman, etc.

[378] Cervelló Autuori (1996: 166).
[379] Hornung (1999: 130-131).
[380] A good example of this situation was reflected in the Lamentations of Ipu-wer, dated in the First (or Second) Intermediate Period. See for example, E. Bresciani (1969: 102-117).

[381] See Schäfter (1902: 15 2-3, 28 5-3).
[382] Except solar cult association (?). Contra, see Cervelló Autuori (1996).
[383] Dualism is a concept developed by many societies. As an introduction, see Hocart (1970: 162-179, 262-290). According to Hornung (1999: 221), the order established by the Creator is characterised by the duality, which both together are the totality.

As archaeology has shown, two late predynastic political entities (circumscribed only in the two geographical regions of Egypt –i.e. Upper Egypt and the Delta-) never existed, just one Upper Egyptian proto-kingdom.[384] The Upper Egyptian kingdom founded sites in the Eastern Delta in the late Naqada II period, while in the Western Delta there was an indigenous material (and political?) culture. Epigraphy has shown that the administrative division of Upper and Lower Egypt occurred shortly before the First Dynasty[385] (see figure 13).

Fig. 13: Ink inscriptions on pottery vessels found in the tomb of Horus Ka at Abydos. The inscriptions record the provenence of goods from Upper Egypt (above) and Lower Egypt (below). Not to scale.

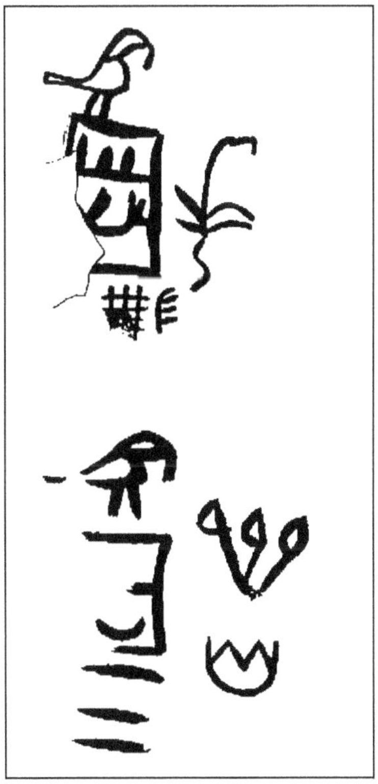

Thus, although the dualistic perception of many aspects of the world is an unquestionable fact in Late Predynastic and Early Dynastic Egypt, the concept of a dual country was developed little by little and, surely, as a political consequence in the first half of the First Dynasty.[386] From that moment until the end of the Second Dynasty, many symbols, which have religious and political meanings, were re-defined: the Red Crown, whose origin seems to be in the Naqada region,[387] became the Lower Egyptian emblem. The *zwt* plant, which symbolised the Predynastic Upper Egyptian kingdom with all its colonies in the Eastern Delta, became the Upper Egyptian emblem and the phonogram of king. The *bjtj*, symbol of the proto-kingdom of Sais (?), became the Lower Egyptian emblem. Horus, who was the god of Hierakonpolis (and other Egyptian cities), became the national god of Lower Egypt,[388] while Seth, the god of Ombos/Naqada, was converted into the Upper Egyptian god *par excellence* in that age.[389] It does not seem strange that those changes affected religion, because it was intimately connected with the monarchy.

At least from the beginning of the First Dynasty and until the end of the Second, there was a redefinition of many of the elements, which symbolised the Egyptian monarchy. This redefinition was a consequence of the administrative reorganisation of the new State, but it was also due to political situations (in some cases internal conflicts), which even influenced the religion. The (creative) method was very simple: elements or gods (i.e. Wadjet from Buto and Nekhbet from el-Kab) from an important city of a geographical - *versus* political - region lost their local[390] meaning and proceeded to have a regional meaning.[391]

Surely, one of the first concepts created was the ceremony of "Uniting Upper and Lower Egypt". But, before the creation of this concept, it is necessary to seek the real meaning of this

[384] Recently, Wilkinson (2000a: 390-392 & fig. 4) has pointed out five: Buto, Helwan, Tarkhan, Abydos, and Hierakonpolis.

[385] In Abydos, Petrie found many pot-marks of Horus Ka, which showed the origin of the offerings. They can be summarised in two groups: Lower Egypt –Petrie (1902: pl. III) - and Upper Egypt –Petrie (1902: pls. I-II).

About the dual administration, see Wilkinson (1999: 192-194 & Figure 6.2), with references.

[386] Jiménez Serrano (in press).

[387] Midant-Reynes (1992: 174-175, fig. 8a-b), with reference.

[388] Cervelló Autuori (1996: 219-220).

[389] Cervelló Autuori (1996: 203).

[390] Here we understand as "local", the towns and their close and/or dependent areas, but smaller than later nomes. The term "regional" is used here as a group of later nomes that share geographic and cultural features (i. e. Kemp's Upper Egyptian proto-state). The term "national" refers to Egypt: the Nile Valley and the Delta (from Elephantine to the Mediterranean Sea).

[391] Jiménez Serrano (in press).

ceremony in the earliest times. It is well known that the Upper Egyptian kingdom established settlements in the Delta, which means that there was an Upper Egyptian occupation of the eastern part of the Delta. At that time, it seems certain that those settlements were dependent on the Upper Egyptian kingdom. However, the status of the cities of the western part of the Delta is still unknown. Although the native material culture in Buto changes into the Upper Egyptian material culture at the end of Naqada II, this is not a definitive argument for considering this city as a part of the Upper Egyptian kingdom. The existence of many royal representations earlier than the First Dynasty in Lower Egypt and in the northern part of Upper Egypt that are completely different to their contemporary Upper Egyptian representations could be the key for the resolution of this problem. These *serekhs* and palace-façades show that some areas in the Delta could have been ruled by different leaders.[392]

In addition, Hans Goedicke[393] has argued "For the "Union of the Two Lands" this implies the equal status of both parts of Egypt in the venture, ruling out the possibility of domination of one over the other. Translated into political terms it results that an event denoted as *zmꜣ-tꜣwj* can only indicate by the union of two equal partners in a union".

To summarise, in the Naqada III period the Delta was divided into at least two areas. In the east of the Delta, numerous Upper Egyptian settlements have been detected and studied.[394] In contrast, the west of the Delta and perhaps some zones surrounding the Fayum Lake were under the control of other political entities.[395] At the moment when Egypt was unified under one single ruler, the territory was divided into two different regions, depending on their geographical features. Thus, it is possible to consider that at the beginning, in the ceremony of "Uniting the Upper and Lower Egypt" the king took possession of both administrative entities.[396]

Much later, the concept of Menes as king was created, he who unified Upper and Lower Egypt and founded Memphis.[397]

The ceremony of the "Circuit of the Wall" was related to the symbolic taking possession of the land.[398] As will be dealt with below, this ritual was very common in many festivals and the meaning was the same in all of them. After the foundation of Memphis, this concept was assimilated into the king's domination over the Two Lands, because the new city was situated at the junction of the Valley and the Delta. The king ran the perimeter of the royal capital, which symbolised the whole country. It is impossible to confirm if the allusions on the Palermo Stone referred to Memphis (*Jnbw ḥḏ*, "The White Walls") or another place. The earliest mention of this ceremony in the Palermo Stone is usually dated in the reign of Djer.[399]

The "Appearance of the King"[400] is an obscure ceremony that could be celebrated not only at the time of the enthronement, but also repeated during the reign. This ritual could be celebrated in three different ways: the appearance of the king as *nzwt* (king of Upper Egypt), as *bjt* (king of Lower Egypt) or as *nzwt-bjtj* (king of Upper and Lower Egypt). Again, the latter is attested in mid First Dynasty (surely Den), confirming the development of the "new duality concept".

---

392 Jiménez Serrano (2000a: 153-159); also *íd.* (2001a; 2002a).

393 (1985: 308).

394 Van den Brink (ed.) (1988; 1992).

395 Dreyer (1992b: 260) has suggested that Horus Crocodile was king of the Fayum area.

396 Jiménez Serrano (in press).

According to Goedicke (1985: 322) the unification of Egypt was based on negotiation rather than actions of force. The combining of Upper and Lower Egypt should not be envisaged as a military triumph of the south over the north.

397 This follows the argument of Allen (1992: 20-22), who holds that Menes derives from the name of Memphis. According to him, Memphis derived from the name of the city area, which was situated beside the pyramid of king Pepi, which was called *mry-rꜥ* (Pepi) *mn-nfr*. As the language has a tendency to shorten names, Memphis was called Mennefer, and from it, his founder had to be named Men/Menes. Anyway, Allen's is one among many interpretations of the name and position of Menes.

398 For a discussion of other meanings, see Goedicke (1985: 317 & n. 50), also with references.

The king could take possession of Egypt symbolically or in reality (travelling to the main regions and temples of Egypt), Cervelló Autuori (1996: 171).

399 For example, Helck (1987: 150-151).

400 Millet (1990) interpreted the Narmer mace-head as the depiction of the ceremony of the "Appearance of the king of Lower Egypt". Against this interpretation, see the chapter on the *sed* festival.

Fig. 14: The ceremonies of the "Appearance of the king of Upper Egypt and appearance of the king of Lower Egypt" and the *sed* festival recorded on the Palermo Stone (certainly in the reign of Den). Not to scale.

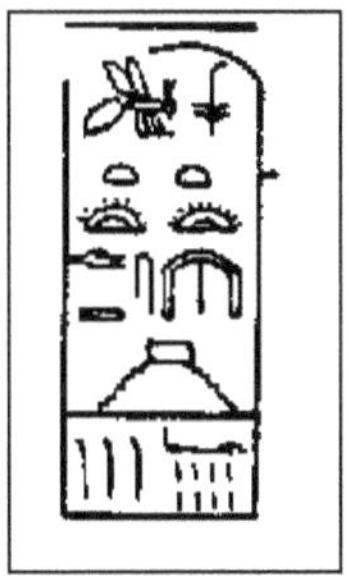

- **Conclusion**

In Ancient Egypt, the ceremonies of the enthronement were full of symbols and political tradition. The first two ceremonies, the enthronement with the white and the red crowns, might well have appeared during the formation of the Upper Egyptian proto-kingdom. At that moment, the king of the Upper Egyptian proto-kingdom was the king of Naqada on being crowned with the red crown, and king of Hierakonpolis on being crowned with the white crown. At the beginning of the First Dynasty, it was necessary to create another ceremony that justified the unique power over the whole country (Lower and Upper Egypt). The symbology was addressed to this main target: taking possession of the Land(s) of Egypt. On the one hand, the king united symbolically the Two Lands (receiving homage from both countries) and, on the other, he ran over the whole land of Egypt (again symbolically around the walls of Memphis). It might be suggested that the first ceremony ("Uniting Upper and Lower Egypt") had some economic and power features, whereas the second one ("Circuit of the Wall") was more related to the symbol and definition of the sacred space, in which *maat* had to rule.

Through the enthronement, the king achieves divine aspects. The king is not a god, but a testimony of the power of the Creator.

It can only be surmised that the ceremonies of the "Appearance of the King" are related to a sort of royal cycle of revitalisation, in other words, a "petit" *sed* festival.[401]

[401] In this regard, see Bleeker (1967: 112).

B) *SED* FESTIVAL

B. 1) Definition and genesis

The *sed* (or Jubilee) festival was regarded as one of the most important events of the king's reign. Although there are many mentions of this festival throughout Egyptian history, it is impossible to reconstruct all the ceremonies and rituals as well as the meaning of certain parts, for most of them the meaning remains obscure for scholars.

Many authors[402] have related this festival to African rituals or myths of regeneration. It is probable that this festival has also to be related to a god called Sed,[403] who was a jackal-god. This god accompanied and preceded the king from the First Dynasty or even earlier. In the Third Dynasty, Sed gained the epithet Wepwawet "Opener of the Ways",[404] because he opened the way in procession for the king together with other gods (Horus, Seth and the royal placenta).[405] As Florence D. Friedman[406] has held, "Pyramid Texts make clear that Wepwawet is not only a form of the living king but specifically a manifestation of the king on the day he ascends to the throne".

The festival could be celebrated several times during the reign. In most cases, the first time coincided with the 30th year of the reign; after this, it could be celebrated every three years. But many kings celebrated this festival before their 30th regnal year, and many of them lived during the Old Kingdom and even earlier.[407] This means that, in origin, these festivals had no fixed year of celebration in the reign.

In some reigns of the First Dynasty, the *sed* festival was celebrated more than once. "The first time" was in Early Egyptian *zp tpj*, although the decisive indication in relation to sed festivals is the occurrence of zp 2, because that suggests that the festival was really celebrated more than once. In this regard Murnane[408] has noted that the Jubilee formula *zp tpj* (or 2) *sd* "First (or second) occasion of the Jubilee" initially described the occasion of an actual *sed* festival. The formula retained this significance in the Old Kingdom (and by extension, in the Early Dynastic period too) and later indicated that the king had already celebrated a Jubilee. *zp tpj* refers also to creation (see p. 27) and evoked the magic that radiates from every beginning. This designation was perceived not as a single event, but instead as something that entailed constant repetition.[409] Thus, this formula used in those terms had the explicit meaning of a continuing principle. This idea is part of *maat*.

The origin of the *sed* festival lies surely in prehistoric times, but the first time that it is attested in Egypt is (at least) in the reign of Narmer. For this ceremony, the king dressed in a special tunic; for this reason, Bleeker[410] suggested that the denomination of this festival, *sd*, was related to this tunic, which in ancient Egyptian was also *sd* "cloth"; because this festival was the re-investiture of the king. On the basis of this argument, it is possible to suggest a link between this tunic and the one used at births to swaddle babies. The *sed* festival would be a game of words, in which the god Sed, the god connected with death (which could be seen as a re-birth), was

---

402 For a deeper discussion, see Cervelló Autuori (1996: 208-216) who also mentions many interpretations. For the regicide see also *idem* (1996: 152-161), with a deep discussion and references.

403 Quirke (1992: 90) is one of the scholars who relates the word *sed* with the meaning of "tail", and expresses his doubts about its real origin in this context, which could be "the bull's tail shown at the back of the royal kilt to denote his creative force in potency". However, Gohary (1992: 2-3) has argued that is a misinterpretation of the determinative. According to her, *sed* in some way referred to a period of time such as a generation or a man's expected life-span.

In general, for a presentation of all the theories, see Gohary (1992: 2), with references.

404 F. D. Friedman (1995: 5).

405 For a deep study of standards, see Cervelló Autuori (1997). About the standard interpreted as a placenta, see also Posener (1965).

406 (1995: 36).

407 Fairman (1958: 83-84); Gohary (1992: 3-4). Edwards (1971: 27), referring to the references of the *sed* festival during the reign of Den, affirmed that the festival occurred early in the second half of a reign, which may have exceeded fifty-five years. Godron (1990: 183-184) suggested the possibility that those ceremonies were celebrated every ten years and during the inundation. But, the closest example to the Late Predynastic and Early Dynastic kings is Netjerikhet, who celebrated his *sed* festival, and his reign was no longer than 20 years, F. D. Friedman (1995: 8).

408 (1981: 375). Against Hornung & Staehelin (1974), who considered that this formula expressed the hope of celebrating one or more such festivals.

409 Hornung (1992: 39).

410 (1967: 120).

(deliberately?) mistaken in his use of the word "tunic", which has at least the same transliteration.[411]

The *sed* festival was an occasion for renewal of kingly potency and the reaffirmation of the divine descent of the king and thus the confirmation of his right to the throne.[412] It has also been suggested that the *sed* festival was a ceremony which avoided the murder of the king before he began to grow old and lose his cosmic powers.[413]

B.2) Preliminary phases and localization of the *sed* festival

Before the celebration of the *sed* Festival, there was a proclamation of the feast (*sr ḥb-sd*) by a high official in various major centres throughout Egypt. This would give time for the accumulation of gifts.[414] Then, many statues of the main gods were taken to the place in which the festival was going to be celebrated.[415] The festival began, after long preparations, on the first day of the inundation season,[416] a fact that for Pérez Largacha[417] has great relevance because, according to him, the king tried to show his power over the natural forces.

Concerning the location where the *sed* festivals were celebrated, Gohary[418] has summarised the main suggestions made by scholars. In Gardiner's opinion,[419] the *sed* festivals were normally celebrated at Memphis, on the basis that certain "jubilee mansions" (*ḥwt ḥb-sd*) were situated there. However, Gohary[420] prefers to locate the celebrations of the *sed* festival at Memphis only in the Old Kingdom, when the capital was situated there. According to her, in the Middle Kingdom the *sed* festivals would have taken place at Itj-tawy or (even) Heliopolis. In the New Kingdom, the place where these festivals would be celebrated was at Karnak, Thebes, and, under Ramesses II, Per-Ramesse. Later, it was at Bubastis, in the Twenty-second Dynasty, and Memphis (and Alexandria?), in the Ptolemaic period.[421] As a conclusion about the location where the *sed* festivals were celebrated, it is possible to argue that they took place in the current capitals or in cities with a special religious meaning. In Late Predynastic and Early Dynastic periods, there are four cities that could have witnessed those festivals: Hierakonpolis, Abydos, Memphis and Buto.

B. 3) Localization of the *sed* festivals in the Late Predynastic and Early Dynastic periods

It seems likely that Netjerikhet (first king of the Third Dynasty) celebrated his *sed* festival in the Step Pyramid complex at Saqqara[422] (Figure 16). Due to the similar shape of this complex and the necessity of a large space, it might be suggested that the funerary enclosures found at Abydos and Saqqara (Figures 8 and 10) were used for this purpose in the First and Second Dynasty. But, there are other similar enclosures that could have been used at least at the beginning of the First Dynasty and at the end of the Second Dynasty at Hierakonpolis (see below) (Figures 9 and 11).

---

411 For the *sed* festival, *Wb.* IV, 364; for "cloth", *Wb.* IV, 365.
412 For example, see Gohary (1992: 1).
413 For example, Barta (1975: 62-70), with earlier references; *contra*, Griffiths (1980: 170). Perhaps, connected with this concept is the annual enthronement of a falcon at Edfu mentioned by Fairman (1958: 80), which, according to him, represented the king (and Horus).
414 Gohary (1992: 4).
415 Sauneron (1962: 48).
416 All festivals in Ancient Egypt began by coinciding with a natural phenomenon, which could be the inundation, solstice or lunar phase. For an example, see the calendar of the festivals at Esna, Sauneron (1962: 5-8).

According to Fairman (1958: 78), the enthronement (and the festival *sed*) could be celebrated at the beginning of one of the three seasons. The most favoured date was the first day of the first month of the winter (the fifth month of the Egyptian year).
417 (1993a: 123).
418 (1992: 5).
419 (1944: 27 & n. 2).
420 (1992: 5).
421 For all the evidence that exists of *sed* festivals in Ancient Egypt, see Gohary (1992: 6-9), with references.
422 For example, see F. D. Friedman (1995).

Fig. 15: Structural comparision between different enclosures: (1) Abydos enclosure of Djer; (2) The Hierakonpolis temple enclosure; (3) Abydos enclosure of Khasekhemuy; (4) The first phase of the Netjerikhet complex.

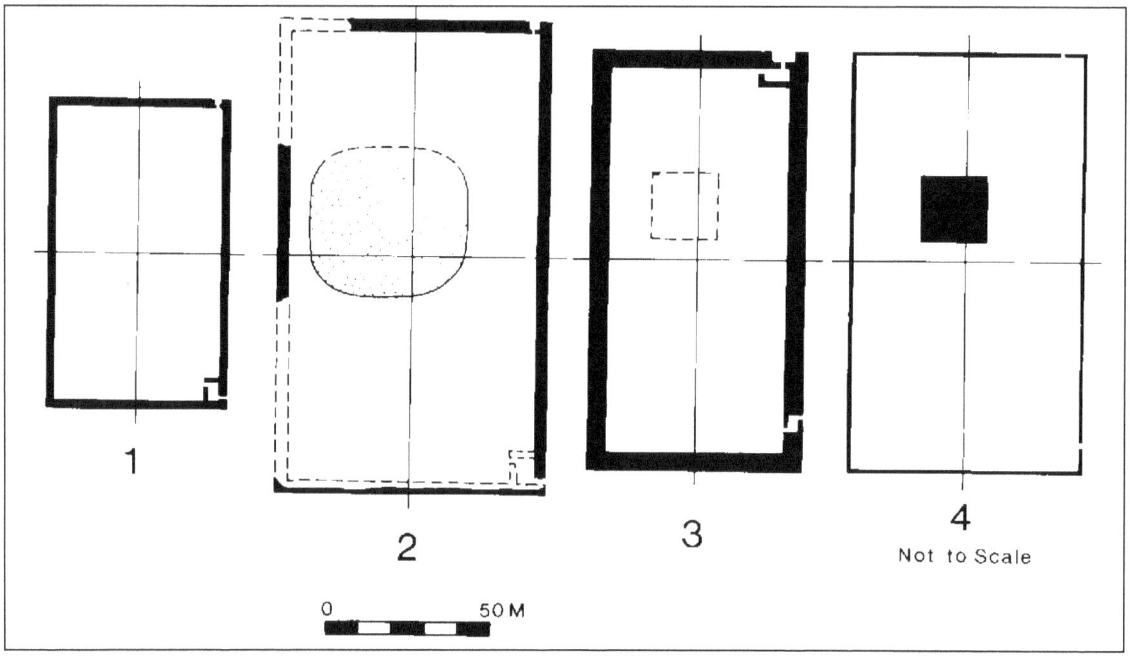

B. 4) Ceremonies of the *sed* festival

Kaiser[423] has revised the order and has commented on the scenes of the *sed* festival at the sun temple of Neuserre at Abu Ghurob. According to the German scholar, it is possible to distinguish twelve ceremonies:

1. - Foundation rites of the building (palace or robing room) constructed specially for the *sed* festival.

2. - Inspection and cattle census.

3. - Start of procession: the king walks along with various attendants, priests and the royal children (*msw nzwt*).

4. - Lion-furniture sequence: according to Kaiser,[424] it is some kind of purification ceremony.

5. - Homage scene I.

6. - Homage scene II: in those scenes (numbers 5 and 6), the king is enthroned in one side of the double pavilion, receiving homage from the dignitaries of Upper and Lower Egypt.

   It is possible to draw a parallel between the meaning of this scene and the offerings presented to the god Horus at Edfu. According to Finnestad [425] the figures of fertility that represent the nomes of Egypt and are headed by the king "represent the life-sustaining capacity of Egypt, their products are presented as gifts to the god, the creator". In the case of the *sed* festival, it is possible to assume that the king represented the creator god.

7. - Min sequence: king's offering to this god (?).

8. - Wepwawet sequence: comprises the *sed* festival dance or running of the ritual course, under the auspices of Wepwawet whose standard is carried before the king.

9. - Driving cattle and its allotment: after this ceremony, the king's feet are washed and he returns to his palace.

[423] Mentioned by Gohary (1992: 10-11 & n. 145), with references to the publication of von Bissing and Kees and Kaiser's discussion.
[424] Mentioned by Gohary (1992: 11).
[425] (1985: 120-121).

Fig. 16: Netjerikhet complex at Saqqara. (A) The southern part of the Step Pyramid. (B) Scene of king Netjerikhet visiting the shrine of Horus of Behdet. (C) Stone platform with double staircase as found at the sed festival court. (D) The double throne.

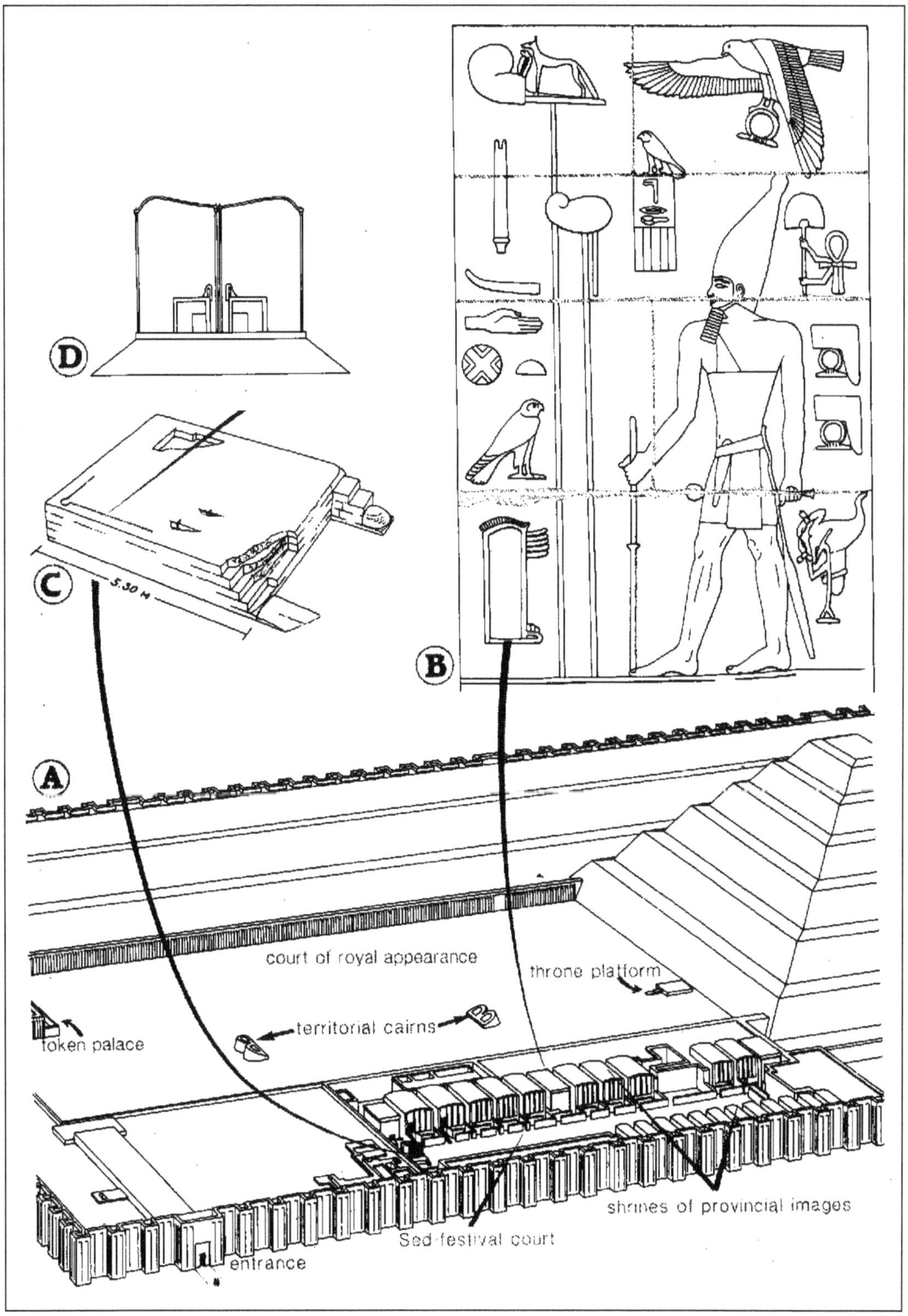

10. - Bringing the palanquin (i. e. carrying-chair).

11. - Mounting the palanquin.

12. - Closing palanquin procession: it is performed once for Upper and once for Lower Egypt.

The Upper Egyptian crown appears in all the ceremonies except number 10, whereas the Lower Egyptian crown appears definitely only in ceremonies number 8 and 12. The queen does not appear very much, she is only depicted with other members of the royal family.[426]

The problem for discussion is that Kaiser's interpretation is based on very badly preserved reliefs.[427] Thus, it is necessary to use later representations of the *sed* festival, not only from Neuserre's reliefs at Abu Gurob, but other reliefs as well (Amenhotep III in Soleb, Akhenaten at Karnak, and Osorkon II at Bubastis)[428] and, mainly, the evidence from Netjerikhet's funerary complex at Saqqara.[429] With all of them, it is possible to reconstruct a reliable version of the *sed* festival in Egypt at the end of the Predynastic and in the Early Dynastic periods. On this basis and with the iconographic evidence discovered at the Late and Early Dynastic sites, it is possible to get a picture of the *sed* festival in those early periods.

After the construction of the "Festival Hall"[430] within an existing sanctuary,[431] the preparation of a Court of Festival and a "Palace" (acting as a robing-chamber), and shrines of primitive Upper and Lower Egyptian type,[432] the celebrations began. The initial proceedings were presided over by the cow-goddess Sekhat-Hor, who suckled the god-king.[433] The main celebrations began with visits of the king to shrines,[434] which were purified and dedicated,[435] and, after receiving pledges of loyalty, he went to pay homage to a god or goddess in the Court of the Great Ones. The king is preceded by the standard of the royal placenta and by a choir-master, a fan-bearer and a door-hinge-bearer.[436] The king was received by a master of ceremonies, a recitation priest, and courtiers, while the "Great Ones of Upper and Lower Egypt" kissed the ground before him, and two courtiers of the rank of "Friend" washed his feet.[437] The king ran round a track four times as the ruler of the South and four times as the ruler of the North, to prove his physical ability to rule.[438] There were more ceremonies, but the interpretation is very complicated,[439] and surely most of these acts were added later. The Followers of Horus were key figures in the sed festival; according to Hassan,[440] "The Followers of Horus represent the notion of royal ancestor worship as a legitimisation of power. Each ruler became a part of this upon his death (...). Closely associated with the Followers of Horus at the Sed festival are the various standards which support the kingship and are shown close to the king at other ceremonies. While still known as the Following of Horus, the ancestors were also called the Souls of Nekhen and Souls of Pe - a system of duality brought together as a result of the unification".[441] Since the times of king Netjerikhet (and possibly earlier),[442] there is evidence that in his *sed* festival a ceremony called *pẖr ḥꜣ jnbw* "circuit of the walls"

[426] Gohary (1992: 10). However, there are some scenes (1, 2 & 3), in which the king does not appear, nor is he wearing the white-crown, nor is his figure complete.
[427] See all the plates of the volume published by von Bissing & Kees (1923, 2).
[428] Summarised by Gohary (1992: 11-39), with references. Also Galán (2000).
[429] F. D. Friedman (1995), with references.
[430] There is a parallel of this construction in the African tribe of the Shilluks. Before the killing of the king of the Shilluks, a special hut was built, and there the king was killed, Cervelló Autuori (1996: 156), with reference.
[431] But not always: for example, Netjerikhet built all the necessary buildings for his *sed* festival in a new complex.
[432] Fairman (1958: 84).
[433] Frankfort (1948: 82); followed by Hassan (1998c: 106).
[434] In those chapels or shrines, the gods (called "The Great Ones") were accommodated to participate in the ceremonies, Frankfort (1948: 80).
[435] Fairman (1958: 84).
[436] According to J. Spencer (personal communication), in fact is a representation of the sky.
[437] Frankfort (1948: 83).
[438] Hassan (1992: 311).
[439] Frankfort (1948: 85-88).
[440] (1992: 311).
[441] Fairman (1958: 85) explains this ritual as a sort of act of homage to the royal ancestors.
[442] There are some examples on the Palermo Stone dated to the First Dynasty, see Schäfer (1902: 15, no. 3,28, no. 8). The ceremony of *pẖr ḥꜣ jnbw* coincides in all of these cases with the enthronement of a new king.

was celebrated.[443] This ceremony was also celebrated during the enthronement (see p. 38). According to Fairman,[444] it symbolised taking possession of the kingdom. He added that it could have connotations of protection (protective rite).

According to Galán,[445] the *sed* festival in the New Kingdom benefited "some religious institutions by exempting them from obligations and demands of various levels of the civil administration", but there is no evidence for the Late Predynastic and Early Dynastic periods.

B. 5) Elements of the *sed* festival

Apart from those chapels or shrines, two more constructions were required: the Festival Hall and the Stone Markers. The first one has already been mentioned: the Festival Hall (*wsẖt*-court),[446] where the Great Throne stood, and the "Palace", in which the king changed his costume and insignia. From the Predynastic period, the Festival Hall was made of reeds, as the Pyramid Texts describe.[447]

The oldest *wsẖt*-court is at Saqqara, in Netjerikhet's complex (Figure 16). As Patricia Spencer[448] confirms, *wsẖt* is a term which occurred in many different contexts (titles, Pyramid Texts, etc.). It is derived from the root *wsẖ* "to be broad". From Old Kingdom texts, it is possible to affirm that the *wsẖt* was a hall in which offerings were made or one from which offerings came. According to Patricia Spencer,[449] "one would expect the *wsẖt* to have been an open court, presumably broader than it was long, surrounding and protecting an important building such as a palace".

According to Gohary,[450] Netjerikhet included in his funerary complex all the buildings used in his *sed* festival, in order that he would able to continue celebrating the festival in eternity.

Netjerikhet's complex presents remains of large stone markers that look like the half-moon markers seen on some Early Dynastic labels. Two were pushed together at the north end and two at the south end of the great *wsẖt*-court. The markers are placed about 55 meters apart, measuring from the straight insides, which are 11 meters long. On the east side of the complex is the smaller *wsẖt*-court lined on both sides with remains of provincial shrines of Upper and Lower Egyptian design. They contain doorways and niches that held statuary, probably much of it of the king, almost none of which has survived. On the west side of the court are ten chapels, including a *zḥ-nṯr* shrine at each end and one in the middle. On the east side are twelve chapels with internal statue niches. At the southern end of the court are the remains of a throne with two sets of stairs, where the monarch sat as King of Upper Egypt on one side and of Lower Egypt on the other.[451]

The stone markers (*ḏnbw*)[452] had a metaphoric meaning. In one of the rituals, the king had to circuit both of them eight times for Lower and Upper Egypt; the markers meant the country of Egypt, as it is possible to conclude from a sentence of the Pyramid Texts: "He has circuited about the two banks". In this way the king reclaimed his royal possession.[453]

In the *sed* festival, the king was not the only actor, there are some primitive designations for officials and priests that took part in the ceremonies: "The Herdsman from Nekhen",[454] "The Man from Hermopolis," and "The Great Ones of Upper and Lower Egypt." The two first titles could disguise members of the government, and the last one apparently consisted of "ten members from each two halves of the country;

[443] Munro (1961: 71). In the case of Netjerikhet, F. D. Friedman (1995: 14) holds that the king went not only around the markers, but also along their axes and out of the funerary complex to circle its walls.
[444] (1958: 79).
[445] (2000).
[446] Spencer (1978: 54, n. 29).
[447] Frankfort (1948: 80).
[448] (1984: 73).
[449] (1984: 73).
[450] (1992: 6).

[451] F. D. Friedman (1995: 11).
[452] Spencer (1978: 52-53) concluded that those markers were called *ḏnbw* (at least since the 19th dynasty) - probably derived from the verb *ḏnb* "to turn away", "to turn round", etc.- In Netjerikhet's complex at Saqqara, as was explained above, the track was denominated *wsẖt*-court and "it seems reasonable to assume that Djoser, like Den, performed a run between the markers", F. D. Friedman (1995: 11). The enclosure of the city temple of Hierakonpolis measures around 100 meters, where there was enough space for the shrine and a ritual area.
[453] F. D. Friedman (1995: 22). Pyr. 406 c. Spencer (1978: 52-53) suggests that the markers could mean 'boundaries' or 'limits' of the land.
[454] Two attendants wearing caps of wolf skin with the head and tail of the wolf-god Wepwawet accompanied this figure, Frankfort (1948: 83).

they alone were present, representing the people, at actual enthronement during the Mystery Play of the Succession". The Royal Princes and the Royal Kinsmen also participated.[455]

As Florence D. Friedman[456] has revealed, in the *sed* festival, the statue of the king played a very important role, because it meant a rebirth of the king. In her study about the six underground panels of Netjerikhet's complex at Saqqara, Friedman wrote that "They [the six underground relief panels of Netjerikhet] concern a living, recrowned king who in statue form strides east and south from the Sed shrines; who runs south and out and around the precinct walls, as well as south and around the *ḏnbw* to reclaim his territory; who is acknowledged by his ancestors and the gods; receives rightful claim over heaven and earth; is dedicated (born) anew in statue form; and assumes eternal lordship of the two lands".[457]

According to Bleeker,[458] the *sed* festival was bipartite: one series of rites concerns Northern Egypt, the other Southern Egypt. However, it has already been assumed that the concept of duality was not completely developed until the middle of the First Dynasty (pp. 38-40). Hence, on the Narmer mace-head and on the other mace-head (Scorpion II?) from Hierakonpolis (pp. 51-57), the king is represented celebrating his *sed* festival, but always wearing the red crown, which permits us to suggest that in this period the crown does not indicate a region, but ritual valour.[459] Later, in the reign of Den, the king appears represented with the two crowns and inside two different chapels, so it is possible to ascribe this to two, possibly similar, ceremonies.

If Bleeker's suggestion[460] is right, the so-called "appearances of king", which have been read on the Palermo Stone, could represent *sed* festivals. Thus, it might be concluded that in those early times the king could have celebrated two different *sed* festivals after the reign of Den, one for Upper Egypt and another for Lower Egypt.[461] The first evidence known, in which the *sed* festival was celebrated for Upper and Lower Egypt, is dated in the reign of Djer. In later examples, this double celebration was reflected in the depiction of the rituals: those dedicated to Lower Egypt (with the king wearing the red crown) were depicted on the northern wall and vice versa.[462]

Many times at least in the reigns of Djer (7th year), and Den (41st (?) year) the so-called "appearances of the king" are followed by the birth (or festival) of Min, the god of vegetation. Bleeker[463] explained it was because that year there was a "successful harvest".

The renewal character of *sed* festivals would be seen in the labels and in other monuments, which bore representations of the *sed*-festivals, where Vikentiev[464] saw three objects that, according to him could be seeds germinating (against, see Item no. 3, pp. 57-60).

The six reliefs found in underground galleries of Netjerikhet's complex at Saqqara refer to rituals of the *sed* festival.[465] They permit us to summarise some of the elements that appeared in those ceremonies at that early date:[466]

a) Enclosure: in the case of Netjerikhet with dummy buildings (west side: ten chapels; east side: twelve chapels with internal statue niches), two *wsḫt*-courtyards with the stone markers (*ḏnbw*), a mound (the pyramid), a platform for the throne at southern end of the court.

b) Sanctuary *ḥḏ* and sanctuary *pr-wr* .

[455] Frankfort (1948: 81-82). In later periods, the "Hereditary Prince" and the Heri Udjeb (*ḥrj wḏb*, "The Master of the (King's) Largesse) took part in the first ceremony. The latter is depicted in tombs of the Old Kingdom.
[456] (1995: 31). See as well note below.
[457] F. Friedman (1995: 40).
[458] (1967: 105).
[459] It seems very plausible that the red crown has its origin in the Naqada region (see p. 39). One of the gods worshipped in that region was Seth, who was associated with the red colour. These coincidences might suggest a different interpretation of the red crown at the end of the Predynastic period.
[460] (1967: 112).
[461] According to Gohary (1992: 9) "Presumably these duplicated rites were to emphasize the king's reassertion of power over both parts of the country".
[462] Gohary (1992: 9 & ns. 141 & 142).
[463] (1967: 112). In this regard, see also Helck (1966).
[464] (1949-1950: 226).
[465] F. D. Friedman (1995: 42).
[466] From the study made by F. D. Friedman (1995), with references.

c) King running (*pḫr ḥ3 jnbw* 'circuit of the walls') between the stone markers. The king holds the *mks*, which is a container that has the *jmt-pr*, which is a document that means 'that which is in the house' (or 'that which constitutes the house').

d) The standard with the representation of the jackal-god Sed (Wepwawet).

e) Stopping of the king before the shrine of Horus Behedetite.

f) Inscribed travertine vessels.[467]

g) Baboons (*wrw*),[468] that refer to the ancestral fathers (the preceding kings).

h) Royal statues, that mean the rebirth of the king.

i) Horus *ḫnty ḫm* (Letopolis).[469]

j) Different elements such as fans held by *ʿnḫ* and *w3s*, Horus extends, etc.[470]

B.6) Material evidence of the *sed* festival in the Late Predynastic and Early Dynastic periods

Before a discussion in depth, it is necessary to enumerate all the items that will be studied in the following pages:

1.- Anonymous fragment of mace-head from Hierakonpolis.

2.- Narmer mace-head.

3.- Aha wooden label from Abydos.

4.- Aha fragmentary ebony label from Abydos.

5.- Djer ivory label from Abydos and Saqqara.

6.- Djer seal-impression from Abydos.

7.- Djer seal-impression.

8.- Djet ivory label from Saqqara.

9.- Wooden label of Den from Abydos.

10.- Den seal-impression from Hemaka's tomb.

11.- Fragment of a wooden label of Den from Abydos.

12.- Two similar fragments of ivory labels of Den from Abydos.

13.- Fragment of a wooden label of Den from Abydos.

14.- Anonymous limestone slab from Saqqara.

15.- Anedjib's vessels from Saqqara.

16.- Qaa's vessel from Saqqara.

[467] According to Murnane (1981: 374), those vases must be seen as utilitarian rather than strictly votive objects. Baines (personal communication) assumes that the inscribed festival vessels are late Old Kingdom.

The *zp tpj* (or 2) *sd* "first (or second) occasion of the Jubilee" formula that appears on the surface of some of these vases served as a date.

[468] Helck (1972: 97; 1986a: 1221) claimed that baboons were called *wrw* (singular *wr*) 'The Great Ones' and represented the deceased kings or deified ancestors.

[469] Letopolis was the place where Horus defeated Seth definitively, see Altenmüller (1980: 43).

[470] Summarised by F. D. Friedman (1995: fig. 22).

Fig. 17: Relief panels from the complex of Netjerikhet. Above the relief panels under the pyramid and below, the relief panels under the south tomb. Not to scale.

Fig. 18: The king's mace-head from Hierakonpolis. Not to scale.

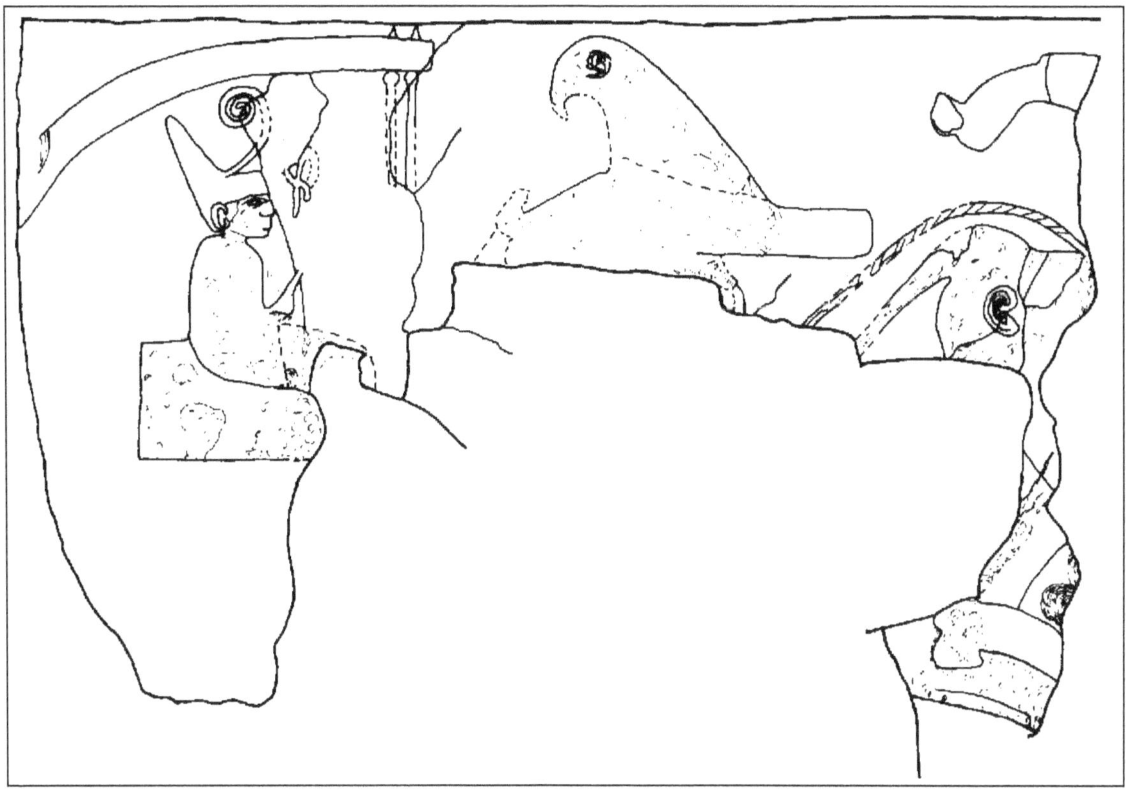

- **Before the First Dynasty (?)**

Before the study of the monuments that represent some ceremonies of the *sed* festival, it is necessary to discuss some possible *sed* festivals detected some years ago. Williams and Logan[471] studied the Metropolitan Museum knife handle (dated by Pérez Largacha[472] to Naqada III period). They related some elements represented on this handle to other Late Predynastic and Early Dynastic objects such as, for example, the Hierakonpolis Tomb 100 painting,[473] painted linen from Gebelein,[474] the Narmer palette (see below). According to them, it is possible to reconstruct a royal cycle, in which barks and palace-façades are the main elements. In some cases, they also connected barks and palace-façades with the *sed* festival. However, this connection with the *sed* festival is not satisfactorily explained, neither were the features and ends of cycle, that they attempt to characterise, adequately described. They referred only to an ethereal royal cycle supported merely by evidence clearly related to different festivals, for example, the hippopotamus hunting or royal processions in barks.[475] In the case of the Hierakonpolis Tomb 100 painting (dated by Pérez Largacha[476] to Naqada IIB-C), Williams and Logan[477] recognised the "*Heb-Sed dance*", which probably refers to the running of the king (see p. 46). However, it seems very difficult for us to accept this interpretation because of the poor state of the painting in this particular scene. The only discernible feature in this scene is a man holding the *ḥqꜣ* sceptre[478] in front of another figure with at least one uplifted arm, which might be his double, a woman, or even an enemy.

Item no. 1 (Figure 18). There is a **mace-head from Hierakonpolis**,[479] in which Arkell[480] tried to re-construct King Scorpion's name. However, it is too fragmentary to confirm his hypothesis. The

[471] (1987).
[472] (1993a: 114-115).
[473] Case & Payne (1962); Pérez Largacha (1993a: 105-112), with more references; Cialowicz (1998).
[474] Pérez Largacha (1993a: 102-104), with references.

[475] Royal processions in barks are very difficult to relate to later festivals and the meaning remains obscure for us.
[476] (1993a: 110).
[477] (1987: 255).
[478] There is evidence of another *ḥqꜣ* sceptre found at Umm el-Qaab and dated to Naqada IID period, see Dreyer *et alii* (1996: 21, Taf. 6c).
[479] Quibell (1900: pl. XXVIA).
[480] Arkell (1963).

only certain evidence is that the king appears seated beneath a canopy supported at the front by two poles. He was represented wearing the red crown and dressed in a long garment and one of his hands is exposed at waist level and holds a rod, which is broken at the end. This scene is practically the same as the one represented on Narmer's mace-head. The position and shape (with rectangular tail) of the falcon Horus is very similar to that in the "Archaic Horus incense burner" of Qustul.[481] From the scene in which the king appears, Hornung and Staehelin[482] concluded that this mace-head represents the *sed* festival, as in the Narmer mace-head (see below).

Cialowicz[483] and Gautier and Midant-Reynes[484] have proposed new reconstructions of the Scorpion mace-head. According to the latter two authors, on the right side of the king, in the middle register, they reconstruct the figure of the Falcon of Nekhen and consider that the fragment of mace-head deposited at UCL (item 1) was part of the Scorpion mace-head. It seems difficult for us to accept this last hypothesis, mainly because the theme of both mace-heads is completely different. The UCL fragment would have a similar representation to the Narmer mace-head, in other words, the festival *sed* (see below).

- The first Dynasty

Item no. 2 (Fig. 19). The Narmer mace-head:[485] The focus of the scene is the figure of the king. He sits under a canopy erected on a high dais, wearing the Red Crown and holding the flail, his body swathed in a long cloak. The royal personage is attended by the minor figures of fan-bearers, bodyguards with long staves, and the skin-clad official. Before Narmer three bearded men run a race towards him between the stone markers, while in a higher register a figure faces him from a litter. Over this personage is a simple enclosure within which stand a cow and calf. Above the runners stands a rank of four variously clad men carrying standards, also facing the throne. Behind and beneath the running men are ideograms with numbers: cattle, 400,000, goats (?), 1,422,000. To the right, and separated by a vertical line from the foregoing, are a bound man and the number 120,000. Together with all these scenes, there is the depiction of a shrine, which appears on Aha's label (see Item no. 3), and below this structure there is an enclosure with goats.

Since the discovery of this mace-head, scholars have proposed different explanations for it. Petrie[486] suggested that it commemorated the symbolic wedding of the king to the heiress of the crown of Lower Egypt and the legitimisation by marriage of his military conquest of Lower Egypt. Vandier[487] argued that it represented the *sed* festival, and he compared it to one scene of the Eighteenth dynasty, in which there was a representation of a funerary ritual, in which the animals, after the sacrifice, were interred in a burial pit near a sanctuary. Millet[488] expresses his view that the scene represents the ceremony "Appearance of the King of Lower Egypt" (*ḫ*ᶜ*t-bjty*) and it was celebrated in Buto, because Sethe[489] identified the shrine as the temple at *ḏb*ᶜ*wt* (the old name of one of the sanctuaries of Buto). He also proposes that the figure in the litter is a female "Child of the king", representing the female relatives of the king, and the amount of people and cattle is "the purest fantasy". According to Baines,[490] it "seems to show the presentation of captives and booty to the king in the context of a public *sed*-festival ritual. The whole probably relates to the separate shrine, which may legitimise ritual and conquest while also forming the ultimate destination of the wealth acquired." Baines adds that it "is a prospective ritual or a commemoration rather than a specific event." In accordance with Reneé Friedman[491] (following Michael Hoffman), given the continued activity at Hk29A (see *infra*) into the First Dynasty, it is tempting to suggest that the structure of the Narmer mace-head is not just similar to, but could be a representation of this ceremonial complex as well.

---

481 Williams (1986: pl. 33).
Arkell (1963) saw the traces of a rosette on the surface of the mace, as in the other incense burner of Qustul -Williams (1986: pl. 34)-, but Adams (1974a: 3) admitted that she could not find it.
482 (1974: 16).
483 (1987).
484 (1995).
485 About the disposition of the scenes of the mace-head, see Godron (1957: 194-195), with a discussion of the earlier interpretations and references.

486 (1939: 78-79), also followed by Emery (1961: 45-47) and Hoffman (1979: 322-323).
487 (1952, 1, I: 602-605); also Bleeker (1967: 99).
488 (1990: 56-58).
489 (1930: 138-139).
490 (1995: 118-119).
491 (1996: 33-34).

Fig. 19: The Narmer mace-head from Hierakonpolis. Not to scale.

However, it is possible to offer a new interpretation, based on the preceding discussions and some re-considerations. The Narmer mace-head records the *sed* festival (as already interpreted by Vandier).[492] This interpretation finds support in the track that is built in front of the enthroned king, as Kemp[493] related. Ahead of the track, there is the figure of a *tekenu.*[494] As has already been discussed, in the *sed* festival there was a ritual death and birth. Thus the *tekenu*, in this case, means those parts of the royal body that were not treated after the ritual death.

In addition, there are more coincident elements between the Narmer mace-head and Niuserre *sed* festival reliefs:[495]

(1) The sandal and seal bearer is represented beside the pavilion;[496]
(2) the four standards;
(3) a retainer;[497]
(4) fan bearers;
(5) three running men and the *ḏnbw*; from Niuserre *sed* festival reliefs, Logan interprets these three running men as the Great Ones (*wrw*) of Upper and Lower Egypt. Doubtless, the meaning of them in the early sed festival remains obscure for us.
(6) the king and the royal canopy.
(7) The presence of the cattle is important on the mace-head, and could be related to the census of cattle in later *sed* festivals. There are three different representations: the easiest to read is the one that is below the track, because it gives the number; the second is above the track and shows two bovines inside an enclosure. The third one is below a depiction of a temple. Following Renée Friedman (and M. A. Hoffman), the *sed* festival took place in the Locality Hk29A. This site was discovered by Michael Hoffman a few years before his death. In the second half of the 1980s, the Anglo-American expedition at Hierakonpolis discovered a ceremonial centre at Locality Hk29A[498].

This complex was used at different periods: the earliest was during Naqada IIc-d, and after that, the complex appears to have been abandoned for a period of time. Although ceramics datable to Naqada IIIB/First Dynasty were found,[499] this occupation appears to date to a period after the complex had fallen into disrepair. The next occupation was early in the First Dynasty: Aha and Djer, as the pottery

[492] Also Logan (1999: 265).
[493] (1989: 57-62, fig. 20); also Bleeker (1967: 98).
[494] In later times, the *tekenu* were containers of the parts of the body that were not mummified, Hornung (1992: 170). About *tekenu*, see Helck (1986b: 308-309). It is possible to see *tekenu* in the reliefs of the *sed* festival in the temple of the sun built by Neuserre, see von Bissing & Kess (1923, 2: Bl. 18, 44d & Bl 21, 50a).
[495] Logan (1999: 262-265).
[496] Von Bissing & Kees (1963, 2: Bl. 10, 24).
[497] Logan (1999) confirms that "is difficult to be sure who this might be among the multitude of officials in the Niuserra *sed*-festival reliefs but the *sm*-priest wears a similar garment with a fail."
[498] Friedman (1996); see also Adams (1995).
[499] R. Friedman (1996: 29).

found in a pit shows.[500] Inside this pit, many different kinds of ceramics were discovered: Egyptian vases, incense burners, pottery imported from the Delta and E.B. II Palestine pottery. "Either prior to or shortly after this event, the complex was intentionally deconstructed. The fill of the large post-holes indicates that these rare wooden features were not allowed to rot in place and there is further evidence to suggest that other wooden features (wall posts, poles, etc.) and cultic items were removed to the new complex being built in the sacred precinct at Nekhen".[501]

Many elements (lithics, ground stone, faunal and ceramics) indicated that the ceremonial function of the Hk29A complex need not be determined on the basis of the monumental architectural features alone. In this guise, it was possible to show that butchery was taking place at the site.[502] Also large (2 metres) Nile perch (*Lates niloticus*), crocodile and turtle bones have been found, a fact that reinforces the impression that large and, in some cases, dangerous aquatic fauna were being caught specifically for use in the complex. The great quantity of lithic tools and beads suggested a craft function for the subsidiary buildings on the northern perimeter of the complex. A great quantity of potsherds were found, not only Egyptian, but also Nubian, limestone-tempered pottery imported from Palestine, incised and impressed pottery possibly from Lower Egypt, and shale-tempered ceramics perhaps from the Eastern Desert[503].

The temple had a monumental door with large post-holes. Opposite, smaller post-holes were found. The convex roof, in the form of a tent, was made with vegetable materials (wood and reeds), drawing a geometric motif, perhaps with horns and tail.[504] Friedman[505] holds that the Hk29A ceremonial complex was the *pr-wr*. In the representations, the *pr-wr* (in Hierakonpolis) is shown without an enclosure or with only a small fence in front of it, most often on a sledge; due to this, Williams[506] argued that it might depict a small shrine rather than a temple. However, the representations on which Williams bases his suggestion are of a later date or are sanctuaries built for special ceremonies such as the *sed* festival. After the Third Dynasty, the *pr-wr* represents the emblematic Upper Egyptian shrine.[507]

Against Friedman's view, it will be argued here that the temple depicted on the right of the mace-head corresponds with the primitive city temple of Hierakonpolis[508] (Nekhen), built over in a later period (in the Middle Kingdom?). Although part of her argument is accepted —that it represented a *sed* festival celebrated at Hierakonpolis—, it is preferable to locate the *sed* festival in the city-temple enclosure.[509] The arguments for this assertion are:

- On the Narmer mace-head a temple is depicted which is also represented in a label of Horus Aha's reign, the same shrine appears depicted and there are many references that prove that it was located at Hierakonpolis (see Item no. 3 – reign of Aha-).

- Many depictions of this type of temple were found very near or at the Main Deposit of Hierakonpolis.[510]

- In the depictions of the Narmer mace-head and the label from the Horus Aha's tomb, a bird appears over the roof of the shrine. In this regard, more fragmentary depictions of this bird (probably forming a group with the shrine) have been found at Hierakonpolis.[511]

500 However, Adams (1999: 26) dates the last use to the reign of Narmer or Horus Aha. She affirms (personal communication) that pottery from this level is similar to that from Tomb 1 (= contemporary to Narmer) at Hierakonpolis (Locality 6).

501 Friedman (1996: 29-30).

502 Thus, it is possible to explain the link between the great quantity of animal bones that have been discovered at that locality and the large number of animals present on the Narmer mace-head.

503 Friedman (1996: 24, 29).

504 Vandier (1952: 556-557); Adams (1995: 58).

505 (1996: 33-34).

506 (1988: 48).

507 Vandier (1952: 559).

508 As Baines (1990: 11) affirms "These compositions are not organised as scenes of unified passages, but they are constituted by a juxtaposition of significative or representative elements on a plane surface".

509 It seems clear that the Upper Egyptian temple  *pr wr* was located in Locality Hk29a, see Friedman (1996).

510 Adams (1995: front cover illustration). Faience model, see Adams (1974a: 30, pl. 22, no. 148); compare it with Kemp (1989: fig. 33-34).

511 Hathor bowl, see Burgess & Arkell (1958), Adams (1974a: 50; 1974b: 14). Other examples: Adams (1974a: pl. 38, 39, 44).

Fig. 20: A provisional reconstruction of the HK29A complex by M. A. Hoffman.

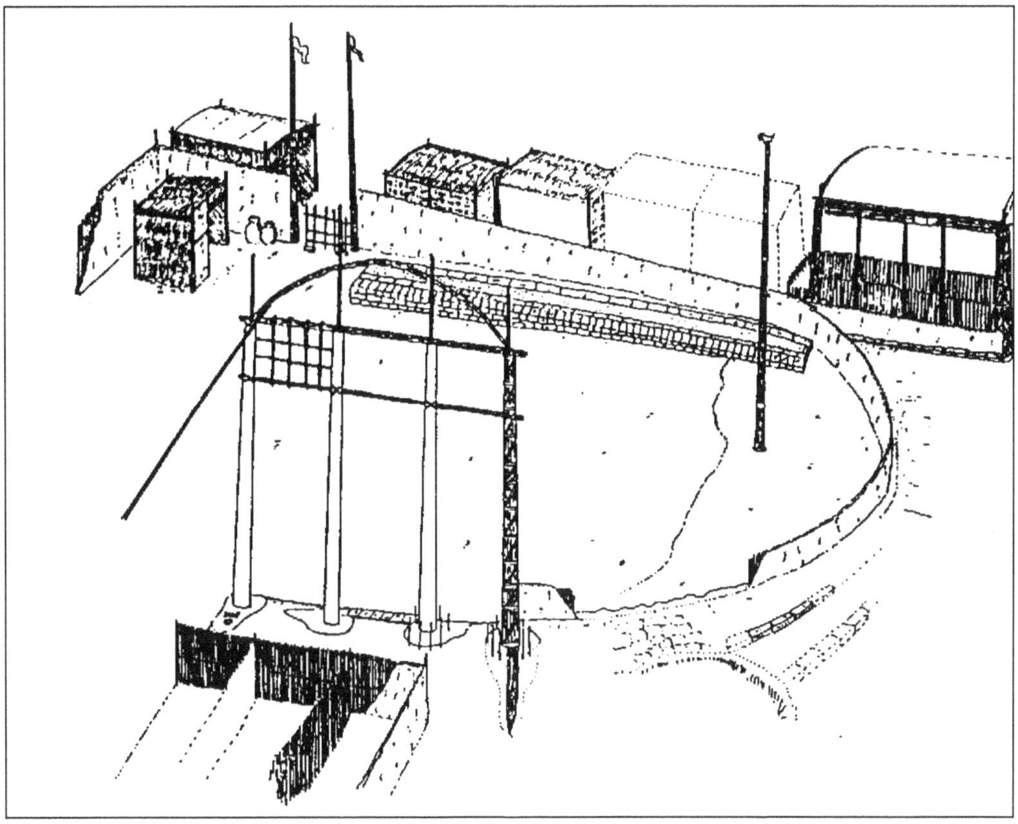

- In Wadi Maghara in Sinai, one inscription was found dated to the reign of Sanakht (Third Dynasty),[512] in which a falcon determinative surmounts a small mound that was connected with a pole to a representation of a façade of a temple. This façade is very similar to those represented on the Narmer mace-head and Aha's label.[513]

- Two kneeling statues of enemies were found 2 m. apart from the Main Deposit. As is well-known, the sacrifice of enemies in the *sed* festival was one of the most important rituals.

- As O'Connor[514] noted, the type of the city-temple enclosure was very similar to those at Abydos and Saqqara. Thus, the temple of Hierakonpolis (Nekhen) might have served as a model for the later enclosures built at Abydos and Saqqara.

- The mace-head was found at Hierakonpolis.

Therefore, the city-temple of Hierakonpolis (Nekhen) was built in the Lower Egyptian style: rectangular body and curved roof with two gables. This could be explained as a consequence of the cultural interchange between Upper and Lower Egypt before the First Dynasty and unknown religious reasons. Moreover, there is evidence of a Lower Egyptian temple type in Upper Egypt. The temple of Herakleopolis (20th nome of Upper Egypt) appears represented on two fragmentary labels from the tomb of Den and on the Palermo Stone (?).[515] In both cases, it appears depicted as a typical Lower Egyptian temple.[516]

---

512 See, for example, Weill (1908: 137).
513 Kahl (1994: 887) accepted the transcription offered by the *Wb.* (II, 310.14), n<u>h</u>n.j.
514 (1992).
515 Schäfer (1902: 20, no. x+9).
516 For an interpretation, Weill (1961, 1: 61-65); the contradiction between the two kind of temples was pointed out by the same author (1961, 1: 87-88).

Fig. 21: Reconstruction and situation of the temples at Hierakonpolis.

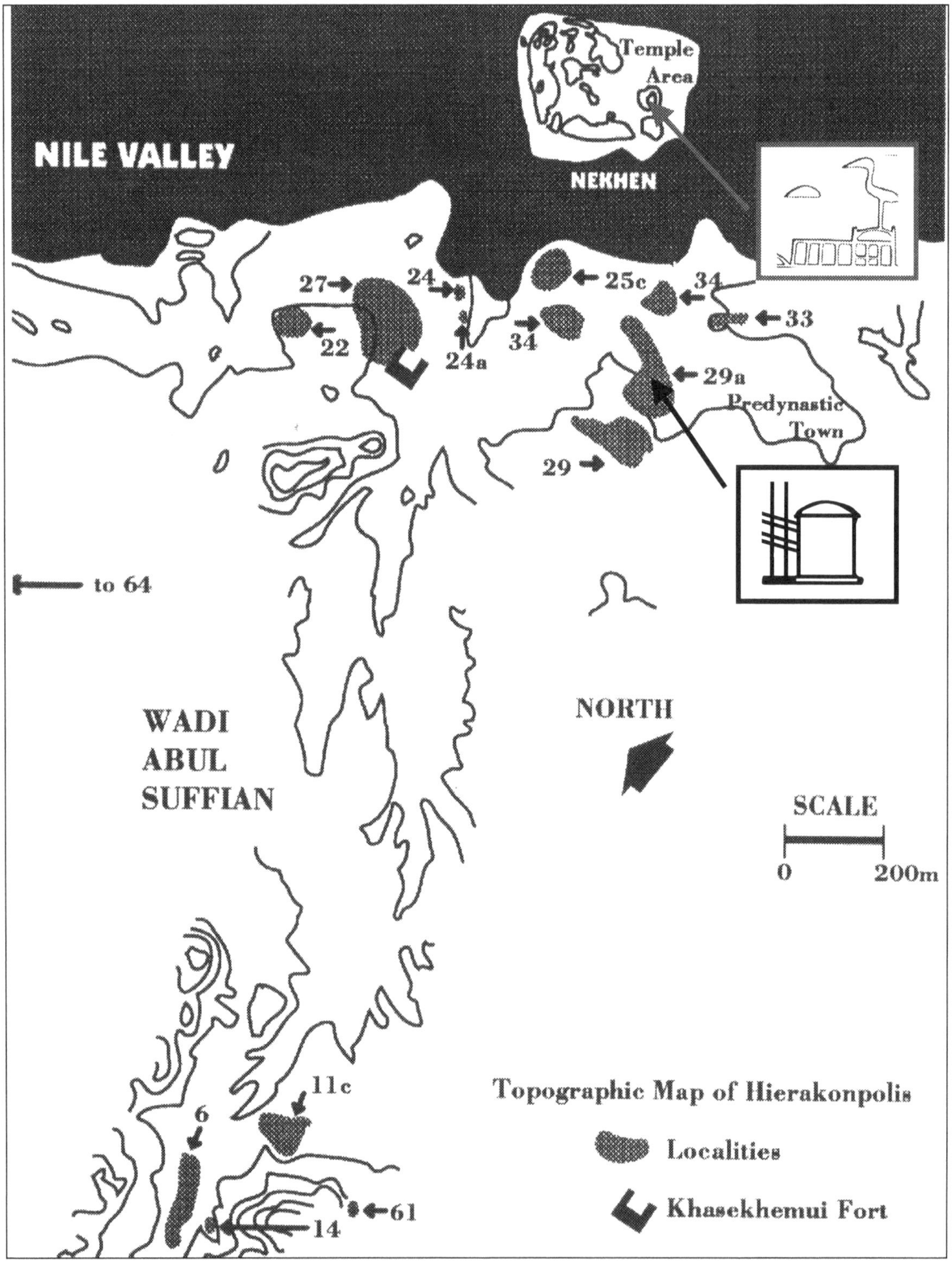

Possibly, the conclusion from all of this is that the two "national" shrines in the *sed* festivals owe their presence to the disposition of the sacred spaces at Hierakonpolis. Probably, both temples played a liturgical role during the whole festival (see Figure 21). The period of coincidence between them was very short (from the beginning of Naqada IIIB (?) period to Aha),[517] but it was enough time to be accepted as part of the stated ceremony of the *sed* festival.

For further support for this identification, it is necessary to re-interpret a label that was found by Petrie[518] at Umm el-Qaab, which was later identified by Dreyer as part of the funerary equipment of the early tomb U-j, as other parallels have proved.[519] Dreyer[520] suggested that this depiction could represent a temple of Buto (*ḏbꜥwt*). However, after the re-interpretation made above, it seems clear that it refers to the city temple of Hierakonpolis (Nekhen). Moreover, if those labels were offerings from Buto, it would mean that Buto was under some kind of Upper Egyptian domination in the Naqada IIIA period, which seems less probable. However, it would be more plausible if the depiction of this temple refers to the city temple of Hierakonpolis, which could have been built in this shape a little earlier. The first mention of the *ḏbꜥwt* temple is dated in the reign of Userkaf (Fifth Dynasty).[521] The next mention occurred in the Pyramid Texts.[522] On all occasions, *ḏbꜥwt* is represented by an ideogram ( ), which shows a bird on the top of a pole. This pole has a triangular base, but is not a building or anything comparable to a building as appeared on the Narmer mace-head (see Fig. 19, top left) or Aha's labels (see Figs. 23-24). The bird represented is also different, whilst in the First Dynasty depictions it is clearly shown in a standing position, in the later depictions it is represented with the legs completely flexed.

Item no. 3. Horus Aha wooden label from Abydos (Figure 23).[523] Vandier[524] claimed that this was the most important label that has been found from Aha's reign, because of the potential information that it can provide. For this reason, many scholars have interpreted this label in different ways.

Petrie[525] read in the first row the name of Aha, "Born of Amiut", as well as two sacred barks and a shrine and temenos of Neith. In the second row, Petrie noted a man making an offering, with two signs above, which read as "alone". Behind him, is a bull running over bumpy ground into a net stretched between two poles. Petrie noticed that the shrine of this label and the one that appears on the Narmer mace-head are very similar. In the third row, Petrie saw three boats on a canal or river passing between certain places, that could be *Biu*, a disctrict of Memphis, *Pa She*, the "dwelling of the lake, capital of the Fayum, and the canal of Mer or Bahr Yusuf, divided in two, above and below the Fayum."

According to Legge's[526] interpretation, in the first row it was possible to read "On the foundation of the temple to Neith, at the funeral ceremonies of the Horus Aha." In the second row, the bull represents a foundation act, the man in front of the bull "is the king scaattering sand from a winnowing-fan in order to mark the path traced out by the bull. The signs above him I should be inclined to read 𓇓𓆤 or *sutten bat*, a variant of the expression *suten seshf* (...) denoting that this part of the ceremony had to be performed by "the king himself". (...) the signs underearth (...) are numerals denoting the number of times the bull's journey was made, and the half-erased circular sign may be a primitive form of the place sign ⊗..." The third row "shows a procession of the three boats (...) proceeding from a city, bearing the same bird (...) and which may be Hermopolis, the city of Thot. One of them seems to journey towards another city denoted by the nome sign 𓈈 (...).

[517] Renée Friedman (1996: 29-30) suggests re-use in the reigns of Aha and Djer on the basis of the pottery, but this is not a definitive argument.

It is possible to assume that the city-temple (Nekhen) was constructed shortly before the First Dynasty. It could have been built in the period of Naqada IIIA-B, when the Locality HK29a seems to have been abandoned – R. Friedman (1996: 29)-; obviously, Hierakonpolis needed a temple, and if there is an abandonment between Naqada IIIA period and the beginning of the First Dynasty, where was the cult developed? The only answer is in another building, in another place: the city-temple.

[518] (1901: pl. III, no. 12).

[519] Dreyer (1998: Abb. 80, nos. 127-129).

[520] (1998: 142). Followed by Wilkinson (1999: 318-319).

[521] Schäfer (1902: 34).

[522] Faulkner (1969: 327). The hieroglyphic version could be consulted in *Wb*. V, 567.

[523] Petrie (1901: pls. IIIA, nos. 5 & 6, X, no. 2, XI, no. 2).

[524] (1952, 1, II: 836).

[525] (1901: 21).

[526] (1907: 21-23).

Fig. 22: The city temple of Hierakonpolis (Nekhen) according to the depictions found at Abydos. Not to scale.

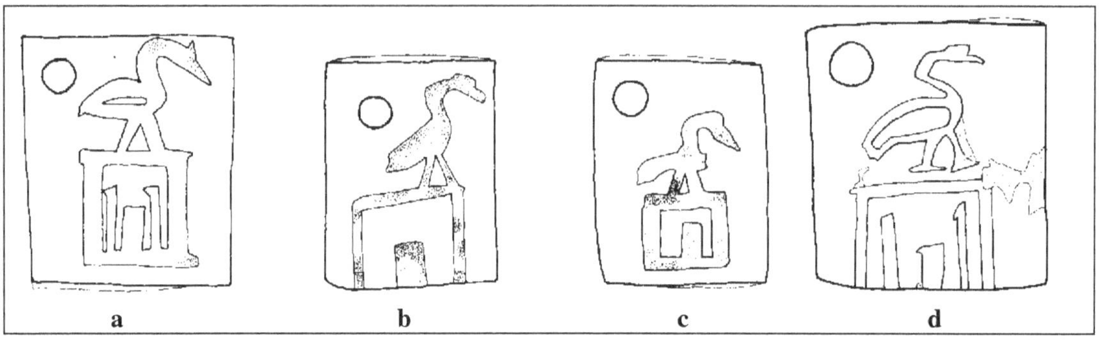

Fig. 23: Horus Aha wooden label from Abydos. Not to scale.

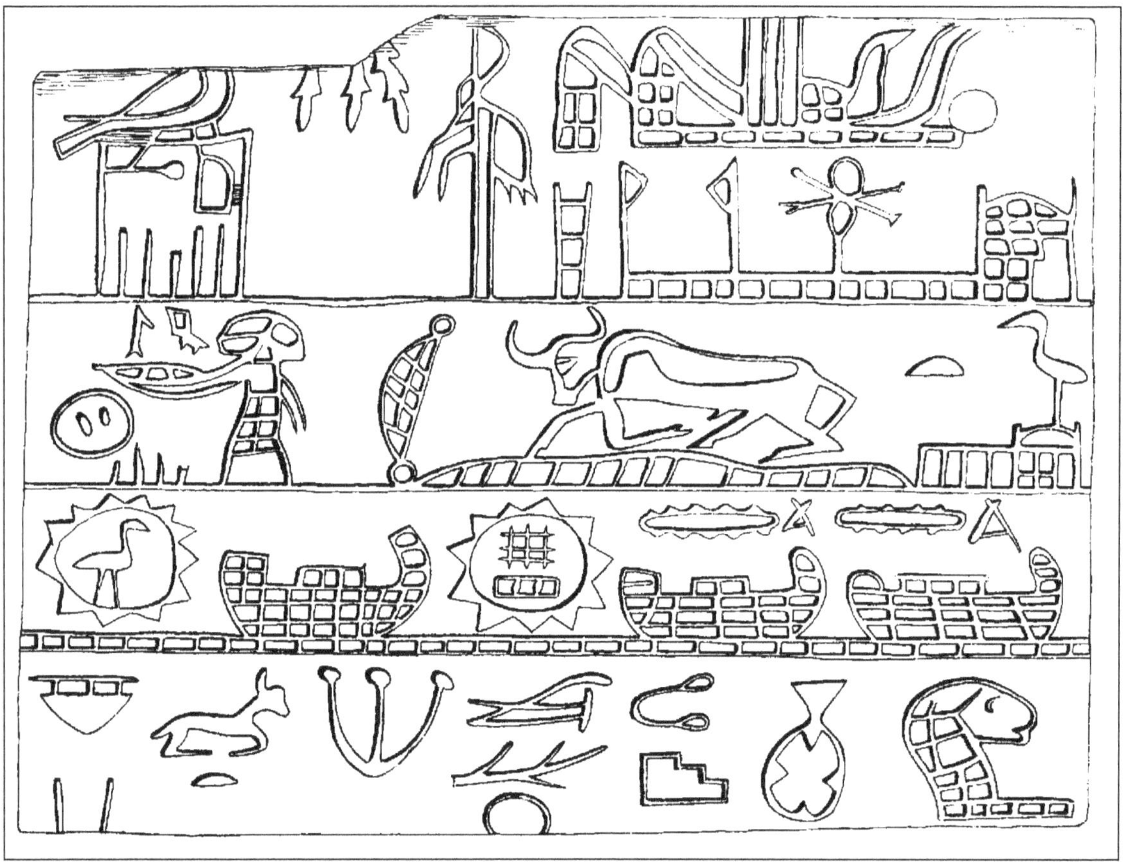

Does this refer to the Fayoum? The other two are journeying past two islands ▭ which, contrary to custom, have the serrated edges of a city cartouche, and the hoe-sign *mer* in front of them. Does the whole register susgested that the king's benefactions to the temple were brought in barges from the city of Thoth? I am unable to suggest any other explanation." In the fourth row, Legge read "At the foundation of the City of Neith (?) the Horus gave to the temple a hundred measures of wood, vegetables, meat, loaves, and jars of wine."[527]

Vandier[528] interpreted the first register as the navigation of the king Aha to a sanctuary of Neith, probably at Sais. In the second row, he saw a ceremony in which the king was represented by a bull, beside him a sanctuary and a man with a basket or offerings. The lower row would be the return trip of the king and the lowest row is connected with the lowest register of the label of Naqada.

Weill[529] read the first two rows: 1.- Birth of Anubis, river procession and (royal) visit to the temple of Neith. 2 .- Presentation of aliments *sm*, by the *sm* priest (vegetables?), sacrifices *smꜣ·t* (and everything) nutricious plenitude."

Helck[530] read the first row "Birth of Imiut. Travel on two ships and stay in the temple of Neith at Sais. Second row: Catching and shooting of the desert animal, four times in *ḏbꜥwt* by (the priest) *Sem*. Fourth row: (Fetching of) *mr* and *ꜥš*-wood fro *Pš* and arrival of ships from the Bird-Land."

Logan[531] reads the first row as "the fashioning of an *jmy-wt* fetish, erecting the temple of Neith." The offering depicted on the left side of the second row would be related to the foundation of a temple, meanwhile the bull running constitutes another scene that is related to the running of Apis. According to him, the third register shows a royal inspection tour where two walled towns are named. In the fourth row, the commodity to which the label was attached is mentioned, namely *sty-ḥrw* oil. According to Longan,[532] "Since the tax is from Lower Egypt and the cult of Neith has been traditionally identified as originating in Sais, and the same ships in the same register are interpreted as seaworthy, the accepted interpretation of a visit by the king to the Delta seems to be likely."

It seems clear that the temple represented in the first register of this label was dedicated to the goddess Neith.[533] It could be read: "Horus Aha. Fashioning (ms[.t]) [534] of Imyut. Erecting the (sacred) bark of the temple of Neith."[535] The fetish of the *jmj-wt* used to be represented, in later periods, adjuncts to the *ms.t* ceremony, enthronement, *sed* festival and royal burial.[536] As will be dealt with below, this ceremony could be connected with the *sed* festival, the first conclusion being that the *sed* festival, although celebrated in one specific place, had associated rituals all around the country. In the second register, it will be suggested that the ceremony of the *sed* festival was depicted and that it was celebrated at Hierakonpolis. This argument is based on the hieroglyphic sign of Hierakonpolis (◎) that appears besides a person (probably, the

[527] For the other label (or tablet), he read the triple number of wood, Legge (1907: 24).

[528] (1952, 1, II: 836-840).

[529] (1961, 2: 1-5)

[530] (1987: 148).

[531] (1990: 64).

[532] (1990: 65).

[533] For example, Jéquier (1908: 27-31); El-Sayed (1982: 225-226), with some references. Baines (1991: 35, fig. 6), who mentions formalised successors in the late and Graeco-Roman periods.

[534] Schott (1972: 35) translated the sign *ms* as "dedication" (of a statue). Previously, Sethe (1914: 235) had proposed the meaning "to form", "to model".

[535] Surely, the localisation of this temple could be Sais. However, there are other alternatives: Vandier (1952: 560) suggested that this temple could have been built at Abydos, showing, in this way, the devotion for this goddess in the Upper Egyptian capital. Neith had been worshipped at Kommer since the Ptolemaic period. Kommer was a locality between Hierakonpolis and Esna. During the festival of Khoiak at Esna, many statues of gods visited and joined in the rituals. One of these gods was Neith of Kommer, see Sauneron (1962: 48-52), with references. But, Neith played a very important role in the ritual at Esna (and, obviously, at Sais), Sauneron (1962: 249-251).

About this first row, Vikentiev (1948: 667) proposed to identify this temple with the inscription *pr kꜣ Nt* "the house of the goddess Neith", see Petrie (1914: 74-75).

[536] Logan (1990: 61), with references.

Among many ceremonies that were celebrated at Sais, can be cited the funerary ritual, see Málek (1984: 355). Perhaps Imiut in this representation was connected with one of them.

king or a *sem*[537] priest) that brings his offerings. Above the basket, there are two uncertain signs. Below the basket, there are four protuberances that Vikentiev[538] proposed as symbols of fertilisation, although it is preferable to interpret them as the four times (four for Upper Egypt and four for the Lower Egypt) that the ruler had to run around the track.[539] This running was possibly represented in the same register: the Predynastic Egyptian ruler was depicted several times as a bull and he even had some titles that related him to bulls or cows.[540] Finally, to the right of the running bull, it is thought that the primitive temple of Hierakonpolis is depicted.[541] In the third row, there are three boats that seem to be going somewhere. If this interpretation is correct, these barks are going to Hierakonpolis (in the left-hand enclosure, the bird that appears depicted is the same as that on the roof of the primitive temple of Hierakonpolis). Perhaps, this scene is related to an Utterance (§409) of the Pyramid Texts, which Faulkner[542] translated: "The king is the bull of the Ennead, possessor of five meals, three in the sky and two on the earth; it is the Night- and Day-barks which convey this to the King from the *nẖn*-shrine of the god". This is a spell that relates the king to the "*nẖn*-shrine" (Nekhen, the city temple of Hierakonpolis) and food. This last element is basic in all the festivals and ceremonies, as part of the offerings and also as celebrations.

Following the interpretation of the third row, it is necessary to mention the central enclosure, which has two hieroglyphs in its interior, which represent the two religious capitals of Egypt: Pe (□) and Nekheb (⊂⊃),[543] where the goddesses Wadjet and Nekhbet had their respective origins.[544] It is also possible that the boats were made of *meru*-wood.[545]

A **similar label**, also from Abydos, is incomplete (BM 35.518) (Figure 24).[546] The two registers conserved are practically identical, except for the inscription in the lower part: the oil is *stj-ḥr* and is accompanied by the numeral 300.[547] It is very difficult to translate the fourth row of these two labels. Both of them begin with the formula "Finest of...", and perhaps are making reference to wood (with flowers determinative) and pottery (with oil or wine).

[537] Godron (1957: 195), Vikentiev (1949/1950: 202) and Ogdon (1981: 62) read *sm* too.

[538] (1949/1950: 202).

[539] Hassan (1992); also Bleeker (1967: 101). Hence, it is difficult to agree with Rowe (1941: 342-343) who thought that the running bull could be the determinative in the place name *Mtwn* (Methun), "The Fighting Place of the Bulls", mentioned in the mastaba of Nefer-Maat at Meidum.

[540] The figure of the king associated with animals is very common in different cultures, see for example Hocart (1970: 90-92), with references.

[541] This representation of the temple has been interpreted as the temple of Buto, see for example Wilkinson (1999: 319, fig. 8.10) or even the temple of Thot, Smith (1946: 120). Barta (1982) interprets these oval signs as a type of building called *wnt* and described in Huni's autobiography. However, Ogdon (1983: 58-59) suggests that they represent temples located on the fringe of the desert.

[542] (1969: 134).

[543] For the identification of Nekheb, see Ogdon (1982a: 44). The two hieroglyphs together could also make reference to *(p) chi*, Gauthier (1928: 112), a locality of the 4th nome in Upper Egypt.

[544] However, Ogdon (1981: 62) holds that the procession of the ships is taking place between two fortified enclosures, and it would be "some sort of religious navigation that the two unnamed "towns" were founded".

[545] In this regard, O'Connor (1987: 33) interprets the return of a sea-going expedition from Lebanon with a load of the coniferous *meru* wood, and in the bottom row, he reads "fragrance of the god Horus".

[546] Petrie (1901: pl. IIIA, 6; pl. XI, 2); Spencer (1980: 64, no. 455, pl. 48, 52).

[547] Kaplony (1963, t. I: 313); Spencer (1980: 64, n. 3).

Fig. 24: Fragmentary wooden label from Abydos. Not to scale.

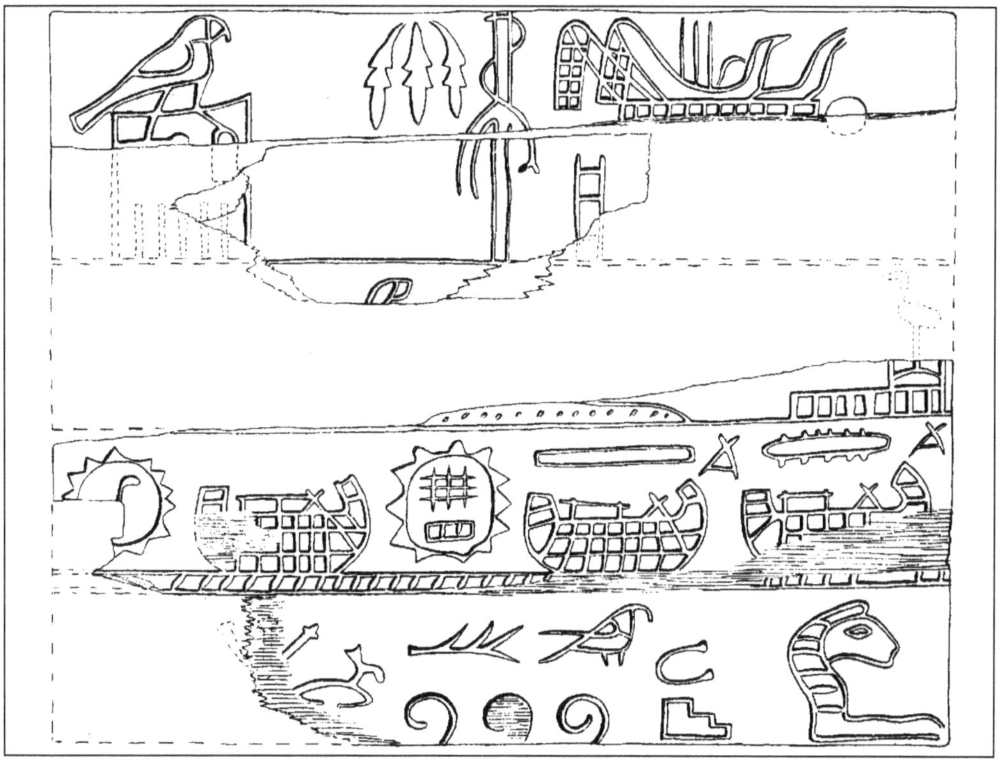

Item no. 4. Hor Aha fragmentary ebony labels from Abydos (Figure 25).[548] Petrie found two fragments of the same label. In the final report, he placed the pictures of both labels one above the other. They are included below. In the upper label (Petrie's no. 4), Petrie[549] saw a scene in which the king was receiving the captives of the south and the north.[550] In the other label (Petrie's no. 6), he saw a superintendent standing, and a man seated, apparently stabbing a seated captive in the breast, which for him suggested a scene of a captive being sacrificed at the royal funeral. He could also read the title "born of Horus and Amiut" (Anubis). According to Vandier[551], the king is going to kill a prisoner and this ceremony is related to a feast dedicated to Horus and Anubis ("*nébride*"). Vikentiev[552] correctly related this fragmentary label to one with a similar representation bearing the *serekh* of Djer and found at Saqqara. Logan[553] interprets both fragments of the same label as "the scene as the king observing a sacrificial scene accompanied by the *šzp šmʿw mḥw*[554] and the "fashioning of an *jmj-wt* fetish."

It is possible that these labels might be related to the *sed* festival, as Vikentiev[555] pointed out. The victim of the sacrifice might be a Nubian captured in the course of the Egyptian expeditions that took place during both reigns (see Gebel Sheikh Suleiman, pp. 89-90).[556] The victim could be related to other scenes of *sed* festivals in which a prisoner become an essential part of the ceremonial, playing the role as a substitutive victim of the king. In this sense, it might explain the presence of the gods Horus and Anubis (Imiut); Horus represents the king and Anubis guarantees the immortality of the dead king.[557] The represented scene would be one of the ceremonies in which the king also receives the homage (*šzp šmʿw mḥw*) of Upper and Lower Egypt. Moreover, the royal palace appears depicted between the *serekh* and a human figure (the king?).

---

548 Petrie (1901: 20, pl. III, nos. 4 & 6) noticed that they were duplicated.
549 (1901: 20).
550 Griffith, in Petrie (1901: 49), had a different interpretation "receiving the princes of the North and South" or "receiving the kingdom of the North and South".
551 (1952, 1, II: 835).
552 (1949-1950: 189-194)
553 (1990: 66).
554 "Receive Upper and Lower Egypt".
555 (1949-1950: 171, 195).
556 See Jiménez-Serrano (forthcoming).
557 As in the royal tombs in the Kings Valley (New Kingdom), see Costa *et alii* (1999: 105).

Fig. 25: Two fragmentary ebony labels found in the tomb of Horus Aha at Abydos. Not to scale.

Fig. 26: A reconstruction of the plan of the enclosure of Djer, where the *sed* festival could be celebrated.

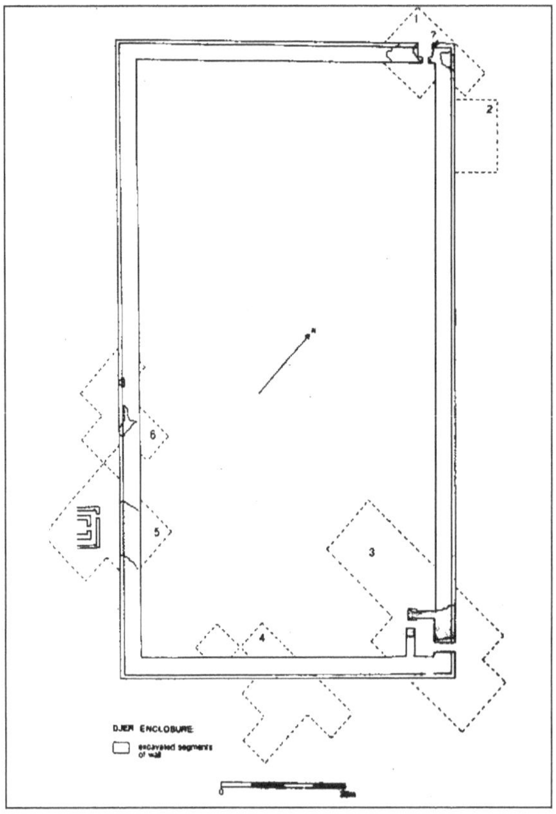

Item no. 5. Djer ivory labels from Abydos[558] and Saqqara[559] (Figure 27). Both of them have the same depiction, except in the fourth row. The second one is almost unknown and was discovered in a tomb dated to the middle of the First Dynasty.[560] This fact can be explained as a gift that an official received at the beginning of his career during the reign of Djer, although he built his tomb in the middle of the First Dynasty. The brief description written by Quibell[561] does not permit one to know the owner of the tomb, although surely it was Netjermu.

Legge[562] interpreted the first register as a festival celebrated by the king at the foundation of some building. The second register appears to describe the queen's pavilion belonging to the crown of Lower Egypt, in a city situated in the nome of the jackal, and containing a temple dedicated to Safkit.[563] In the third register, he wondered whether in this row it was possible to interpret "the feast of Heb-sed was held for the North and South for the fifth time in the city of Thot". The fourth register reads: "At the foundation, the Horus gave the temple trees (?), the thousand jars of royal wine from the South, loaves of bread and wine..."

For Emery[564], it records a visit of the king to Buto and Sais, and Vandier[565] adds Hermopolis, as well as from these two cities.

Helck[566] translated: "1. - Horus Djer, (behind him) *Mn*; staying in *P* and 'opening' (Upper Egypt) of the seat of Horus the harpooner in Buto. 2. - (visit) of the royal court, in the royal shrine in *Dp* and stay in *smr-nṯrw* with birth of *Sd*, death of the queen, sacrifice (?) and standing on the throne. 3. - Arrival of barks of *mrw*-wood from the bird town. 4.- In Upper and Lower Egypt... of every *rẖyt*'.

Fig. 27: Ivory label of Djer from Abydos. Not to scale.

First of all, it is necessary to discuss the orientation of characters in this piece. All the registers must be read from left to right. However, there is an exception; in the second row, the name of Buto (*dp*) is written with the hand in uncommon direction. This might be explained by the fact that the shrine is below an imaginary axis around which the word is depicted:

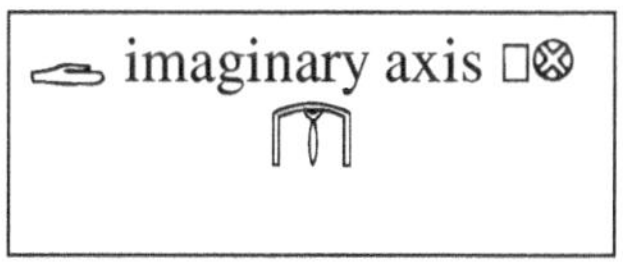

In addition, it would be possible to give a different interpretation, considering that there are pictorial elements and hieroglyphic signs: in the first row of the labels, can be read: *mn* (), the royal *serekh*, a mast () over the sign of city (), an enclosure with four signs: lower mandible with a falcon on the top, and the king's name.[567] On the top of this enclosure there are two signs: the standard of and the sign (?). Gauthier[568] mentioned an unidentified locality in the Fourth nome of Lower Egypt called *ᶜḥᶜ wrt*, which would

[558] Amélineau (1904, 3: pl. XV, no. 19). A good depiction in Emery (1961: 20) or Helck (1987: 152).
[559] Quibell (1923: pl. XI, nos. 2, 3). Tomb 2171.
[560] According to the characteristics -this tomb has a portcullis- published by Emery (1961: 141-142) for the tombs of the Early Dynastic period.
[561] (1923: 6, 23-24)
[562] (1907: 71-73).
[563] Legge (1907: 72) affirmed that this explanation did not convince him at all.
When he referred to Safkit, he meant Seshat.
[564] (1961: 59).
[565] (1952, 1, II: 841).
[566] (1987: 152).
[567] There is a curious parallel in Central Africa; Cervelló Autuori (1996: 144) –with references- mentions that in the funerary temples of the kings of the Baganda from Uganda the priests emit oracles of the dead kings. Funerary temples and tombs are separated, but in the funerary temple a part of the body of the dead king has remained: his mandible. Together with this is the royal placenta, which is considered a twin brother of the new-born king. The main feature of this "twin brother" of the king is that he was born dead. The royal placenta is one of the standards in the Late Predynastic and Early Dynastic periods in Egypt.
[568] (1925, 1: 156).

be close geographically to Buto (see below) and phonetically to the hieroglyphs [hieroglyphs] *ꜥḥꜥ wr*. It is impossible to know if the depicted signs refer to this locality close to Buto, but the possibility has not been rejected that king Djer made a royal foundation in Lower Egypt called 'Horus Djer's jaw' the same year that he visited Buto for the celebration of his *sed* festival (see below). Besides, some palm trees with some buildings (?) and a channel (?) have been represented, which, according to Dina Faltings,[569] represent the two areas which formed Buto, Pe and Dep. The meaning of the whole row would be '*Mn* (a title), Horus Djer, (visits) *ꜥḥꜥ wrt* (and founded the royal state of) *ḥr ꜥrt ḏr* (Horus Djer's jaw). (Visit) Buto'. There is also another possible reading: *mn ḥr ḏr ꜥḥꜥ njwt r wr(w) ḥr ḏr ꜥrt* 'Mn, Horus Djer, rise the city to the "Great Ones" (called) "Horus Djer's jaw"'. The second row may be divided into two parts for its analysis. Two thirds (on the left side) seem to represent an enclosure where the standard of the god Sed (Wepwawet) is depicted over the perch, three posts, a *tekenu*, a man running (?), a rosette, the goddess Hathor or a bovine goddess[570], a stairway ([hieroglyph]) with a mast ([hieroglyph]). The last third of the row represents very interesting elements, some of them also appear depicted in the Narmer mace-head: the shrine (in this case with signs [hieroglyph] *nbty* 'The Two Ladies', referring to Wadjet and Nekhbet), [hieroglyphs], *dp*, Buto,[571] and the red crown surrounded by a spiral.[572] Those elements make it seem likely that in this register the *sed* festival at Buto was represented.[573] The confirmation is given by the elements that are depicted: a special enclosure, the rosette, the shrine, the standard of the god Sed, the red crown, the man running and the *tekenu*. The third register depicts a falcon surrounded by walls, a bark and hieroglyphs that can be translated as "Upper and Lower Egypt give the (statue (?) of) alabaster (?) to Thot." The fourth register presents a problematic reading and the fourth register of the label from Saqqara is unreadable.

Item no. 6. A **seal-impression of Djer from Abydos**[574] **(Figure 28)** was interpreted by Hornung and Staehelin[575] as a representation of one of the ceremonies of the *sed* festival, because Djer was represented twice, with the god-jackal Sed (Wepwawet), seated with different crowns (the red and white) and with the robe. This is the first time in which a king is depicted with both crowns in this ceremony. It has to be understood as a new step in the development of the concept of duality. At least from this moment, there is evidence, which permits us to relate the crowns with the two regions of Egypt (in accordance with the later iconography of the *sed* festival).[576]

Fig. 28: Seal-impression from Abydos. Not to scale.

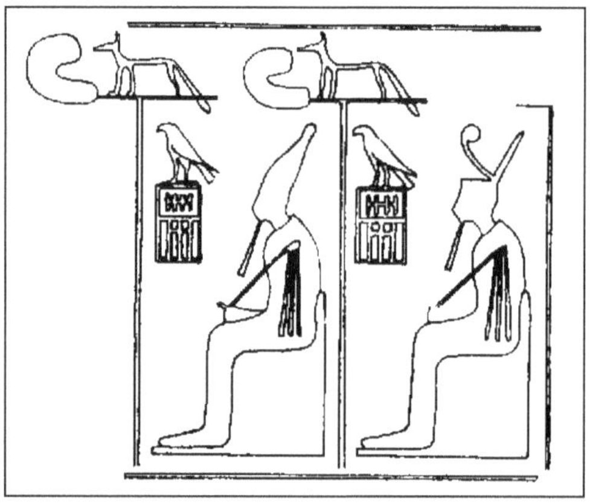

Item no. 7. In another **seal-impression**[577] **(Figure 29),** the king Djer was represented running with the *mks* besides a building called *zḥ-(-nṯr)* and traces of a platform. Kaplony[578] related it to a festival, Hornung and Staehelin[579] connected it with the *sed* festival and F. D. Friedman,[580] following this last interpretation, distinguishes the building as a funerary shrine and the figure of the running king as a possible representation of a royal statue.[581] The scene clearly represents elements of the *sed* festival: the palace ([hieroglyph])the building is *zḥ-nṯr* ([hieroglyph]) the king running (with the white crown and the *mks*), and the stairway of the pavilion ([hieroglyph]).

569 (Personal communication).
570 See Hassan (1992).
571 Dina Faltings (personal communication) interprets it as Dep, one of the names of Buto. See *Wb* 5, 443.
572 According to Baines (personal communication), it may represent a ground plan formed to make the interior invisible from outside.
573 Monnet-Saleh (1969: 177) suggested this possibility as well.
574 Petrie (1901: pl. XV, no. 108).
575 (1974: 16).
576 See for example, R. H. Wilkinson (1992: 146, fig. 2).
577 Kaplony (1964: Taf. 19, no. 1032).
578 (1964: 23-24, Taf. 19, no. 1032).
579 (1974: 16).
580 (1995: 32, n. 171).
581 Eaton-Krauss (1984: n. 484) admitted her doubts.

Fig. 29: Reconstruction of a seal-impression. Not to scale.

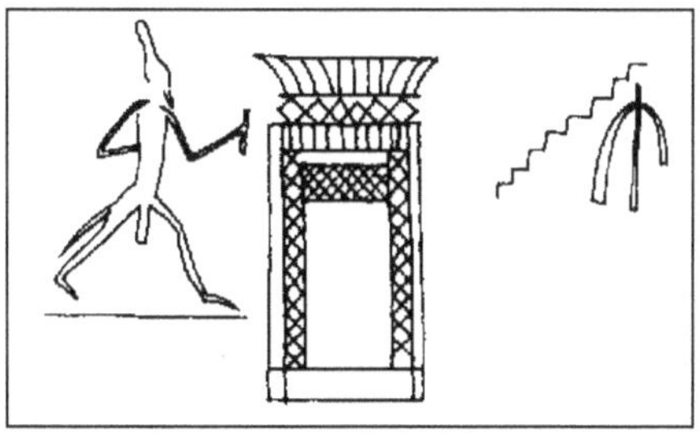

Item no. 8. An ivory label of Djet from Saqqara (tomb 3504)[582] **(Figure 30)**. Emery[583] read "Year of taking (*šzp*) the ... (fortress?) of the North. The making of a statue of Thoth" (below there is a group for which he could find no parallel, and he wondered if it might represent some ritual object raised on a standard). Beside the royal *serekh*, there is a group of signs that he interpreted as a personal name Sekhemkay (*sḫm-kꜣ·(j)*) and a title "treasurer" (*sḏ(ꜣwty)*). In the bottom right-hand corner, "the shrine of (or protected by) the goddess of Upper Egypt; the shrine of (or protected by) the goddess of Lower Egypt". The rest of the signs to the left of the *kheker*-topped structure indicated the articles or substances contained in the box or bag to which the label was attached, and it could mean "gift (or allotment) of the king, 1100..."

Gardiner[584] presumed that it made reference to the domination over both Upper and Lower Egypt, based on the representations of the temples that appear in the enclosure with the signs . According to him, the two buildings depicted in the interior of the enclosure were the *jtrtj*.[585]

Helck[586] read "Year: Planning (?) of the foundation of the two fortresses; birth of two signs of bud lotus; standing in the royal shrine of the Two Ladies".

Fig. 30: Ivory label from Saqqara. Not to scale.

However, this label can also be read as follows: *rnpt sꜣḫ jnb (?) mḥw* "Year of the approaching to a fortress of Lower Egypt"; *ms(.t) ḏḥwty* "Making the statue of Thot". Below them, are two signs that have no parallel with other hieroglyphs.[587] They could be sacred items for the cult of Thot, used only in that period. As Gardiner suggested, the most interesting part of this label is the bottom right side. It is possible to suggest that it could represent the funerary enclosure that was also used for the *sed* festival, because there are many elements that are coincident: the palace , the vulture (goddess Nekhbet) [588], the red crown ,[589] *nbtj* (connected surely with the two above), a palace façade , and the *pr nw* . But, apart from some elements related to the *sed* festival, there is no evidence to prove the celebration of such a ceremony during the reign of king Djet. Thus, it could be the record of the foundation of the royal enclosure at Abydos. For the rest of the label, here we follow Emery's reading.

Den celebrated at least two *sed* festivals according to a fragment of vessel discovered at Abydos (Figure 31). It mentions "the second occasion of the *sed*-festival"[590].

[582] Emery (1954: 102, fig. 105 & pl. XXXV).
There is another label (practically a duplicate of the last one) of uncertain provenance. Vikentiev (1959: 9-16), who analysed it, emphasised the stimulant character of this resin gum from Libya mentioned on this label.
[583] (1954: 102-103).
[584] (1958).
[585] According to Gardiner (1958: 39), *jtrty* referred to two opposite lines of shrines specially built for the *sed* festival. He also argued that these buildings represented Hierakonpolis and Buto.
[586] (1987: 155).

[587] Kahl (1994: 592, m17) defines them as flowerbuds.
[588] Compare with the Narmer mace-head, where the vulture (goddess Nekhbet) appears flying.
[589] It might be considered as the red crown (*dšrt*) or the representation of Lower Egypt (*bjty*), see Gardiner (1957: 504)
[590] Dreyer (1990: 80, Abb. 9, taf. 26d).

Fig. 31: Fragment of vessel from Abydos. Not to scale.

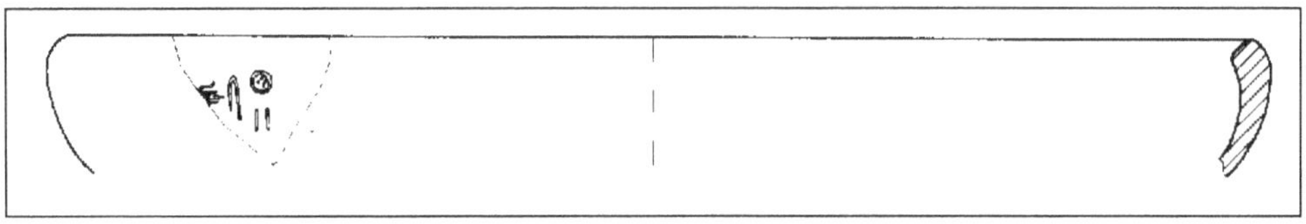

Item no. 9. Wooden label of Den from Abydos[591] (Figure 32). Although a part of this label is missing, most scholars support that the right side of this label was originally divided into four registers.[592]

According to Griffith,[593] the scene in which it is possible to distinguish the king running (right side), represents a ceremony for the worship of the gods; the figure of the canopy can hardly be intended for Osiris, as the running figure is turned away from it. Griffith read the second register as "Opening the gate of the foreign lands to those that desire". The third row, which was related to another fragment of label[594], was read "The Master comes, the King of Upper and Lower Egypt Semty, having seized thirty nomes (or territories)". On the left-hand side, he read the names and title of the chancellor Hemaka and Ka-sa, who "held the same position as Hemaka under Den, but an earlier period". Also, he could translate the title "who took the throne of Horus".[595] For the next group of signs, he offered three possibilities of interpretation: "Sheikh of the Libyans", "*hatet*-oil of the Libyans", and the city of This (Thinis)[596]. The enclosure with the man pounding was interpreted as "governor of the quarry city of Het-nub" and below it is "the Residence of the King of Upper Egypt", which he placed a little north of the latitude of Oxyrhynchus. He finished the analysis of this label by recognising a "royal smith" or "axe maker" and a group of signs that he could not read.

Sethe[597] read in the second register of the right-hand side "Open the Fortress, "the beautiful door", destroy the walls of.... and get into the kings (?) by the *Sm*-priest in front of the temple".

Legge[598] read in this label: "In the year when the Sed festival was celebrated in the thrice captured and rebuilt city of..... Hemaka being chancellor of Lower Egypt, the royal residence for Upper Egypt was built by the royal architects.[599] (Formula.) At the foundation the Horus gave to the temple the thousand jars of water, two hundred measures of wood, and two (?) *hin* of strong wine".

Kaplony[600] reads the name of Den and the seal-bearer of the King of Lower Egypt, Hemaka, together with the name of another official, Iti-sen, who bore the title *mḏḥtj-nzwt*.[601] Beside his name are two signs of uncertain reading. Beneath the king's name is the designation of the kind of oil to which this label referred, together with its quantity, although part of the number is missing. On the right-hand side of the label, the inscriptions in the four registers are bordered by a large hieroglyph (𓆳, *rnpt*), "year". He interprets the top of the register as the *sed* festival, in which the king is running as part of a ritual and seated on the throne in a booth. The meaning of the lower register is not so clear for him, affirming only that it includes references to the destruction of a stronghold and the taking of captives.

Helck[602] interpreted "1- Festival Sed. 2. - Opening the fortress in beautiful arch;[603] disease

591 Petrie (1900: pls. XI, no. 14, XV, no. 16).
592 For all the interpretations see Godron (1990: 32) with references.
593 In Petrie (1900: 40-42).
594 Petrie (1900: pl. XV, no. 18).
595 , *yṯ ys.t ḥrw*, Griffith, in Petrie (1900: 41).
596 In Petrie (1900: 41).
597 (1905: 66).

598 (1907: 105).
599 Vandier (1952, 1, II: 853) agreed with the theory that affirms that the *sed* festival is represented in the first register on the right-hand side (also the identification of Hemaka, the royal carpenter, and the royal palace), but in the second he interpreted the inscription as "running around the wall" (probably Memphis). However, Vikentiev (1949/1950: 203) interpreted the second row on the right as "transport of the cereals (into) *Khent*" (*jn (t) smw (m) ẖnt*).
600 (1963, I-III: 300, 313 -the name for the oil is *sṯj-ḥr*, 439, 1004 (n 1607), 1005-1007 (n. 1610).
601 Kaplony (1963, 1: 300) read *mḏḥ-mḏḥ(w) nsw*.
602 (1987: 159).
603 Ogdon (1981: 62-63) translated "to open the door (?) with the picks", "to bring the *dꜣj*-drug in the portative (sic.) -chest", and mentions specific religious rituals.

of the virgin; fetching of Sem *ḫntj*-box. 3. - King of Upper and Lower Egypt *ḫ3stj* (before)..."

According to Fischer[604], it represents a enthronement or a royal jubilee in the first register; below, the sign means "opening" (referred to a settlement) and the sign is "smiting" (referred to its inhabitants). The three strokes could indicate the plural or scattered bricks. The rest of the section is difficult to interpret except for a mention of the king's name, Khasty. On the left side of the label is the *serekh* of Den, behind which is the name of Hemaka. Below, there is a designation of the product to which it was affixed; then, after an obscure phrase, it is possible to read "the best of olive oil, 1200". The column of signs on the left is difficult to read for this author, but he offers the possibility that it could be "the king's mansion" in which the oil is prepared, as well as the name and the title of the supervising official.

Godron[605] translates: "(1st register right) Sed Festival[606]. (2nd register) sending an expedition (or expeditions). Dismantling the fortress *ꜥ3ꜥn* ("the beautiful door"). Smiting the *ỉwnwt*. Capturing (lit. conducting) with (the god) Sopdou, who preside the Mines (Sinai?). (3rd right) Hunting birds with boomerang by the king of Upper and Lower Egypt Khasty. Representation of the hunted birds in their thickets.[607] Harpooning <the fish>. Representation of the king harpooning the fish in their marshlands (4th right) Harpooning (lit. throwing) the hippopotamus[608] by the king of Upper and Lower Egypt Khasty. <making the statue of> *ḥmw*. (Left side) Horus Den's serekh. The chancellor of the Lower Egyptian king, Hemaka. The royal palace: the palace of the casters, the carpenters and the constructors (?) *ṯj-jwntj* (??). The throne of Horus. The mention of a certain quantity of oil from Libya."[609]

The label can be interpreted as Godron did for the right side, but another reading would be possible for the left side: Horus Den. The chancellor of Lower Egypt, Hemaka. The finest olive oil from Libya, 1200 (?). Grinding olives (?). From the *ḥwt-njswt*, the royal carpenter *ṯj-wnty* (?).

Wooden label of Den painted with red and black ink from Abydos[610] (Figure 33). This label was discovered in tomb 83, situated to the south-west of the tomb of Djer.[611] According to Godron's[612] reconstruction, this label must have been very similar to the previous one. Thus, for an interpretation of this label, see reference to the preceding label.

---

604 (1989: 70).

605 (1990: 39, 61, 64, 66, & 74).

606 Godron (1990: 41) saw the king identified with Osiris in the seated figure.

607 In recent years, a new fragment of a label has been discovered in which the king appeared running in the celebration of the *sed* festival, with captured birds, see Dreyer *et alii* (1998: 163, taf. 12f).

608 A fragment of a label as found in recent years in cemetery B at Abydos, representing probably the hunt of the hippopotamus, see Dreyer *et alii* (1998: 163, taf. 12d) and Figures 43-44.

609 Newberry (1912: 282) read the oil as *ḥ3.t ṯḥnw* (Libya).

610 Amélineau (1905, pl. XXXVII, no. 3); for clear photographs and a reconstruction, see Godron (1990: pls. I, nos. 1 & 2, II, 3 & 4, III, 6). As Legge (1907: 150) pointed out the quality of the photography in Amélineau's publication is very poor. As Legge did not have access to a good image, his interpretation has not been used in this case.

611 Godron (1990: 27).

612 (1990: pl. III, no. 6).

Fig. 32: Wooden label of Den from Abydos. Not to scale.

Fig. 33: Wooden painted label of Den from Abydos. Not to scale.

Item no. 10. Emery[613] found in the tomb of Hemaka, a **seal-impression** (Figure 34), which represented two scenes. In the first one appeared the phonogram *p* and a running bull, behind is the running king with the red crown and his *serekh*. In the second scene, an enthroned baboon offers a bowl to a running king preceded by a standard with Wepwawet (?). The king, on this occasion, wears the white crown and behind him is his *serekh*. According to Hornung and Staehelin,[614] those images must be connected with the *sed* festival, Kaplony[615] related them to the Cairo fragment that mentions a festival honouring the god Hedjwer, and, finally, according to Eaton-Krauss[616] they are the representation of two running *sed* statues in accordance with the short bases that appear like plinths. Although it seems likely that the images of the king were his statues, there is only one element that could be related to the *sed* festival and that is the image of the baboon. There could be a second, a standard of the god Sed,[617] but the only preserved part cannot permit such an assertion. However, the representation of a bull running and the only conserved hieroglyph □, *p*, make one suspect that this seal impression refers to the running of the Apis bull. In the Palermo Stone, there are two references to the running of the Apis bull in the reign of Den.[618] The verb used for *pḥrr*[619] and the ancient Egyptian name of Apis was *ḥp*. Both words are formed with the phonogram *p*, but it would be possible to read the verb *pḥrr*, because the disposition of the hieroglyphs in the Palermo Stone is the same.[620] Thus, it is possible to propose that this seal-impression represents the fashioning of a royal statue for the *sed* festival and the running of the Apis bull. Moreover, according to the Palermo Stone, these two different events, the *sed* festival and the running of the Apis bull, happened in two successive years.[621]

Item no. 11. Fragment of a wooden label of Den from Abydos[622] (Figure 35). Griffith[623] recognised a *Sed* canopy in the top of the register, with the name *Sed* "rudely engraved" and in the second register, he distinguished a hawk and an ibis. Legge[624] saw the following signs: a "year name", the double staircase of the *sed* festival with two signs in front, a post with something on the top, a bird on a standard (one of the nome-standards carried before the king at his enthronement?), the *ms*-sign (without the top sprouts), the ibis of Thoth, the *serekh* of Den and the signs, which were translated by Griffith[625] as "the royal chancellor of Lower Egypt" (seal-bearer). Vandier[626] read the name of Hemaka, saw the *sed* festival pavilion and a festival of Thoth. Helck[627] translated this fragment (also followed by us): "Birth of (Wepwawet), x festival of Sed, epidemic in the West Delta; supply (??); Birth of the ibis".

Item no. 13. A variant of this label has been discovered at Abydos (Figure 36). The fragmentary inscription, which says *(zp) t(pj) ḥb-sd sḏ3wty bjtj* "First time of the sed festival; seal-bearer of Lower Egypt") is related to the festival *sed* and appeared with the title of seal-bearer of Lower Egypt.[628]

Together with this, there are some scenes that surely referred to the *sed* festival,[629] because in one case the king appears running and seated in a pavilion with the ceremonial robe, and in the other two cases the king is seated and in front of him are depicted three Lower Egyptian type shrines[630] surrounded by an enclosure (Figure 37). It seems likely that those three shrines were the shrines of the provincial images, as in the case of Netjerikhet complex at Saqqara (see Figure 16).

[613] (1938: 64, fig. 26).
[614] (1974: 17). They followed the opinion already expressed by Kees and Blackman in the late 1930s. For references see Hornung & Staehelin (1974: 43, n. 3).
[615] (1966: 98).
[616] (1984: 90-91); followed by F. D. Friedman (1995: 32).
[617] Compare to the one in the Palermo Stone, Schäfer (1902: 21, Nr. 11, x+11).
[618] Schäfer (1902: 19, Nr. 3, x+3, & 21, Nr. 12, x+12).
[619] *Wb*. 1, 541, B, a.
[620] According to Baines (personal communication), it would probably suit better a writing of *ḥp* 'Apis' with the normal *ḥp* sign and *p* as a complement.
[621] Years x+11 and x+12, Schäffer (1902: 21).
[622] Petrie (1900: pls. XI, no. 5, XIV, no. 12).
[623] In Petrie (1900: 41).
[624] (1907: 105).
[625] (1898), mentioned by Legge (1907: 104-105).
[626] (1952, 1, II: 853).
[627] (1987: 160).
[628] Dreyer (1990: 80, taf. 26a).
[629] Dreyer *et alii* (1998: Taf. 12f, g & h).
[630] According to Dreyer *et alii* (1998: 163-164), the shrines represent the city of Buto.

Fig. 34: Seal impression from the tomb of Hemaka at Saqqara. Not to scale.

Fig. 35: A fragment of label from the tomb of Den at Abydos. Not to scale.

Fig. 36: Fragment of label from Abydos. Not to scale.

Fig. 37: Fragmentary labels from Abydos. Not to scale.

Item no. 14. At Saqqara, Emery[631] found an **anonymous limestone slab** (Figure 38) bearing elements from a scene of the *sed* festival, carved in low relief. The slab was found reused in the wall of a Third Dynasty tomb shaft, which had been cut into tomb 3507, dated to the reign of Den. In the relief, the king was represented twice[632] with the red crown, clad in the short robe and holding a flail in the left hand and the *ḥts* in the right. In front of the leading figure, is a baboon seated on a pedestal very similar to the hieroglyph *mꜣꜥt.* Four birds surround the baboon, one of them is clearly an owl. The other three are conserved in poor condition, but it would be possible to suggest that they could be the three birds used for the word *wrw* "The Great Ones", which always appear together with the baboon.

Item no. 15. In Netjerikhet's underground galleries, some **fragmentary stone vessels** were found showing the name of **Anedjib** (Figure 39). All of them[633] would have had the same representation in their origin: a hall used in the *sed* festival 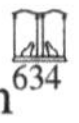 with an unreadable inscription on its platform[634] ( *mr(y) n nṯr*, "beloved of god" (?)). Over the hall, it is possible to read *zp tpy sd* "First time of the sed festival". In addition, different names of royal dominions (depending on the case) are mentioned.[635]

631 (1958: 72, 84). See also Spencer (1980: 16, pls. 8 & 9).
632 Surely because it is a practice piece.
633 Firth & Quibell (1936: pl. 105, nos. 7-9); Lacau & Lauer (1959: pl. III, no. 4; 1961: 19-21). There is an identical depiction in a fragmentary vessel found by Petrie at Umm el-Qaab, Petrie (1900: pls. VII, nos. 5, 7, 8). As Hornung & Staehelin (1974: 43, n. 4) noted, a fragment previously attributed to Anedjib was classified and published by Petrie (1900: pl. VII, no. 5) as belonging to the reign of Semerkhet, Anedjib's successor. But there is no problem with this attribution, because in the tomb of Semerkhet at Abydos fragments of an inscribed stone vessel with the name of Anedjib have appeared. The most surprising thing is that the two joined fragments bear, partially-erased, the *serekh* of Anedjib - see Petrie (1900: 20, pl. IV); Kaplony (1965: 13, pls. 23-25); Spencer (1980: 41-42, no. 269) - or with the *nzwt bjtj* of this king, *Mr-pj-bjꜣ.* Two fragments of an inscribed stone vessel, see Petrie (1900: 20, pl. VI, no. 5); Spencer (1980: 42, no. 270).

There is another fragment that would have had the same representation, see Kaplony (1965: 14, Abb. 30).
634 Lacau & Lauer (1961: 20).
635 Lacau & Lauer (1961: 20).

Fig. 38: Anonymous relief from Saqqara. Not to scale.

Fig. 39: Different inscriptions of Anedjib found in the underground galleries of the Step Pyramid. Not to scale.

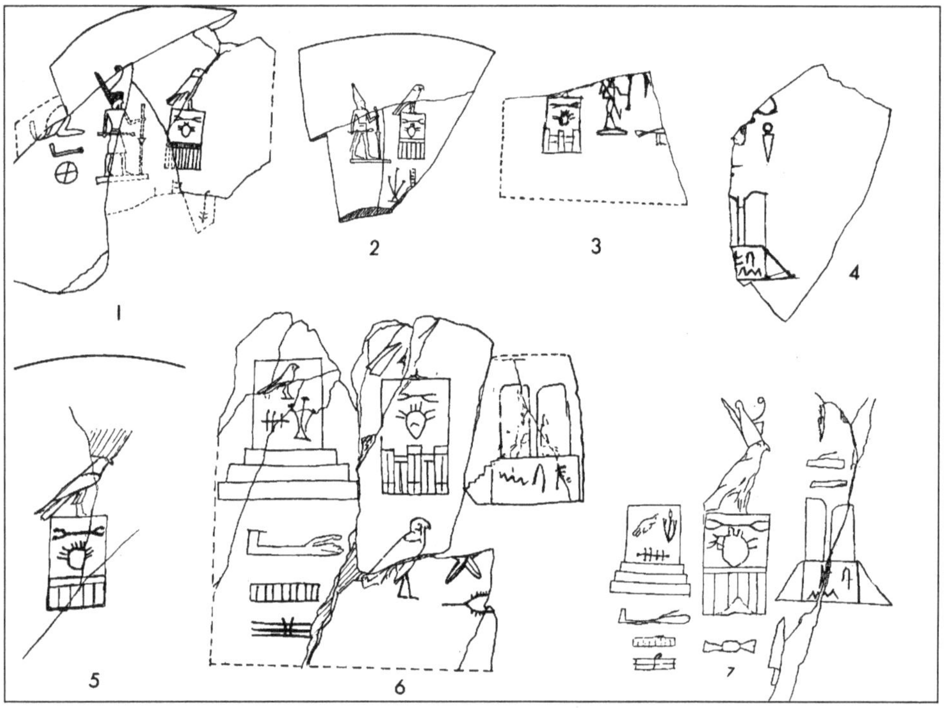

Semerkhet.- Petrie[636] read in a fragment of crystal bowl found in the tomb of Semerkhet at Abydos the *sed* festival of this king. (**Figure 40**, not to scale).

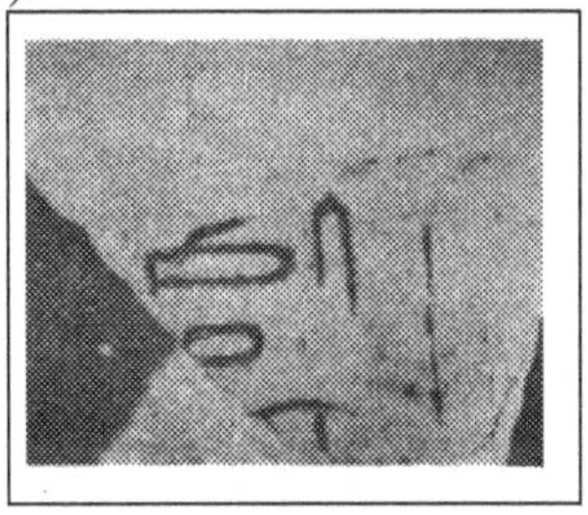

Inscription of the reign of Qaa on the surface of a stone vessel found in the Step Pyramid, Saqqara[637] **(Figure 41)**. Lacau and Lauer[638] read "Second *sed*-festival".

Fig. 41: Inscription of the "second occasion of the sed festival" of Qaa. Not to scale.

Item no. 16. Petrie[639] found three fragments of different vessels (?) which mention the *sed* festival of king Qaa or have the representation of the hall of the *sed* festival . From Saqqara, Lacau and Lauer[640] published a fragment with a similar inscription.

---

[636] (1900: 20, pl. VII, no. 6).
[637] Lacau & Lauer (1959, 1: pl. 8, no. 41).
[638] (1959, 1: 12).
[639] (1900: pl. VIII, nos. 6-8).
[640] (1959: pl. IV, no. 4).

TABLE 2: COMMON ELEMENTS SEEN ON DEPICTIONS OF THE *SED* FESTIVAL FROM THE FIRST DYNASTY AND THE REIGN OF NETJERIKHET																	
	Unknown	**Narmer**	**Aha**		**Djer**			**Djet**	**Den**						**Anedjib**	**Qaa**	**Netjerikhet**
	1	2	3	4	5	6	7	8	9	10	11	12	13	14	15	16	17
	*	*			*	*		*	*	*	*			*	*		*
King with robe		*				*			*		*	*		*			*[641]
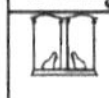	*	*			*				*		*		*		*	*	
		*			*		*		*		*		*		*	*	*
		*	*		*		*		*		*						*
ḏnbw		*	*						*		*						*
Tekenu		*			*												
		*		*													
Offerings		*	*														
		*			*			*									
		*	*					*				*					*
Sandal & seal bearer		*							*				*				
Homage			*	*													
				*			*	*									*
					*							*					*
Wepwawet		*			*	*				*			*(?)				*
		*			*												
						*	*		*						*		*
mks							*		*								*
							*										
Baboon										*				*			*
wrw														*			*
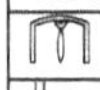																*	
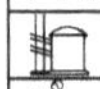																	*
															*	*	*

1.- Mace-head from Hierakonpolis.
2.- Narmer mace-head.
3.- Aha wooden label from Abydos.
4.- Aha fragmentary ebony label from Abydos.
5.- Djer ivory label from Abydos and Saqqara.
6. - Djer seal-impression from Abydos.
7.- Djer seal-impression.
8.- Djet ivory label from Saqqara.
9.- Wooden label of Den from Abydos.
10.- Den seal-impression from Hemaka's tomb.
11.- Fragment of a wooden label of Den from Abydos.
12.- Two similar fragments of ivory labels of Den from Abydos.
13.- Fragment of a wooden label of Den from Abydos.
14.- Limestone slab from Saqqara.
15.- Anedjib's vessels from Saqqara.
16.- Qaa's vessel from Saqqara.
17.- Reliefs from the subterranean rooms of Netjerikhet's complex.

641 Statue found in the *serdab*, see Baines & Málek (1980: 173).

- Appendix A: The *sed* festival in the Second Dynasty

The inscriptions and evidence dated to the Second Dynasty decrease dramatically in comparison to the First Dynasty. Due to this, our knowledge and the possibility of reconstructing more *sed* festivals are reduced considerably. However, this lack of evidence does not mean the absence of those rituals during this period. There are only a few pieces of evidence that suggested the celebration of the *sed* festival in two reigns: Ninetjer (third king of the Second Dynasty) and Khasekhem/Khasekhemui (last king of the Second Dynasty).

There is a small statue that shows king Ninetjer[642] seated with the robe, with the white crown, and the sceptre . Traditionally, it has been interpreted as a statue that represents the king in the *sed* festival.[643]

According to the Palermo Stone,[644] Khasekhem/Khasekhemui ruled for seventeen years, however, it seems clear that he celebrated his *sed* festival on the basis of the following evidence:

a) (As Khasekhemui) The Shunet el-Zebib: the biggest Early Dynastic enclosure at Abydos[645] (see Figure 8).

b) (As Khasekhem) Two statues from the Main Deposit of Hierakonpolis, in which the king wears the robe, and the white crown. On the pedestal are engraved figures of dead northern enemies with the inscription: 47.209 (number of enemies).[646]

According to Kaiser,[647] Khasekhem changed his enthronement name to Khasekhemui, in an attempt at a national renewal after a political crisis. Although there are no other examples of early kings who changed their names after celebrating their *sed* festival, it seems a good occasion to do it, especially since Khasekhemui's reign was relatively brief.

[642] Simpson (1956).
[643] Simpson (1956: 45).
[644] Schäfer (1902: 27), recently accepted and followed by Wilkinson (1999: 94).
[645] Ayrton *et alii* (1904).
[646] Quibell (1900: pl. XXXIX); Petrie, in Quibell (1900: 11).
[647] (1992: 184-185, n. 44).

- Appendix B: The *Sed* festival in Lower Nubia at the end of the fourth millennium BC?

Williams and Logan[648] related the **Siali seal-impressions**[649] to the *sed* festival. These seal-impressions were found in an A-Group storage pit at Siali in Northern Lower Nubia. Williams[650] dated them to the early Naqada IIIA period. Apart from other elements, such as incense burners, three dogs (?),[651] the bow (*tꜣ-stj*,[652]) and two (?) falcons surmounting twice as many buildings, it is possible to see a seated human figure facing a major building. This building seems to be surmounted by a falcon, which is flanked by two *ḏnbw* or stone markers (see p. 47). The place in which these seal-impressions were found is near the Egyptian border. This implies that this area were more "Egyptianised" than other parts of Lower Nubia.[653] Egyptian rituals could be copied by Lower Nubians or be part of a common Nilotic tradition, in which some elements –such as incense burners or the dogs- were active elements of a different evolution of the same ritual. It is very significant to note the connection of this Nubian ritual –close to the Egyptian *sed* festival- with a building, which appears in other major Nubian monuments.[654] Similarly, a close connection between the Egyptian *sed* festival and some specific temples basic in the rituals (see above) has been commented on.

[648] (1987: 270); also Williams (1986: 169-171, figs. 58a, 59).
[649] Kaplony (1964: 3, pls. 1-2, no. 885).
[650] (1986: 169).
[651] One of them, standing on a pedestal was interpreted -with some reservations- by Williams (1986: 169) as a bovine.
[652] Earliest Egyptian name for Lower Nubia, for example see Faulkner (1962: 293, 253).
[653] Williams (1980; 1986; 1987) held that the rulers buried at Cemetery L of Qustul initiated the unification of Egypt. However, the current evidence found at Umm el-Qaab refutes this hypothesis, see for example Dreyer (1998).
[654] For a deeper discussion of Nubian buildings in Nubian monuments, see Jiménez Serrano (2000a; 2002a).

Fig. 42: Williams' reconstruction of the Siali seal-impressions. Not to scale.

B. 7) Conclusions

It can be assumed that *sed* festivals have their origin in the Predynastic period, although the first artistic examples are dated at the beginning of the First Dynasty. It is also a ceremony connected with the African background of ancient Egyptian kingship, because many similar ceremonies were, and are, performed in African societies.

Sed festivals had at least two defining characteristics. On the one hand, they were religious rituals connected to the cosmic potency of the king, on which the whole country depended. On the other hand, as the main actor was the king, those festivals became an occasion for all the people to honour the institution of kingship. The king, as head of the state, re-took[655] possession of the country symbolically. He delimited the area under his power and under natural order (*maat*).

Sed festivals are attested in almost all the reigns of kings of the First Dynasty and in some cases there is evidence that permits the confirmation that there were at least two. That means that they were not celebrated under a determined periodicity (for example, thirty years, as would later become the case), because not every reign of the First Dynasty would have been longer than thirty years. In those early stages, it is possible to argue that *sed* festivals would have been celebrated for many reasons:

- Honouring the king as an act to strengthen the links between the monarchy and the provincial élite. There is no evidence concerning the year in which the first *sed* festival of any reign was celebrated, but surely it was some years after the enthronement. In *sed* festivals, the king would be reconfirmed not only as the integrator role in his person of earth and heaven, but the king would also strengthen the ties with the provincial élite. He was the supreme ruler of the earth; he could even incarnate the figure of the creator god. For that reason, he received offerings from all over Egypt and possibly the neighbouring regions (Libya, Canaan, etc.). That was a good occasion for obtaining part of the royal funerary equipment.[656] But at the same time, the king could redistribute part of these goods among some officials (i. e. Hemaka) as recompense for services, loyalty, and so on.[657]

- Destructive floods,[658] plagues, etc. The climate at the end of the Predynastic and Early Dynastic periods evolved dramatically into drier conditions, which severely affected the environment of the Nile Valley and neighbouring regions.[659] The king as guarantor of *maat* had to restore favourable conditions again, renewing his cosmic powers with a festival.

- The *sed* festival was a unique occasion for taking the census of the country, above all if the country had suffered droughts or plagues. One of the most important elements was the cattle census. The importance of it in the *sed* festival was so considerable that one of the most important titles of the officials that took part in the rituals was the "Herdsman from Nekhen".

The *sed* festival was celebrated from the Late Predynastic and Early Dynastic periods in different areas in Egypt: Hierakonpolis, Abydos and Saqqara. They were the consecutive capitals (or the cemeteries of the capitals) of Egypt, from the Late Predynastic period to the end of the Early Dynastic period. In all these sites, great enclosures have been found in which took place the different rituals that were performed in a *sed* festival. The enclosures were located relatively close to the royal tombs, but also close to the city temple.

In the reign of Narmer and Aha (and probably earlier), Hierakonpolis was the place where the *sed* festivals were celebrated (at least

---

[655] He had already taken possession of the country through the enthronement.

[656] It is interesting to note that most of the labels mentioned the *sed* festival, instead of other festivals or events that we know that were celebrated, according to the Palermo Stone or other sources.

At the same time, the labels representing the *sed* festivals were buried in the tomb and the deceased was helped by the magical depictions, which had a sense of re-birth.

[657] In contrast, Baines (personal communication) suggests that since many of them come from royal tombs, they are more likely to be the result of gifts to the king than from him to the others. However, the appearance of the names of the high officials (such as Hemaka) in some labels might be explained by the charge that they held and their labours in the supply of the royal tomb, for example.

[658] The only mention of a *sed* festival in the Palermo Stone is under the reign of Den, Schäfer (1902: 19 3). This year the levels of the Nile flood reached eight cubits and three fingers, the highest level recorded on the monument.

[659] Hassan (1993a; 1993b), with many references. Destructive floods have always happened in Egypt, even when the climate conditions were dryer and dryer. It is in those moments when high floods are even more devastating.

one in each reign). In the ceremonies two different sacred areas were used. Hk29A (*pr-wr*) was located in the Predynastic town. The city temple (Nekhen) was an enclosure whose later design was imitated in the royal enclosures of the First Dynasty. Some elements found at this temple can be ascribed to the paraphernalia used in the rituals and ceremonies. Clear examples that are related to elements seen in the *sed* festival are:[660] the polished red pottery lion,[661] statues in ivory with the white crown,[662] statues in ivory with the typical robe of the *sed* festival,[663] and ivory statues of captives.[664]

The sacred topography of Hierakonpolis defined the basic elements for the performance of the *sed* festival. The coincidence of two major temples at Hierakonpolis influenced the future structure and organisation of the *sed* festival. Surely, the kings at the start of the First Dynasty (if not earlier) included in the ritual both temples, which would represent an earlier stage of development of the concept of duality (see pp. 38-40), as well as relating this ceremony to the royal ancestors buried at the Locality 6 (see Figure 21).

- Afterwards, enclosures were built successively, first at Abydos (from Djer[665] to the end of the First Dynasty) and later at Saqqara (the beginning of the Second Dynasty?), and returning later to Abydos (Horus Sekhemib-Seth Peribsen and Khasekhem-Khasekhemui). One of the consequences of this change of site was the definitive abandonment of the original *pr wr* (Locality Hk29A) after the reigns of Aha or Djer. The reason is because of the new enclosures at Abydos, the *pr nw* and the *pr wr* were built with every new enclosure. The enclosure with all the elements, very close to the royal tomb, becomes a magic place where the king might regenerate himself through new festivals after his death.

From the remains of the majority of the enclosures, it can be suggested that all of them followed a model created at the Hierakonpolis city temple (Nekhen).[666]

There are several elements that defined the *sed* festival in the depictions. The scene repeated most times is the running of the king. Obviously, the king must prove his physical vitality by running. Another element is the pedestal with the festival booth, which was only used for this ceremony. Later, its shape evolved to a double booth, because the *sed* festival had to be a performance for Upper and Lower Egypt: a consequence of the development of the concept of duality.

On the other hand, it is possible to mention elements that lost their unique value or acquired a larger field of meanings at a later date. One of those examples could be the Red Crown. It is the only crown that appears in the first depictions of the *sed* festival, but later (at least from the reign of Djer) it was accompanied by the white crown. This change of iconography was due to the development of the concept of duality, which implied that both lands had their own crown (red[667] for Lower and white[668] for Upper Egypt), their own symbol (the bee[669] for Lower and the papyrus for Upper Egypt), and their own goddess (Uadjet for Lower and Nekhbet for Upper).

---

660 According to Frankfort (1948: chap. 7), in the *pr-wr* and the *pr-nw* were the souls of Nekhen and Pe, who certainly were the ancestors (*wrw*). All their sacred objects were kept with them.

661 Quibell (1900: pl. XLIV). Could this statue be related to the lion furniture sequence that Kaiser mentioned? See p. 44.

There is another example of unknown origin said to have been found in the Abydos region, see Needler (1984: 351-352, figs. 280a-b).

662 Quibell (1900: pl. VII). This statue wears the white crown and later examples always represent the royal statue with the white crown, see F. D. Friedman (1995: figs. 13 & 15).

663 Quibell (1900: IX).

664 Quibell (1900: pl. XI).

665 Aha's enclosure?, O'Connor (1989).

666 See O'Connor (1992).

667 The pottery dated in the period of Naqada I found in the Upper Egyptian site of Naqada is well known, see Baines (1995: 95-96, fig. 3.1).

668 The white crown is associated with the goddess from el-Kab, Nekhbet, in the Pyramid Texts, see Faulkner (1969: 135, pass. 729, & 157, pass. 900).

669 The bee was related to the goddess Neith of Sais – Leclant (1975: 788)-, where there could have been an independent kingdom in the Predynastic period. Thus a part of the Delta is considered the whole of the region.

C) FESTIVALS OF VICTORY

C.1) The king harpooning a hippopotamus[670]

Although the texts concerning this festival are very late (Ptolemaic period), the antiquity of this ritual goes back to the early stages of Egyptian political development. This conclusion is based on the references that appear in the Pyramid Texts, where Horus' harpoon is used to protect the bark of Ra from an evil hippopotamus.[671]

The festival was celebrated at Edfu from the 21st to the 25th of the second month of winter (the sixth month of the year). According to the reliefs, it could be divided into two parts: the first register is the abbreviated text of a sacred drama[672] and the second is known as the Legend of the Winged Disk.[673]

The texts commemorate the victory of Horus over his enemies, his enthronement as king of Upper and Lower Egypt, and his final triumph before a divine tribunal. As Fairman[674] pointed out, the meaning of this festival could be summarised as follows: Horus is the figure of the king, and his victories are the victories of the king.

There are five scenes that represent the Harpooning Ritual of a male hippopotamus (which receives ten harpoons)[675]. In the following scene, Horus is crowned and invested with the royal insignia, and in the last scene the dismemberment of the animal (Seth) is repeated twice. According to Fairman,[676] in the last two scenes, it is possible to see the dualistic conception of the drama. The triumph of Horus inaugurates a new era. According to Säve-Söderbergh, the rising of the star *Sothis*, which marked the beginning of the New Year and was originally thought to bring the inundation of the Nile, may therefore parallel the appearance of Horus on the scene.[677]

In Late Predynastic and Early Dynastic periods, the harpooning of the hippopotamus can be seen as a victory over all evil powers, the maintenance of order by the king. The earliest record of the hippopotamus hunt is dated in the period of Naqada I,[678] which surely reflects the human domination of the environment. However, although it seems difficult to relate it to this festival, those early depictions create a precedent in the mind of those early societies, which would be the nucleus of the later ceremonial.

An impression of the royal seal of Den[679]. Petrie[680] read the *ka* name Den with the hawk above, the king standing, an inscription *m s jb nbtj*,[681] Den having hooked a crocodile is drawing him up out of the water, and preparing to spear him, the king's personal name, *Setui* or *Semti*, the king wrestling with a hippopotamus. There are many fragmentary representations in which the king is a hunter of hippopotamus or crocodiles.[682] Clearly, those impressions commemorated the ritual hunt of the hippopotamus, but according to Godron,[683] the figures of the king represent statues, not the king himself.[684]

According to Säve-Söderbergh,[685] "The scene on the right illustrates the superhuman strength of the king, who is seen wrestling with the hippopotamus. On the left we see the almost

[670] About the translation of the original texts, see Fairman (1935); Blackman & Fairman (1942; 1943; 1944).
[671] Säve-Söderbergh (1953: 33). Pyr. Text. 1211-1212.
[672] About the discussion of whether it was a sacred drama or not, see Fairman (1958: 92, n. 2), with references.
[673] According to Fairman (1958: 93): "The Legend of the Winged Disk is a propagandistic recital, accompanied by innumerable and tedious puns of the progress of the struggle between Horus and Seth, and invested with a spurious historicity by being couched in the form of an historical document and given a mythological date, the year 363 of the king of Upper and Lower Egypt Re`-Harakhte." It is necessary to notice the evil powers appear represented as a red hippopotamus, see Säve-Söderbergh (1953: 26).
[674] (1958: 92).
[675] For the types of harpoons in Ancient Egypt, see Säve-Söderbergh (1953: fig. 2).
[676] (1958: 93).
[677] (1953: 27).
[678] Säve-Söderbergh (1953: 17, n. 1, Fig. 8) mentioned all the Predynastic representations of men and hippopotami together.
[679] Petrie (1901: pl. VII, nos., 5 & 6). A drawing of it, in Säve-Söderbergh (1953: fig. 7).
[680] (1901: 25).
[681] Petrie originally transcribed *em se ab en ... nebti*.
[682] Petrie (1900: pl. XIV, no. 8; 1901: pl. VII, nos. 5, 6, 11).
[683] (1957: 195-196).
[684] Recently, F. D. Friedman (1995: 26-33 & figs. 15-19) insists on the same argument. See also Eaton-Krauss (1984: 90-91).
[685] (1953: 16-17).

equally impossible act of the king harpooning an hippopotamus by himself. He wears the crown of Lower Egypt, which makes it probable that the hunt takes place in the Delta, and he stands on a raft with a prow of the type which we find in the New Kingdom scenes".

The original seal would be divided into three scenes. The first would be the one that opens the royal *serekh*, which is followed by a representation of a royal statue (made of gold, *nbw*) with the inscription *ḥr jb.sn nb nbtj*, "Horus, Lord of the their heart, the Two Ladies". Then, there are two more scenes separated by the royal *semti* name. In the first one, the king is harpooning a crocodile (?)[686] and, in the second, he fights with a hippopotamus. As Newberry and Wainwright[687] already suggested, those scenes can be related to one frame of the Palermo Stone, which was read by Schäfer[688] "(...). Killing the hippopotamus". Obviously, this hunting had ritual meaning, which was commented upon above.

Recently, the German team working at Abydos has found a new fragment of a label that might represent the same theme.[689] In fact, there was a very similar fragment of this label found by Petrie,[690] one century before.

C.2) Military victories

Warfare in Ancient Egypt shared some features with other Mediterranean civilisations. This was because Egypt had no professional army until at least the Middle Kingdom,[691] so had to recruit troops when necessary. Most soldiers would be peasants. This may explain why military campaigns were conducted after the harvest or when the Egyptian "black land" began to be inundated. In other words, warfare was subordinated to general economic interests. Military campaigns were also of short duration. This meant that conflicts between different entities were not solved rapidly.[692] According to Pérez Largacha,[693] warfare and trading routes were related aspects, because the Egyptian state had to ensure the safe arrival of the trading goods to their destiny. Due to this, Egyptian kings campaigned more often in the Way of Horus or in the interior valleys in Canaan.[694] In those places, Egyptian kings had to show their power to ensure the protection of caravans.

It is assumed that every mention of a victory or campaign against the enemies of the crown was followed by religious ceremonies, in which the king and gods were honoured. It is also possible to understand that royal defeat in the battlefield was not mentioned or recorded.[695] Sometimes there are mentions of Egyptian military campaigns, which surely never took place[696] as well as other campaigns, which were surely conducted. All of them are discussed with the same perspective. For this chapter of the book, the historicity of these events is less important than the representation of them and their symbolic message.

The "Minor" relief at Gebel Sheikh Suleiman. During the expedition of the Egypt Exploration Society at Buhen between 1962 and 1963, Winifred Needler discovered a rock drawing very close to the well-known Gebel Sheikh Suleiman relief. That relief represented a scorpion in the top centre, facing left. It held between its claws a prisoner dangling from a rope, while a second figure, a little below and to the left, brandishes a weapon, which could be a mace-head. Below the scorpion, there is a third man (upside down) who is pointing with a bow and arrow towards the prisoner. Needler[697] suggested that this relief commemorates Scorpion (II)'s victory over Nubia.

---

686 It seems likely that might be also a hippopotamus.
687 (1914: fig. 6 & 7).
688 (1902: 20 3-8).
689 Dreyer *et alii* (1998: Taf. 12d).
690 (1900: pl. XIV, no. 8).
691 Berlev (1971).
692 Pérez Largacha (1994: 63-64).
693 (1994: 65-66).
694 More examples might be added for the Late Predynastic and Early Dynastic periods: Wadi Hammamat, Aswan or Gebel Sheikh Suleiman (Second Cataract).
695 A deeper discussion in Pérez Largacha (1994: 62).
696 For example, Tutankhamun, who was represented defeating enemies but fairly certainly never participated in any combat.
697 (1967: 90-91).

Fig. 43 : King Den harpooning a hippopotamus. Not to scale.

Fig. 44: Two fragments of labels found atg Abydos and probably depicting the same scene: the harpooning of the hippopotamus. Not to scale.

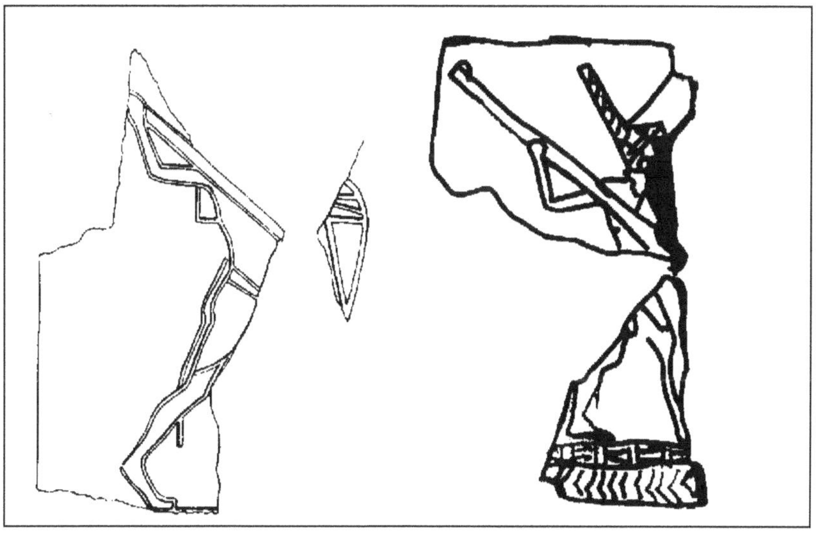

Fig. 45: The "minor" relief at Gebel Sheikh Suleiman. Not to scale.

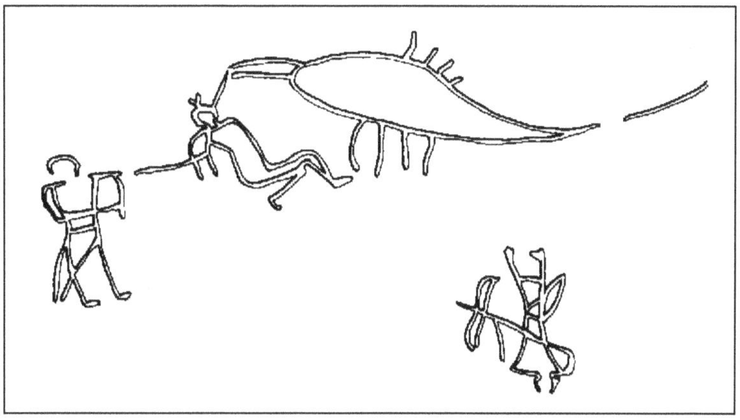

Fig. 46: The Narmer palette. Not to scale.

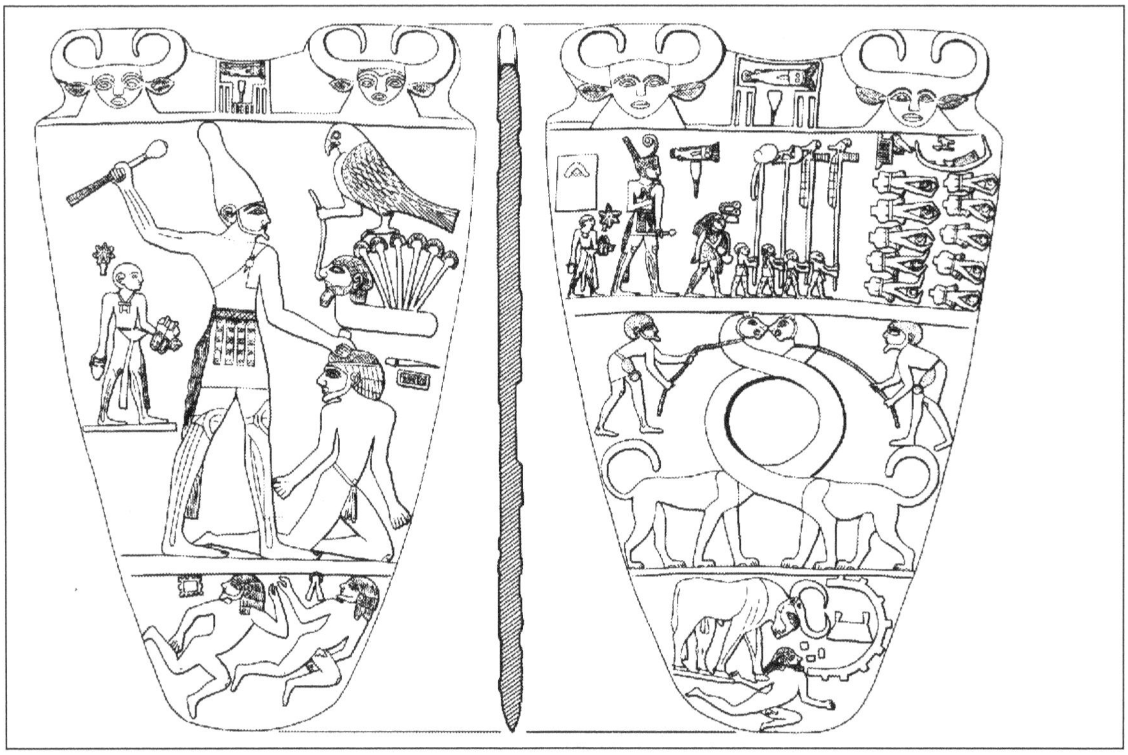

The Narmer palette (Figure 46). - This was discovered by Quibell[698] and although the excavation reports claimed that it came from the Main Deposit, Green's field notes pointed out that it came from a spot one or two metres away.[699] In his report, Green even stated that the Narmer palette was directly associated with the Early Dynastic temple.[700]

I agree with Dreyer,[701] who holds that an ivory label from Abydos (Figure 47), which was found in the spoil from old excavations, represents the same event as the one depicted on Narmer's famous palette. In this label, the catfish (one of the two phonograms of Narmer's name) is holding a mace and grasping at papyrus plants growing from the head of a fallen enemy and a possible reading is "Victory over the papyrus people". Underneath that scene, there is the inscription of the content (oil) and its number (300).

The Narmer palette has been interpreted in different ways by many authors, although it is possible to arrange them in three groups:

a) A victory by Narmer over the Delta:

Gardiner[702] considered that this monument was one of the first connections between pictorial art and hieroglyphs. First, he pointed out that every stalk (𓆼, *ḫꜣ*) with a flower meant a "thousand" (total six thousand). Above them, Gardiner saw a falcon (Horus) and beneath them a foreign prisoner plus the land sign (𓇾, *tꜣ*). Part of the main scene of the *recto* was translated: "Horus brings to the Pharaoh six thousand foreigners captured within their land". Afterwards, Gardiner changed his opinion, and he interpreted the plants as six papyrus plants: "The falcon-god Horus (i. e. Narmer) leads captive the inhabitants of the papyrus country".[703] He also proposed that the signs beside the kneeling captive could be read as his name *wꜥšj* (Washi).[704] He[705] interpreted the

[698] (1900).

[699] Adams (1974b); Hoffman (1976: 36).

[700] Quibell & Green (1902: 13).

[701] Dreyer *et alii* (1998: 139, Abb. 29).

[702] (1915: 72-74). He mistook it verso for recto. In his book *Egypt of the Pharaohs* (1961), he corrected his error, pl. XXI-XXII.

[703] Gardiner (1961: 404).

According to Edwards (1971: 7), the falcon over the papyrus means "Horus brings (to the king) captives of Lower Egypt". Millet (1990: 59) reads the scene of the triumphant king (*recto*) as "Year of Smiting the Northland (*rnpt sqr tꜣ-mḥw*)".

[704] Gardiner (1915: 74); Kaiser (1964: 89) also interpreted it as a name.

[705] Gardiner (1961: 404).

verso as Narmer inspecting the results of his victory; in front of him are the standards of his confederates and a ship, which seems to have brought him to the place where his decapitated enemies are still lying. The two long-necked felines appear to be restrained from fighting by a bearded man on each side. The group of signs (𓍿𓏏, ṯt) have been translated as spelling *Thaty* (*ṯ(ꜣ)tj*, later written 𓅾𓏏 *ṯꜣt*) the word for "vizier"[706] or "offpring" *wṯtw.*[707]

One of the most surprising readings of the Narmer palette has been proposed recently. Whitney Davis[708] interprets the human-cow heads on the top edge of the palette as human-faced bulls, which would represent the ruler's power as a bull. He based his argument on many elements, which define the king as a bull in this palette: a great bull attacking an enemy's citadel, the bull's tail that the king wears while he is smiting an enemy and, in the same scene, the belt of the king, which is decorated with bulls' heads. According to him, the narrative construction of the palette is organised by presenting the earlier scenes/events at the bottom and the later scenes/events at the top. His reading begins in an opposite way, in other words, according to him, the verso is the part that has to read first, and would follow an inverse chronological order (from later to earlier). This chaotic and hyper-complex reading can be summarised as follows: He reads the second row on the verso as the celebration of Narmer's victory. This scene is related to the group in which a falcon is shown above the Delta land. The falcon would be interpreted as meaning that the ruler (as a falcon or protected by him) has defeated his enemies and prepares them for their judgment or destruction. The next scene is the one in which a bull[709] attacks a fortress. The subsequent scene would be that one on the opposite side, where two enemies are fleeing in panic from the fortress.

b) A victory of Narmer over foreign peoples (Nubia and Libya):

Walter Fairservis[710] proposed one of the most original interpretations of this palette. However, scholars have not followed his reading, because it would mean that the Narmer mace-head was composed with a cryptographic system. He read (recto) "Lord "Charging Bull" (the fearsome) foremost (among) great bulls. Commander of thousands, *ṯbwty ꜥnḫ* (the sandal 'bearer') who follows (the ruler) and gathers the troops. The mace-wielding chief of the East, the bearer of the powerful robe (sacred robe), who makes enemies tremble. The (great) Hawk (who) binds the people of the papyrus land (Nile land?). (The mace wielding chief) who (seizes) the land of the ruler of Elephantine. Na`rmer causes all the people of the papyrus (Nile Valley) to flee (or) be captured". (Verso) "Lord charging Bull (the fearsome) foremost (among) great bulls. District of Edfu. Commander of thousands, *ṯbwty ꜥnḫ* (the sandal bearer) who follows (the ruler) and gathers the troops. Nar`mer ruler of the West, the one who rules and captures hundreds, the mace-wielder, the protector. The queen *tt(y).* Defeater of foes, the governor (of) the two lands (East and West) of *ḥr.* The all powerful, the one *ḥr* who (with) the warship(s) (of Neith) beheads (destroys) the chiefs of the Medja(y). Uniter of the peoples of the two banks of the Nile (in Nubia?). Narmer demolishes the fortress(es) and loots the storehouses (granaries) of the "long-haired"". This reading is erroneous for us because:

- All elements are considered signs, used as a cryptographic system of writing.
- There are no comparisons with contemporaneous monuments.
- Fairservis interpreted some elements that have no contemporary correspondence (for example, Medyau, who are mentioned for the first time at the end of the Old Kingdom –1000 years later!).

Schulman[711] interprets the palette as representing the victory of Narmer over the Libyans. He considers that the Egyptians saw the people from Southern Canaan as Libyans. In the main scene, Narmer kills Washa, the Libyan chief. The rest of his interpretation elaborates on the idea that this could be an early version of the motif of the Libyan family captured by the king, as it is possible to see in other later reliefs, which he mentioned.

706 Massoulard (1949: 449), with references in p. 470, n. 69.
707 Wilkinson (2000c: 30).
708 (1992: 165-173).
709 Whitney Davis (1992: 169) regards the bull "as an aspect, double, or representation of the ruler".
710 (1991: 18).

711 (1991/1992: 81, 85, 87-88, pls. 2-6).

Fig. 47: Ivory label of Narmer. Not to scale.

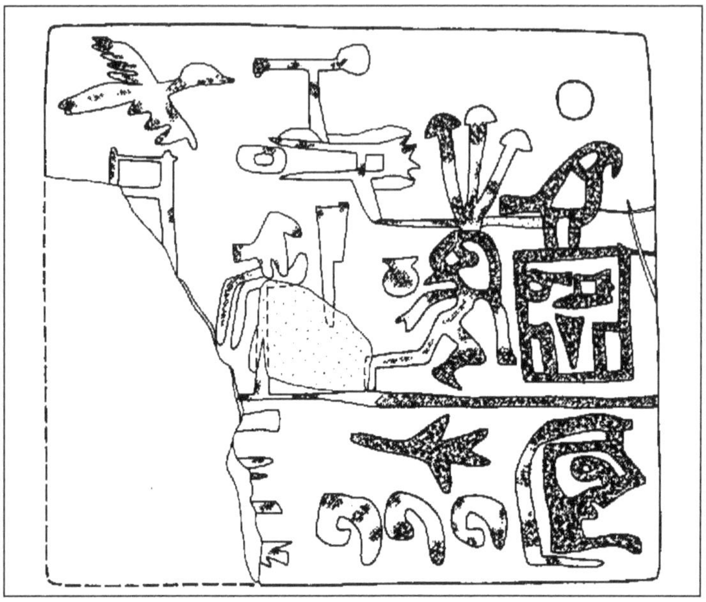

Goldwasser,[712] after analysing only the *recto*, holds that this side of the palette relates the victory of the king over certain Asiatics in two scenes, as a human and as a falcon. She considered that the two men that appear beneath the central register are dead and the unreadable signs are hieroglyphs that probably indicate their origin.

c) Ritual affirmation:

Baines[713] considers that the two principal scenes might be read as a military victory as indicated by the decapitated corpses, followed by the ritual execution of the enemies' leader. The groups at the bottom, which are emblematic in terms of later iconography, could have a similar sequence, but cannot be linked directly with the main part. The captions seem to refer to specific people, events and places, and the enemies have no clear foreign ethnic markers, thus an internal victory of south over north appears to be shown. According to him, it is better to see the composition as a ritual affirmation of conquest, not a real event.

Although it is not an interpretation, it is interesting to mention Vivian Davies and Renée Friedman's [714] summary. For them, the message of the palette can be reduced to a few words: "Narmer, the King, is the undeniable victor. Eternal death, unremembered, is the fate of those who defy him".

The last interpretation of the palette presented here is very old and it is missing in recent studies. However, it is believed here that it could represent the starting point of a new interpretation. Newberry[715] pointed out that on Narmer's palette it is possible to see twice the same sign (the primitive), and it is always beside or over the defeated enemies of the king[716]. He related this sign to the later nome of the Harpoon, that, in the Third Dynasty, was situated in the north-western corner of the Delta, on the shore of the Mediterranean Sea (afterwards the seventh lower Egyptian nome, between Sais and the actual Bolbinitic branch). Its capital appears to have been Senti-nefer, and the cult object of its inhabitants the Harpoon.[717] This Harpoon deity was mentioned in the Pyramid Texts and in other religious works, and the Harpoon itself was also a word-sign for *wʿ*, "one", although its true significance has not generally been recognised. Apart from more or less erratic interpretations of the papyrus sign (he made the same mistake as Gardiner, see p. 83) or the identity of Menes, Newberry compared the falcon on the Harpoon with the sign ,[718] which he translated as "Horus

[712] (1992: 68).
[713] (1995: 119-120)
[714] (1998: 22).

[715] (1908). Sethe (1905: 14) referred to the "Petty-Kingdom of the Harpoon".
[716] Once over the sign (marshland?) and the other under the falcon (the king?).
[717] However, Montet (1957, 1: 70) only mentioned the god *ḥȝ* (later ḥw).
[718] There are many contemporary parallels, which show a falcon surmounting another sign or emblem, see Kahl (1994: 887-888), with references.

conqueror of Nubt (Ombos, Naqada)." He also recognised two signs (*ꜥꜣ-wr*, "the Great Door", or "Port[719]"), which are followed by a bark. He held that those scenes corresponded to the last steps of the unification and he identified Narmer with Menes.

As has been mentioned above, Newberry's interpretation is the base for our proposal for a new reading of the Narmer palette presented here. This new interpretation is based on recent interpretations summarised above and personal re-interpretations, which try to offer a new vision of this monument. We support the idea that the Narmer palette represents a military victory (as Baines affirmed) and was a real event (as supported by the new label discovered at Abydos). On both sides of the palette, a victory over Bedouins, together with ritual ceremonies after the battle, were depicted. On both sides, it is possible to see in the upper register the same representation: two human faces with bovine ears and horns, which probably represent the goddess Hathor[720] (or Bat) or Seshat, and between them is the royal *serekh*. As many authors have noted, the bovine goddess is represented on the top of the palette, which could be associated with heaven.[721] On the *recto*, below this row, from left to right, is the sandal-bearer[722] and beside him the rosette (Seshat?) and an unknown sign,[723] which might be read as *ḥm* "priest". Thus, the sandal-bearer holds another title, priest of Seshat. To the right, Narmer, with the white crown, is smiting an enemy. In front of the face of the king there is a falcon (Horus) offering the head of an enemy (who personifies the hieroglyph "land of the Delta")[724] to the king. Under this group, there are two signs that were correctly read by Newberry (7th nome of Lower Egypt), although he did not realise that they could also represent the 8th nome of the Delta,[725] situated in the Eastern Delta, the capital of which bears the modern name Tell el-Maskhuta. It might represent this nome and not the 7th, as Newberry claimed, because all the enemies that appear in the palette are represented with beards and long hair and without feathers (as Libyans used to wear -compare for example, the inscribe palette of Djer from Saqqara-). Moreover, in the *verso* of the palette of Narmer, in the right part of the second row are two signs that Newberry read as *ꜥꜣ-wr* "The Great Door", that made reference to the entrance of Egypt from Asia. The fortress could be one of the cities on the border or one of the settlements surveyed by Oren[726] in North Sinai -The Way of Horus-. It might be added that there was never a mention of Libyan cities. Libya is mentioned in the verso of Cities Palette,[727] whose recto shows some cities. Although in the same monument, Libya and the cities might not be connected, mainly due to the different context that shows the recto and the verso and also because of the fragmentary state of the palette. In the lower register, two naked enemies flee in panic and leave behind a fortress or a city[728].

In the *verso*, under the register with the two goddesses Hathor (or Hathor and Seshat), from left to right, is a rectangle with an unknown sign in its interior (?).[729] Below, the same group that we could see in the *recto*: the sandal-bearer with the rosette and the unknown sign.[730] In front of him, Narmer with the red crown and his name represented without *serekh* (as in the Scorpion II mace-head). Ahead of the king, there is a woman (?, possibly a man) with the signs that can be read

[719] The word 'door' was used in a geographical sense as frontier, Newberry (1908: 21).

[720] Fischer (1989: 67) and Florence D. Friedman (1995: 3) have interpreted the heads as the goddess Bat. The latter author claims that the palette was dedicated to this goddess.

[721] For a commentary about this case, see Hornung (1999: 210), who also compared it with the ivory comb of Djet (see p. 97).

[722] It has been explained by Schott (1950: 23) as *wdpw ḥrw* "butler of Horus", while Helck (1954: 94) has suggested that it may represent *wdpw nṯr* "butler of the god", a title which is mentioned in other ceremonies. Arnett (1982: 40) read 'treasurer'.

[723] This figure also appears on the Narmer mace-head with the same signs.

[724] As Hornung (1999: 113) noted, the representation of a personified sign (or animal) with a human head is atypical in Ancient Egypt, the common representation being a human body with an animal head or a complete human body with a sign (or signs) surmounting the head.

[725] Baines & Málek (1980: 15).

[726] (1973; 1989).

[727] See, for example, W. Davies (1992: fig. 53).

[728] It is very important to note the differences between how Egyptians and Bedouins have been represented. The former are represented dressed -civilised-, while the latter are depicted naked, except the one that is going to be sacrificed. Weill (1961: 20) interpreted them as Asiatics and read the two hieroglyphs as *sṯ·tjw* "The castle of the Asiatics". The first sign seems clear, but it seems difficult to accept that the second is , as Weill proposed.

[729] Arnett (1982: 39) suggested that this sign represented the name of a temple: *per mer* (?).

[730] Whitney Davis (1992: 167) proposes that it could be the ruler's seal.

ṯt, which possibly represent the name (or title) of a queen (it could also be a man).[731] In front of her, there are the four standards of Egypt[732] and ahead of them a group that it might be divided in two subgroups: the upper one is formed by hieroglyphs that mean "The Great Door, Horus conqueror of (*j3bt*) Washi" and a bark. Below this inscription, ten enemies lie tied and beheaded with the head and penis between their legs[733] (Figure 48). In the lower register, there are two long-necked felines that are compared -among others- by Campagno[734] with the animals that appear on the palette from Hierakonpolis ("Two Dogs" Palette). According to him, those ser<p>opards represent the forces of chaos, which, in the Narmer palette, are under the king's control.[735] In the bottom row, a bull, that clearly represents the king, destroys a fortress and steps on an enemy.[736]

According to the interpretation supported here, the Narmer palette would also represent two different rituals or ceremonies, both differentiated by the crowns that the king bears. The contemporary monuments (Narmer mace-head, Scorpion II mace-head, the mace-head from Hierakonpolis, the ivory label of Djer from Abydos) always represented the king in ceremonies or rituals with different crowns. The first time that a king appears with the two crowns together is in Den's reign (wooden label from Abydos). However, Edwards[737] explained the fact that the king wears the white crown (of Upper Egypt) in the first scene and the red crown (of Lower Egypt) in the second as that this victory marked the final defeat of the northern kingdom and the assumption of its crown by Narmer. But, at that moment, the hegemony of the two countries was shown with the lotus (Upper Egypt) and papyrus (Lower Egypt).

[731] This figure also appears on the Narmer mace-head.
[732] A complete discussion of the standards is made by Wilkinson (1999: 197-199), with many references.
[733] Davies & Friedman (1998: 22).
The depiction of the severed heads and penises could be related to a count of dead enemies after a battle. In this case, Narmer would be witness of the recount of fallen enemies.
[734] (1996: 154).
[735] However, Senk (1952: 27) thought that they represented the Two Lands, and the humans that are beside them holding with strings the necks of the fabulous animals are enemies of Egypt.
[736] A similar image also appears in the so-called Libyan Palette together with a group of other cities that are being founded, Pérez Largacha (1989). The bull is later known as 'the victorious bull' (*k3 nḫt*) and the three rectangles near it represent scattered bricks, Fischer (1989: 69).
[737] (1971: 7).

Fig. 48: Detail of the Narmer Palette of beheaded captives with and without penis. Not to scale.

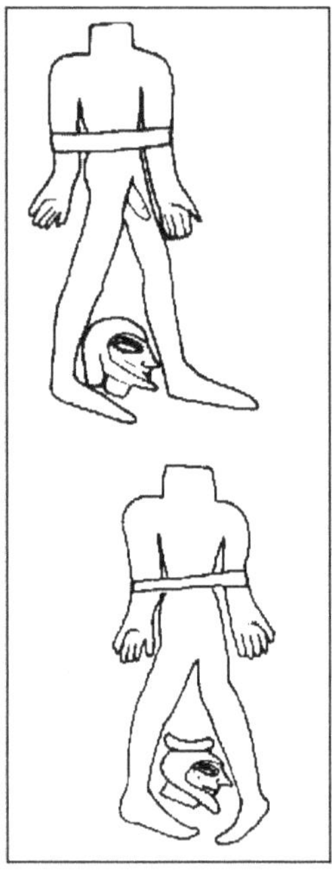

Narmer cylinder seal (Figure 49).[738] It was found at Hierakonpolis together with other similar (unnamed) ivory cylinder seals. It shows one scene in which a personified catfish is holding a stick, which is to be used against seven bounded enemies from Libya. The king (catfish) is protected by Nekhbet and Horus is offering Narmer the sign of life. According to Logan,[739] this cylinder seal might be related to the Cities Palette and both represent the conquest of Libya and the bringing of the tribute, which seems very plausible. He also affirms that this cylinder seal, the Cities Palette and the Narmer palette depict the same event,[740] which cannot be supported here, because in the Narmer palette the enemy is personified as Lower Egypt, as well as in the label found at Umm el-Qaab. Then, it can be stated that Narmer defeated some people in the Delta and, in a different moment, Libyans.

[738] Quibell (1900: pl. 15, 7).
[739] (1999: 276). He also suggests that both monuments could be the precedent of Sahura Libyan reliefs and later copies.
[740] Logan (1999: 270).

Fig. 49: Cylinder seal with Narmer smiting seven enemies. Not to scale.

Hor Aha wooden label from Abydos (Figure 50)[741]. Petrie[742] and Vandier[743] noticed that this label was related to a campaign that this king carried out in Nubia, and the celebration of a festival to Anubis, but they mistook the god Anubis (*Jnpw*) for Khentamentiu. This label does not present any interpretative problem for the scholars who translated it in practically the same way: "Beating the Nubians by Horus Aha; birth of Khentamentiu; Foundation of the fortress *ḥr-pẖr-jḥw*"[744]. Logan[745] partially supports Brovarski's[746] interpretation of this label: "fashioning and opening the mouth of a statue of Anubis". According to Logan, this label is a part of the series of labels commemorating the opening or erecting of a building accompanied by the fetish of Imiut. The bound prisoner would be associated with a ritual killing. However, it seems clear that, together with the *serekh*, there was represented a mace united with the name of the king by an arm (?) – , *ꜥḥꜣ* – "fight" which is complemented with the sign *r* "against"[747] *tꜣ-stj* together with the ideogram of a captive ( ) facing the royal *serekh*. Beside this, there is another column, in which is recorded *ms(.t)*[748] "birth" or "fashioning" of Imiut. Concerning the name of the fortress, Helck[749] added that the wedge-shape sign means "foundation" and F. D. Friedman[750] believes that the sign *pẖr* probably alludes to an early form of the ceremony of *pẖr ḥꜣ jnbw* and the falcon on a standard recalls the glyph for *jmnt* "west". However, it is possible that the fortified enclosure symbolised some other idea; perhaps the original place of the offering: *pẖr ḥr ḥsꜣt* "Horus (the king) encloses (the temple of?) Hesat"[751]. The quantity and the type of the offerings would appear in the missing part of the label.

Fig. 50: Horus Aha wooden label from Abydos. Not to scale.

741 Petrie (1901: pls. III, no. 2, XI, no. 1).
742 (1901: 20).
743 (1952, 1, II: 835).
744 Helck (1987: 145).
745 (1990: 66).
746 Another interpretation was suggested by Brovarski (1977-78: 1). He identified the figure that looks like a prisoner with arms bound behind its back as the ideogram for *twt*, "statue".
747 Faulkner (1962: 46).

748 We interpret this form as infinitive, following similar examples of the Palermo Stone.
749 (1987: 145).
750 (1995: 34).
751 For *pẖr*, see Faulkner (1962: 93). Weill (1961, 2: 31) translated the interior of the enclosure as "circular procession (*šnj·t*) of the cow *ḥsꜣ·t* (or *sḫꜣ·t ḥr*?)".

Fig. 51: The "major" relief of Gebel Sheikh Suleiman. Not to scale.

Gebel Sheikh Suleiman relief[752] (Figure 51). This represents a falcon's head on a *serekh*, that encloses the name of Djer. Alongside, a prisoner facing to the right has his arms bound behind his back, and is holding in his hands the hieroglyph sign *t3-sty*. Further to the right, as Murnane[753] suggested, it is possible to see water, but very roughly shown, perhaps meaning to represent turbulent waters, a cataract (the second cataract?). There are two signs that correspond to Gardiner O 49 (city ideogram), the first surmounted by a bird figure and the other with an unknown sign, which according to Murnane[754] could be a placenta, although it might be a bird without a head. As has already been explained, it would represent the standard of Qustul and his death[755]. The last group of the relief shows another prisoner, facing to the right and seated on the ground, with his arms bound behind his back but without any feature at his hands. An arrow, however, transfixes this man's chest and his neck is connected by a rope to the prow of a ship to the right. The top of this rope also serves as a ground line for a round-topped booth or hut.[756] Below this, between the prisoner and the ship as well as underneath them both, lie four corpses tumbled in death.[757]

[752] Arkell (1950); Murnane (1987).
[753] (1987: 284).
[754] (1987: 283).

[755] Jiménez Serrano (1998b).
[756] Baines (personal communication) suggests that the round-topped booth might well be a later drawing that used the rope as a base line.
[757] Murnane (1987: 283).

There were different interpretations of this document and its meaning. In the early 1950s, Arkell[758] ascribed it to Djer, followed later by Emery.[759] For Emery, the figure that has the Nubia sign represents the Egyptian capture of this region, but he could not confirm if it was merely a punitive raid or a conquest. W. Y. Adams[760] accepts the traditional opinion about this relief and he always dates it in the reign of Djer. His interpretation of the meaning of the relief centres on the symbolic importance that it could have (because it was in Nubian territory), and not on the military consequences. According to him, it was only an attack on two Nubian villages, in which there were not many deaths.

Shinnie[761] presents the actual state of the investigations, in which there are many doubts about the attribution to Djer of this relief. Williams[762] claimed that this relief could be Nubian and it would represent the victory of the A-Group rulers over Egypt, a fact that must be denied because of the discoveries in recent years in Abydos and in the Delta.[763]

The first doubts about the attribution to Djer were expressed by Helck[764], who thought that the relief could have had some later additions (city signs, the falcon and other drawings). He believed that the *serekh* originally did not have any name written inside it, thus it would be dated earlier than Djer's reign. But, according to W. Y. Adams,[765] this would be a speculation.[766] Murnane[767] after having re-analysed the relief *in situ*, confirmed that the *serekh* is earlier than First Dynasty and Djer's sign was made afterwards.[768]

Williams and Logan[769] point out that if Djer's name is eliminated from the *serekh* (because it would be a later addition) and is remade with the falcon, there would not be enough space for any hieroglyph inscription, thus we would have to ascribe it to Kaiser and Dreyer's *Horizont A*. This means that it would be contemporary with the rulers of Qustul. Following Williams and Logan, and Murnane, it is believed that this relief was made in two phases. The first one, at the end of Kaiser and Dreyer's *Horizont A*;[770] it would have been carved when Egypt acted against the Qustul dynasty, which produced a crisis in Qustul. This would be demonstrated by the reliefs that show the man holding the bow besides the *serekh*, the city signs (one crowned by a falcon that would symbolise Egypt and another that represented the bird, which has been considered before[771] as the standard of the Qustul rulers) and the dead men. The fact that this relief is placed on the border (?) of the territory controlled by Qustul shows that the Egyptian monarch ordered these scenes to be carved as a record of power.

The additions that were made afterwards have to be connected with the campaign that Aha waged against the Nubians, as the wooden label showed below. Thus, Djer, Aha's successor, who could well have defeated the last rulers of Qustul, made the modifications.

A fragmentary ivory label from Abydos (Figure 52)[772]. Although the *serekh* has not been conserved, Dreyer suggests that this label could be dated to the reign of Djet, because it was found near the tomb of this king. Dreyer translates the three surviving registers: "1. (...) wrestler, royal *serekh* conserved partially, ///// *ṯ*, Birth of Imiut. 2. Smiting *ṯḥnw*, foundation of the fortress *wḏ-nṯr* (?), ///?-edifice, ? of *mr-nṯr-wy*. 3. Offering), *ṯḥnw*-oil 100 (as) tax from Upper Egypt (*jnw-šmꜥw*)".

---

758 (1950: 28).
759 (1961: 59-60).
760 (1977: 138).
761 (1996: 51).
762 (1986: 171).
763 For a deeper study, see Jiménez Serrano (forthcoming).
764 (1970: 83-85).
765 (1985: 190).
766 W. Y. Adams (1985) and B. Williams (1980; 1986; 1987) debate the role of the Nubian rulers and the origin of the Egyptian State. Williams emphasised the discoveries of Cemetery L at Qustul. According to him, the antiquity of the remains and the motifs, the size of the tombs of Cemetery L and other aspects were evidence of the Nubian origin of the Egyptian State. Adams disagreed and interpreted all this evidence in a major (Nilotic) context. The discoveries at Umm el-Qaab have confirmed Adams' point of view, showing a highly developed élite in Upper Egypt contemporary with the rulers of Qustul.
767 (1987: 284).
768 Cialowicz (1999: 21) suggests that it might date to Scorpion (II)'s reign.
769 (1987: 264).
770 (1982: fig. 14).
771 Jiménez Serrano (1998b).
772 Dreyer *et alii* (1998: 162-163, taf. 12a).

Fig. 52: Djet label from Abydos. Not to scale.

Fig. 53: Den smiting the East. Not to scale.

Perhaps one of the most famous labels of the First Dynasty is the one that represents **Den smiting the East (Figure 51)**[773] (*zp tpy sqr j3bt* 'First time of the Striking of the East'). This depiction might be related to the mention of the Palermo Stone (year x+2) "smiting the Iuntiu".[774]

C. 3) Conclusions

Egypt's foreign enemies were part of the forces of chaos. They were enemies of Egypt because of their strange manners and languages.[775] They did not even follow the rules of warfare. They lived apart from *maat*. However, the Egyptian king was the antithesis of them. He maintained *maat* fighting against all the forces of chaos.

Due to the royal role as defender of *maat*, it is not so important that the representations that have been discussed above could be considered real events or just magic compositions that ensure the maintenance of *maat* in Egypt. Those compositions must be understood in two different ways:

- They are magic depictions that protect Egypt.[776]

- Those representations are part of a plan, which glorified the royal actions. In other words, they are royal propaganda addressed not only against the foreigners, but also the Egyptians. The end of those depictions is to show the power of the king victorious in the battlefield.

The most important moment of the ceremonies would be the death of the enemy, personified in the chief. This ritual assassination is part of the ceremonial but does not mean that the defeated people would have also been killed by the king. The king defeats the enemies in the battlefield (see both reliefs at Gebel Sheikh Suleiman), makes flee in panic the enemies (the Narmer palette), but the king is never cruel with unarmed people (children and women). The king incarnates valour and justice not only in the battlefield but also after the battle, when the chief of the enemies is sacrificed.

---

773 Spencer (1980: pl. 53).

774 Emery (1961: 74). See also Helck (1987: 157, note 18) with more references.

775 Sadly, there is no data about the language that Nubian A-Group spoke. From their artistic representations and the material culture, it is possible to guess that their culture shared many common features with that of the Egyptians. About a hypothesis of A-Group language, see Jiménez Serrano (1998b).

Concerning the manners of 'Asiatics' see *The Instructions Addressed to King Merikare* in Lichtheim (1975: 104).

776 Much later (Middle Kingdom), there are magic spells (execration texts) which associated the name of the tribes with their geographic origin. The purpose was to kill enemies (in doing this it was necessary to show the place they live in), see Belova (1998: 145). They are dated to the Old Kingdom and Middle Kingdom, see for the Old Kingdom, Osing (1976), and for the Middle Kingdom, Koenig (1990).

D. - THE FESTIVAL OF SOKAR

According to the Palermo Stone, some festivals of Sokar were celebrated during the Early Dynastic period.[777] This chapter contains an analysis of the character of this god, a study of the references to celebrations of his festivals and some reflections about the role of this god in this age.

Fig. 54: Four mentions of the festival of Sokar on the Palermo Stone. Not to scale.

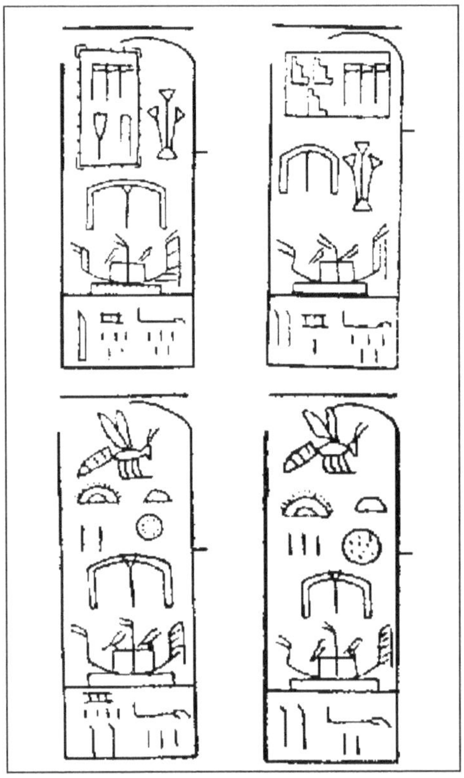

Sokar was the god who generated life in death, who therefore possessed potential life. This assertion could create confusion with Osiris, because he is not only the god of vegetation (in particular of grain), but also of the earth, the Nile or rather the floods which fertilise the grounds. Sokar was the god of death but to a lesser degree the refuge of the souls of the dead.[778] It seems that Sokar was the patron of craftsmen in the Old Kingdom, rather than the god Ptah.[779]

This god was worshipped in many places at the end of the pharaonic period. In the Memphite region, there were three temples or shrines: Shetayet-shrine (at Memphis), Restau (Giza?) and the main temple, Pedju-she, which was at Saqqara, whose name derives from that of the god.[780] But, as Hornung[781] noted, in the Old Kingdom (and obviously before), the topographic element of a god is not so important as in the Late Period. A common feature of some so-called local gods (such as Khnum, Satis, etc.) is their universal aspect.[782]

Sokar was represented as falcon-headed and, in the Pyramid Texts, his name appeared with a boat (called *ḥnw* Henu, 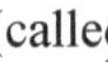), which was a determinative.[783] This suggests that the boat expressed the being of Sokar. The boat of Sokar is known from many representations from the First Dynasty to the Ptolemaic period[784]. Those depictions show the boat resting on a frame, which is held by four legs and placed on a sledge. On the prow, which ends in a gazelle's head facing backwards, there is a ribbed edge. Sometimes behind the gazelle's head is the head of a bull facing forward, from whose mouth hangs a chord. Sometimes a fish hangs out of the gazelle's mouth. On the high, up-curving prow are six falcons. On the stern are attached two or three rudders. In the Pyramid Texts a falcon stands in the boat.[785]

In the four references to the festival of Sokar on the Palermo Stone[786] (Figure 54), all the barks of the god Sokar have been depicted with two falcons, which was explained by Anthes[787] as

[777] Schäfer (1902: 16 2-7, 19 3-6, 23 4-6, 25 4-12).

[778] Bleeker (1967: 56, 69, 75).

About the original nature of this god, see the discussion in Gaballa & Kitchen (1969: 22-23), with references.

In later times, the divine aspects of this god could have been confused by the Egyptians themselves, because in one of the scenes of the reliefs at Medinet Habu, the god appeared named as Ptah-Sokar-Osiris, see Gaballa & Kitchen (1969: 6, scene IV, fig. 2) and also Hornung (1999: 117). The association of those gods could be explained because Ptah and Sokar were gods of the same region (Saqqara and Memphis) and Sokar and Osiris had similar divine aspects. The association of the names of Sokar and Osiris is repeated many more times in the reliefs of Ramesses III, see Gaballa & Kitchen (1969: 11, fig. 3). At the beginning of the Eighteenth Dynasty, the existence of a female form of Sokar was mentioned, see Hornung (1999: 202).

[779] Gaballa & Kitchen (1969: 22), with references.

[780] Gaballa & Kitchen (1969: 20-21).

For the places in which Sokar was worshipped, see Gaballa & Kitchen (1969: 21).

[781] (1999: 208).

[782] Hornung (1999: 208).

[783] Gardiner (1957: 468).

[784] Bleeker (1967: 76)

[785] Bleeker (1967: 79 & fig. 3).

[786] Schäfer (1902: 16 2-7, 19 3-6, 23, 4-6, 25 4-12). The construction of a Maaty bark is also mentioned on the Palermo Stone, see *idem* (1902: 41, x+2).

[787] (1957: 89).

a festival of Sokar (the first falcon) and the king (the second falcon) in relation to the sacred bark (called by him *mꜣʿt(j)*, Maaty).[788] As has been discussed above, the bark of the god Sokar was called the Henu-bark, but this is not contradictory to the fact that in the Late Predynastic and Early Dynastic periods a bark called Maaty was used, because the Pyramid Texts make an explicit connection between Sokar and the Maaty-bark.[789] Anthes[790] held that Maaty-bark was a focus of the cult of Sokar, and not only a processional bark of his.

According to the Palermo Stone, the oldest festival of Sokar is attested since the First Dynasty. In the earliest times, the festival was accompanied by the ceremony of breaking open the ground. It is noteworthy that the festival is mentioned twice in conjunction with the foundation of an important edifice (a temple or a palace)[791] and another two times in accompaniment of the mention of "Appearance of the king" (during the reign of Ninetjer, third king of the Second Dynasty). At that time, this ritual still possessed actual significance and occurred in the month of IIII *akhet* (it probably coincided with the winter solstice).[792]

In the Old Kingdom, the periodicity of this festival was annual, and it probably fell on IIII *Akhet*, day 26.[793] From the end of the Old Kingdom, the festival of Sokar underwent an Osirianization process, which culminated in the New Kingdom.[794]

From the time of Ramesses III, some ceremonies of the Festival of Sokar were carved at Medinet Habu temple.[795] Although some think that the scenes carved in this temple represent a ceremony already incorporated into the Osirian festival,[796] they represent the unique nexus of union with the original festival celebrated in the Early Dynastic period.[797]

The festi val lasted for ten days, from the 21st to the 30th of the month oif *Khoiak*.[798] On the 21st the "Opening of the window in the sanctuary of Sokar"; on the 22nd "The festival of breaking the ground"; on the 23rd "The holding of a procession in the sanctuary of Sokar"; on the 24th "The Placing of Sokar in their midst (of the dead?)"; on the 25th "The *nṯry.t* festival"; on the 26th "the Festival of Sokar"; on the succeeding days were made to Ptah-Sokar-Osiris abd his ennead; on the 30th the erection of the *ḏd*-pillar took place.

Gaballa and Kitchen[799] reconstructed the festival of Sokar before its Osirianization. According to them, it included a funerary role, agricultural significance (season; hoeing) and connections with kingship and incorporated the circuit of the walls of Memphis in the *Henu*-bark on a sledge. It began on the 26th day of 4th *Akhet*, and on this day there was a festival of the *Maaty* bark.

---

788 For the etymology of this word see Anthes (1957: 86) and Gaballa & Kitchen (1969: 14, n. 4).

789 Faulkner (1962: § 1429); Gaballa & Kitchen (1969: 14).

790 (1957: 88).

791 Schäfer (1902: 16-7 & 19-6).

Sokar is a god that has always been related to foundations, as the name of his main temple, Pedju-She, shows, which derives from the verb *pḏ* "to stretch" — *Wb*. 1, 567, I—.

792 Bleeker (1967: 69-71). The month of *Khoiak* was very propitious for the celebration of festivals for different gods, see Sauneron (1962: 47-49).

About the names of the months, there is no evidence, although on the Palermo Stone it is possible to see how Early Dynastic Egyptians compute the time as in later periods, see Schäfer (1902: 15 nos. 2-3, 27 no. 7).

793 Gaballa & Kitchen (1969: 20).

794 Gaballa & Kitchen (1969: 24, 34-36).

795 Commented by Gaballa & Kitchen (1969: 2-13), with references.

796 See Gaballa & Kitchen (1969: 36).

797 The festival lasted for ten days, from the 21st to the 30th of the month of *Khoiak (IIII akhet)* - Bleeker (1967: 82-83), with references. Gaballa & Kitchen (1969: 36) defended the starting date on 18th of 4th *Akhet*, basing their claim on the Pap. Louvre N. 3176. They also give many details of the ceremonies (see *íd*., pp. 38-45).- On the 21st the "Opening of the window in the sanctuary of Sokar"; on the 22nd "The festival of breaking open the ground"; on the 23rd "The holding of a procession in the sanctuary of Sokar"; on the 24th 'The placing of Sokar in their midst (of the dead?)'; on the 25th "The *nṯry.t* festival"; on the 26th "The festival of Sokar"; on the succeeding days offerings were made to Ptah-Sokar-Osiris and his ennead; on the 30th the erection of the *ḏd*-pillar took place.

798 Bleeker (1967: 82-83), with references. Gaballa & Kitchen (1969: 36) defended the starting date on the 18th of 4th Akhet, basing their claim on the Pap. Louvre . 3176. They also give many details of the ceremonies, íd. (pp. 38-45).

799 (1969: 45-48).

The first mention of the festival of Sokar on the Palermo Stone is *ḥꜣ* and a building. *ḥꜣ* was translated[800] as "foundation of the building". According to Gaballa and Kitchen,[801] the right translation would be "around", as in *pẖr ḥꜣ jnbw* "going around the walls." In these two mentions, the scribes would have omitted the verb *pẖr* or similar. According to these authors,[802] "in the First Dynasty, a periodic "feast of the Maaty Barque" involving Sokar and the king may have been (or become) associated with a procession round a royal building linked with the current reign".

Gaballa and Kitchen[803] noted that, in the reign of Ninetjer (Second Dynasty), the festival of Sokar coincides with the *ẖꜥt-bjtj*, "The Appearance of the king of Lower Egypt", and that these festivals have a periodicity of six years. However, on the basis of the oldest mention of this festival on the Palermo Stone, it can be concluded that there was no regular cycle in those festivals.[804] Moreover, *ẖꜥt-bjtj* or *ẖꜥt m bjtj* were roles assumed by the king in rituals (for example, in the ritual recorded in the inscription of Rewer (Urk. I, 232); they need not therefore form part of any particular pattern except in relation to those rituals.[805]

As was said above, it is possible to detect the celebration of this festival during the Early Dynastic period. As in preceding chapters, the major evidence belongs to the First Dynasty.

Horus Aha ivory label from Neithhotep's tomb at Naqada (Figure 55). De Morgan[806] excavated a mastaba, in which he found a fragment of label. The importance of this fragment was such that the Naqada tomb was re-excavated by Garstang with the primary objective of finding a missing fragment. He not only found the missing portion but also recovered a large part of another label of identical design[807] (Figure 55, above). The first scholar that identified the sign *mn* on the label with the mythical Menes was Borchardt, and it was accepted by Petrie, who later changed his mind.[808] Borchardt's interpretation[809] was also rejected by Naville,[810] who preferred to read *mn* as the name of the pavilion.

The traditional belief that Narmer completed the unification of Egypt led many scholars to interpret this label as material evidence of a ceremony that commemorated the unification.[811]

However, there were also other interpretations that saw this label as representing a ceremony. For example, Legge made one of the first readings:[812] "First Register. - At the Sed festival of Horus Aha in his pavilion of repose (y. e., after his death). Second Register. - (Rubric.) The acts done by the king himself (i.e., by the priest who plays his part). The chief of the South mixes the clay for the bricks of the foundation before the Rekhitou and passes through the eating-hall, where tables of offerings of meat, wine, and the like are set before three statues of the gods. Third Register. - At the foundation, the Horus gave to the temple (or had brought by him slaves) two hundred measures of wood and a thousand measures of water (and in the alternative four captives".

800 *Wb*. III, 8, 4.
801 (1969: 15-16).
802 Gaballa & Kitchen (1969: 16).
803 (1969: 16).
804 In the third row (reign of Den), the festival of Sokar is mentioned. If periodicity had existed, the next festival would have been celebrated six years later, but the only events engraved were "Appearance of the King of Lower Egypt. First time of the running of bull Apis", see for example Schäfer (1902: 19 3-6, 21 3-12).
805 Baines (personal communication).
806 (1897). A fragment of a similar label was found at Abydos, Kaiser & Dreyer (1982: Taf. 57c).

807 Garstang (1905).
808 Vandier (1952, 1, II: 828) with references.
809 (1898).
810 (1902:108-112).
811 Garstang (1905: 63) explained the second row "as representing or commemorating the Joining of the Two lands, with some detail of the ceremonial". Vandier (1952, 1, II: 828-834) interpreted the first register as a commemoration of a victory with a ceremony in which is celebrated the unification of the country (second row), while he could not interpret the third register. Later, the same author with Drioton (1952: 138) —and, later, also Emery (1961: 50)— claimed that the scene of the second row represents some ceremony commemorating the Unification of the Two Lands, represented by two human figures performing some function over an unidentified object —the ceremony was called "Receiving the South and the North." Vikentiev (1933: 230) interpreted part of the upper row as *ꜥḥꜣ ꜥḥꜣ bꜣ wnt rꜥ jtrw* "King Aha combatant and destroyer of the fort that is in the mouth of the river." Later, Vikentiev (1948: 680-681) recognised the pavilion *zḥ-nṯr*, which appears in the Pyramid Texts, in the structure that is beside the *serekh*.
812 (1906; especially p. 263).

Gaballa and Kitchen[813] proposed a reading of the upper row: "Hor-'Aha hacking up the earth (or: "opening a channel"?) at X; Hor-'Aha (following) Sokar in his barque and the barque of a goddess".

However, Helck[814] preferred the translation: "[Damaged] Appearance of the fighting hawk and the chopping up of the country with the winding Channel by the fighting hawk; Travel of the 'Hawk in the Bark'; [to found] the crown shrine 'the two ladies are remaining' [by] Horus Aha. Festive sacrifice during the handing over of taxes of Upper Egypt and supply of Lower Egypt" (the taxes would be cattle, bread, wine, olive oil, and beheaded animals).

Fig. 55: Two reconstructions of the Naqada label: above, Gartang's reconstruction; below, Helck's reconstrution. Not to scale.

We believe that it is possible to offer a new reading from the point of view expressed before by some scholars: this label represents a ceremony. The new reading will emphasise in different aspects: the role of the offerings, iconographic interpretations, ... The first row begins with the "Two Ladies" (*nbtj*) name (*mn*)[815]. The Two Ladies must be understood as the appearance of the goddesses of Buto and el-Kab, religious capitals of Egypt, who played an important role in the royal ceremonies. They are followed by Aha's *serekh* and a pair of boats of different size were depicted.[816] The upper one has a falcon in its interior (G7*) which might represent the king (?). Below is the bark that was used for the Festivals of Sokar.[817] To the left is possible to distinguish the titles of the king: Two falcons (*nbwj*, Horus and Seth) forming the name of the king, Aha (fighter). In the second row, a ritual offering is performed in which, on the left side, the different offerings from Lower Egypt are mentioned (votive figurines[818] or baboons, cattle —sacrificed?—, bread, wine, olive oil, and beheaded birds). In the centre of this register, there are two persons smelting or pounding copper ore,

[813] (1969: 18). Gaballa & Kitchen (*id.*), with references, mentioned the possible early agricultural role of Sokar.
[814] (1987: 146).

[815] Among other similar readings and translations, Allen's (1992) reading, *mn-nbtj* 'The Two Ladies Shall Abide', is also very plausible. Johnson (1990: 46-47) also interprets it in the same way; she adds that the cobra, Wadjet, was represented in the form of a hieroglyph, *ḏ*.
[816] Williams & Logan (1987) have claimed the religious importance of the barks in the festivals. However, it should not be forgotten that wooden barks were exclusively transport for royalty and deities. Thus this type of bark (the painted linen from Gebelein, incense burners from Qustul, etc.) represented the monarchy or different gods in a moment of the celebration. The wooden barks would be very rare, and they could only be afforded by the most important temples and the royal palace, with not only a ritual purpose but military as well (see for example the Gebel el-Arak knife handle, in which two different types of barks appear). Thus, barks had a ritual meaning, but at the same time show the power of the king or gods.
[817] See Bleeker (1967) and below. According to Gaballa & Kitchen (1969: 18), the owner of the bark is the god Sokar, but the bark represented on this label would not be the *Henu* or the *Maaty* bark, but *jꜥb-nṯrw* or *jꜥb-sḫmw* barks.
[818] As those found at the temple of Satet in Elephantine, Dreyer (1986), in the temple of Hierakonpolis Quibell (1900), Quibell & Green (1902), or at Abydos, Petrie (1903).

as the inscription shows: *bjꜣ mḥ*[819] plus the ideogram of the verb *ḫwsj* "pound"[820]: "pounding a mineral (surely, copper)." Thus, the figure that is ahead of the building holding a stick is a statue of the king, , the ideogram of the word *ḫntj*, "statue".[821] Moreover, above the statue there is a human figure bowing down () before the figure of the king. Beside this man, it is tempting to read *nsw [n] ḏt.f "the king himself"*[822], which refers to the statue. Inside the palace, there are three people that could be relatives of the king or high functionaries. Thus, the scene can be summarised as an ritual offering to a royal statue. As has been seen before (p. 47), offerings were made in a special court called *wsḫt*. There are many ways to represent this hall, but most show the building of the palace inside,[823] as on this label. For this reason, it is possible that this scene was celebrated in a *wsḫt* court.

Djer.- In the Step Pyramid, fourteen inscribed stone vessels were found. On one of them, it was possible to relate the inscription to one that appears on the Palermo Stone (line 2, no. 7),[824] which was translated by Lacau and Lauer (following Schäfer): "the year of the inauguration (*ḫʿ*) (?), the building (called) 'friend of the gods' in the feast of Sokar"[825].

There is a representation of the god Sokar on his *Henu*-bark on the handle of an **ivory comb (Figure 56, left)**, but there is no reference to any celebration.[826] The god, over a pair of wings, protects the *serekh* of king Djet. In addition, this depiction shows the Egyptian concept of cosmos (figure 56, right), in which heaven is supported by two *wꜣs* sceptres and both were on the earth-sign.

Fig. 56: (Right) Ivory comb of Djet. Not to scale. (Left) Egyptian idea of cosmos.

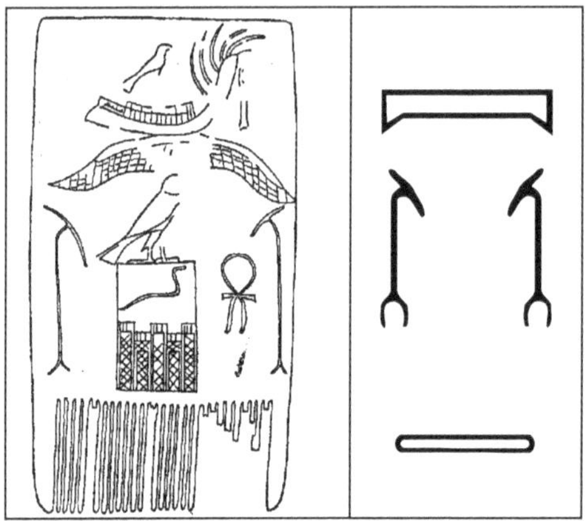

Ivory label (for a container of oil) of Semerkhet from Abydos[827] **(Figure 57).** The inscription is coloured in red and black[828]. Griffith[829] saw, beside the sign of the year, the title of "The Following of Horus", the palace of the Great Ones, the *nebti* titles, a figure that he could not interpret and the text "He who traverses the Pool of Horus, the royal axe-maker, the first, the governor Henu-ka". He found the last three characters obscure. Legge[830] read it: "In the year Sches Hor (sic.), when the royal tribe met in place of the great ones (in the city of Thoth). At the first foundation of *Het suten*, (in the reign of the) King of the North and South, Lord of Diadems, Semerkhet, (when) the royal architects were .... and .... the Horus (gave to the temple) measures of wood and .... jars of wine".

[819] *Wb.* 1, 438, 9 mentions *bjꜣ mḥ* "a mineral". The word *bjꜣ* in ancient Egyptian means also "copper" (apart from a mining region) and the ideogram which accompanies the phonograms was at the beginning , and was later replaced by , Gardiner (1957: 490, 529). is an ideogram used to complement words related to mining works, see, for example, Gardiner (1957: 497).

[820] *Wb.* 3, 248, B, IIb. In this case, the infinitive *ḫwst*.

[821] Gardiner (1957: 444).

It is well known that Egyptian gods were believed to have their flesh made of rich metals, especially gold, see Hornung (1999: 118-124). In this case, it is possible to explain the use of copper instead of gold because gold was rarer than copper in this early period. For copper and gold in the Early Dynastic period, see Emery (1961: 224-228).

[822] See a parallel in Faulkner (1962: 317), who translated *kꜣj n ḏt.j* as "my own ka".

[823] See P. Spencer (1984: 71-72), with many depictions of all periods.

[824] Schäfer (1902: 16).

[825] Lacau & Lauer (1959: pl. 1, no. 2; 1961: 3-6). They were mistaken in the transliteration of the verb and instead of *ḫʿ*, they wrote *ḥʿ*. Moreover, this verb must to be understood as infinitive, *ḫʿ.t*, see Gaballa & Kitchen (1969: 16).

[826] Emery (1961: 248, fig. 146).

[827] Petrie (1900: pls. XII, no. 1, XVII, no. 26); for the name of the label, Spencer (1980: 65, no. 461).

Petrie (1901: pl. VIII, no. 5) found a duplicate of this label in the tomb of Qaa at Abydos. The German Expedition has also recently discovered two similar labels in the tomb of Qaa.

[828] Petrie (1900).

[829] In Petrie (1900: 42-43).

[830] (1907: 245).

According to Spencer[831], beside *rnpt*, the events of a particular year are recorded: the festival *šmsw-ḥr* and *ḥḏ-wrw*. To the left of this, he reads the inscription as *nsw bjtj nbty jry-nṯr* and the name of the official Henuka, who has the title *mḏḥty-nsw*[832]. At the bottom of the label, he recognised the type of oil. The signs at the extreme top-left hand corner were interpreted as an administrative building.[833]

Helck[834] translated the register of the right side: "The Following of Horus; Festival of *ḥḏ-wrw*".

Fig. 57: Label of king Semerkhet found at Abydos. Not to scale.

This label is divided in two parts. On the right, it is possible to read: *rnpt šmsw ḥr ꜥḥ(-ḥḏ)*[835] *wrw*[836] *Zkr* [837] "Year, the Following of Horus, (offerings to) the White Shrine of the Great Ones of the palace (ancestors) in the festival of Sokar."

The left part of the label can be read as *nsw bjtj nbtj smsw* "King of Upper and Lower Egypt, *nebti* (name) Semsu." *tpj jdt* "The best fragrance". *mḏḥ pr nsw ḥꜣt mrw ḥnwkꜣ* "Carpenter of the finest *meru*-wood in the royal palace, Henuka".

A label recently found in the tomb of **Qaa** mentions "The Third time of the festival of Sokar".[838] Thus, there were at least three of these ceremonies in the reign of Qaa. However, the material evidence discussed below does not differentiate which time it is.

- Conclusions

With the foundation of Memphis and its development as the capital of Egypt, the cults established there by the rulers become very important. Although it was once thought that Narmer or Horus Aha founded Memphis, it now seems that it could have been earlier.[839] If Memphis was certainly founded some years earlier than the reign of Aha, it is logical to believe that the transcendence of the festivals of Sokar would begin some years after the foundation of the city. But the key point is that one of the gods of Memphis, such as Sokar, acquired so much importance that its festivals were performed by the king and were recorded as an extraordinary event.

However, it is very difficult to imagine what was the main aim of this festival and why it was so important for the kingship in those early periods. We will stress the later relationship between Sokar and craftsmen. It seems likely that during the First Dynasty this god could represent the image of creator, as Ptah later on.[840] Thus, the king might assume this role, being the re-incarnation of the creator.

The fact that this festival is mentioned on labels found in the royal tombs means that the king received offerings collected in the festival of Sokar. One possible explanation for this is that the king and the god Sokar were identified as one, in the same way that in this age the king is identified with the god Horus. In this regard, it has to be mentioned the close association of king and Sokar

[831] (1980: 65, no. 461).
[832] Kaplony (1963, I: 300) read the title *mḏḥ-mḏḥ(w) nsw*.
[833] Kaplony (1963, I: 299) reads *ḫtjw*.
[834] (1987: 163).
[835] For a close parallel in Netjerikhet's complex, see F. D. Friedman (1995: 24). This author adds (*id.*) that "The *(ꜥḥ)-ḥḏ* of Djoser panel is described in Pyramid Texts as a wooden building that may have been a small shrine for a cult statue", with references.
[836] For a close parallel in a seal impression from Saqqara, see Kaplony (1963, 3: Taf. 59, Abb. 211), and in Netjerikhet's complex, see F. D. Friedman (1995: 24-25). As this author mentions, many baboon temple offerings have been found out at Abydos, Hierakonpolis and Elephantine.
[837] Although this bark has a falcon on the top of the mast instead of two falcons as on the Palermo Stone, the shape of this bark is very similar to Sokar's bark represented on the Palermo Stone.

[838] Dreyer *et alii* (1996: 75). Inventory number Ab K 1443.
[839] Wilkinson (1996a: 347-348); Jiménez-Serrano (2001a).
[840] See the "Memphite Theology", Lichtheim (1975: 51, 54-55).

in the Pyramid Texts.[841] Moreover, both gods, Sokar and Horus, are represented as falcons and it is well known that the Egyptian kings of the Early periods were identified with the falcon. But it must be taken into account that Sokar has a funerary role, as Gaballa and Kitchen noted. As the image of the king, the resurrection of this god on the last day of the festival through the erection of the *ḏd*-pillar might mean the resurrection of the king himself.[842]

The appearance of at least two labels with the mention of the god Sokar in a non-royal tomb (Naqada), means that the king, as the beneficiary of some goods obtained in the festivals of Sokar, could complete the funeral furniture of a relative, as seems to be the case here (Neith-Hotep, Aha's mother?).[843]

[841] Faulkner (1962: §§ 445, 1826).
[842] About the *ḏd*-pillar see R. Wilkinson (1992: 167).
[843] Spencer (1980: 63).

CHAPTER FOUR
GENERAL CONCLUSIONS

1. - Royal festivals in Late Predynastic and Early Dynastic periods

It is easy to conclude that the Egyptian festivals discussed in this book have their origin in Predynastic times. Surely, they are an evolution from prehistoric rites. Those rites are connected to the natural world, as well as to beliefs, which were common to many peoples in the first stages of the Neolithic age in North Africa.[844] But this connection with the natural world must not mask the main objective of this book, the king. Therefore, some of the ceremonies studied here have a political genesis and derive from a political organisation (kingship) more or less articulated in those times.

In Egypt, there is some evidence that seems to support the existence of some festivals in the Naqada II period.[845] However, this book has focused on evidence after the Naqada III period because, from that moment, Egypt shares a common material culture. This fact permits us to suggest that ideological and religious concepts expanded together with the material culture. The characters of the royal festivals are based on those two factors: ideology and religion. The ideology is united with the figure of the king, who from the early First Dynasty at least, ruled over most of Egypt and some neighbouring regions (Southern Canaan,[846] Nubia,[847] etc.). Egyptian kingship was one of the earliest recorded monarchies of the world, which means that kings did not have a local or foreign ideological precedent on which to base their power. The solutions to this problem came from an indigenous development of the figure of the king, who adopted such religious (*nebti*) or political (standards) symbols, and from iconographic elements imported from another area with a similar status of social development.[848]

However, the different religious concepts were not integrated into the royal corpus of iconography. They kept their original independence, although the Egyptian ruler was the high priest of all the cults. Perhaps the possibility that the king could direct the rituals of all the divinities gave a common sense to all the festivals: to guarantee the *maat*.

The king, as high priest, directed the festivals and the beneficiary was the whole of Egypt. Egypt was the people, the land, and the natural world. But Egypt was also the king. The king was the repository of *maat* and Egypt could not exist without the dichotomy king/*maat*. Perhaps this example is clearly illustrated in the *Admonitions of Ipu-wer*, where the chaos is explained as the lack of a strong ruler. Thus, the first beneficiary (together with the gods) of all the festivals was the king, and secondly the whole of Egypt.

The festivals studied in this book shared some features, perhaps as a consequence of the influence of the palace. At first sight, all these festivals seem to have nothing in common, but after a deeper analysis it is possible to detect that the ceremony *pḫr ḥ3 jnbw* ("Circuit of the walls") is part of every festival.[849] Offerings are another important part of the festivals as homage (Enthronement, *sed* festival, and Sokar) or as booty (Victories). The derived conclusion of these coincidences might be a homogenisation process conducted by the palace or an evident imitation of the royal ritual. In addition, religion become the perfect excuse for monarchs to obtain surpluses.

One of the conclusions that can be suggested is that the duality was an existing concept from the Predynastic period, but that it was completely re-defined during the first half of the First Dynasty. The concept of duality affects the policy and the religious areas. Egypt was divided a short time before the First Dynasty into two administrative regions, Upper and Lower Egypt.[850] As a mirror of this administrative division, religious concepts were integrated in the same two different areas. The most noticeable case was the god Horus, who was the god of Hierakonpolis, the most probable winner of the wars that led to the unification of Upper Egypt in the Naqada II period.[851] However, Horus was regarded as the god of Lower Egypt, while Seth was the Upper Egyptian god. However, ancient Egyptians never considered that Horus was born in the Delta.[852]

[844] Cervelló Autuori (1996).
[845] Williams & Logan (1987).
[846] Miroschedji (1998).
[847] Jiménez Serrano (forthcoming).
[848] Pérez Largacha (1993a).

[849] There is no data on the festival of victory; however, the military character of this festival is completely different to the others.
[850] See the hieroglyphics and  depicted on jars from Horus Ka's tomb, Petrie (1902: pls. I-III). See also Figure 13.
[851] Pérez Largacha (1993a).
[852] Cervelló Autuori (1996).

Festivals were major events in Egypt. Because of this, they were recorded on many different objects. The purpose of these representations was not only propaganda, but also magic. Ancient Egyptians believed that images had a powerful magic. This magic was a consequence of the representation of some sacred entities, for example gods, the king, standards, etc. The bias towards that is why most of the information has been found in tombs or in sacred places, such as temples. The role of the magic inscriptions in the tombs is to repeat the sacred ceremonies throughout eternity. In temples, those objects give them a position of respect in relation to other temples, and legitimisation.

But recorded festivals are in debt to the administration. As has been seen, most of the information that has been analysed here comes from labels that were attached to some funerary goods. As from the middle of the First Dynasty, the inscriptions are introduced with *rnpt*, it can be assumed that those goods were obtained during the festivals. This means that festivals were a unique occasion for the king to obtain funerary goods from the whole country as well as a way of individualising the year. It may also be concluded that the king used some of those goods as prizes for high officials (it can be assumed that many of them were part of the royal family), because some of those labels have been found in private tombs.

It seems reasonable that the king obtained goods in the royal festivals, but what happened to those goods obtained in the festivals of Sokar (for example)? A possible explanation is that the king and the god Sokar were identified as the same entity in those early times. Thus, the king, as well as the main temple of the god, was a beneficiary of the offerings.

The other physical consequence was the architecture. Festivals in ancient Egypt were celebrated in temples or special enclosures, depending on the type of ritual that was performed. One common ceremony of most festivals was the foundation of a building. With this ceremony, a new pure place was delimited. In that place, new shrines were built and the rituals were performed.

2. – Symbolic topography and royal festivals

Discoveries of Late Predynastic and Early Dynastic temples are rare in Egypt, and do not permit one to have a general idea about them. However, there is a complete example that has survived at Hierakonpolis.[853] From the plan of its structure, it has been possible to draw parallels with other similar structures built in different places of Egypt. Thus, it is possible to confirm that the architects of the Early Dynastic kings developed a special enclosure, which was used not only as a funerary temple, but also as an area in which some festivals related to the kingship were performed.

As these enclosures were built for the glory of the contemporary king, the propagandistic elements are highly developed: size, location, materials of construction, decorative elements, etc. The size of the whole enclosure is monumental; they are the precedent of the pyramid enclosures. The location is very important, because the royal enclosures are found only at three capitals:

- Hierakonpolis, where Horus was worshipped from prehistoric times and where the ancestral kings of the proto-kingdom of Hierakonpolis were buried.

- Abydos, where the Upper Egyptian kings of the end of the Predynastic period were buried and where the god Khentiamentiu was worshipped.

- Saqqara, where the high officials (surely part of the royal family) of the First Dynasty, and some kings of the Second, were buried. Saqqara was the necropolis of the élite that lived in Memphis from the First Dynasty. It is also noticeable that the festivals of Sokar played an important role during this period.

But royal enclosures also had two different uses:

- During the lifetime of the king, enclosures were used as sacred places where certain ceremonies were celebrated. As a result of some of those ceremonies, the king received different offerings, which were stored in the enclosures. These offerings were deposited in the royal tomb after the death of the king.

- When a king died, his enclosures became his funerary temple, as well as the public part of his tomb.

[853] Another in Buto — von der Way (1997b: 115-172).

The temples were conceived as being in origin the first islands that emerged from the waters of chaos. They conserved this aspect, but, as sacred places, they had an aspect of purity. In ancient Egypt, the myth and the present were always intermixed, thus temples always represented this aspect of islands surrounded by the waters of chaos. Due to this, the presence of sacred barks in the areas (where the temples were) would not be unusual.[854] In this way, the gods could always sail over these waters of chaos.

The Egyptian kings developed a complex system of ceremonies and rituals that served them as a form of expression before society. As we have seen, the ways were also complex and varied, but so effective that most of these festivals continued to be performed during a period of more than three thousand years.

---

[854] Beside the enclosures at Abydos, see O'Connor (1991). At Saqqara, beside some of the tombs of the high officials, see Emery (1961: 131 & fig. 78). At Helwan, Saad (1969: 74-75, pls. 105-106).

Abbreviations

Anc. Eg.	Ancient Egypt.
ASAE	Annales du Service des Antiquités de L'Egypte.
BAEDE	Boletín de la Asociación Española de Egiptología.
BAEO	Boletín de la Asociación Española de Orientalistas.
BASOR	Bulletin of the American Schools of Oriental Research.
BES	Bulletin of the Egyptological Seminar.
BIE	Bulletin de l'Institut d'Égypte.
BIFAO	Bulletin de l'Institut Français d'Archéologie Orientale au Caire.
BiOr	Bibliotheca Orientalis.
BSFE	Bulletin de la Société Française d'Égyptologie.
CdE	Chronique d'Égypte.
CRAIBL	Comptes Rendus à l'Academie des Inscriptions et Belles-Lettres.
CRIPEL	Cahiers de Recherche de l'Institut de Papyrologie et d'Égytologie de Lille.
DE	Discussions in Egyptology.
GM	Göttinger Miszellen.
IEJ	Israel Exploration Journal.
JARCE	Journal of the American Research Center in Egypt.
JEA	Journal of Egyptian Archaeology.
JESHO	Journal of Economic and Social History of the Orient.
JHE	Journal of Human Evolution.
JNES	Journal Near Eastern Studies.
JRAI	Journal of the Royal Anthropological Institute of Great Britain and Ireland.
JSSEA	Journal of the Society for the Study of Egyptian Antiquities.
JWP	Journal of World Prehistory.
LAAA	Annals of Archaeology and Anthropology.
LdÄ	Lexikon der Ägyptologie. Wiesbaden.
MDAIK	Mitteilungen des Deutschen Archäologischen Instituts Abteilung Kairo.
Mon. Piot.	Monuments et Mémoires Publiés par l'Académie des Inscriptions et Belles-Lettres.
PSBA	Proceedings of the Society of Biblical Archaeology.
Rec. Trav.	Recueil de Travaux Relatifs à la Philologie et à l'Archéologie Égyptiennes et Assyriennes.
RdE	Revue d'Égyptologie.
SAK	Studien zur Altägyptischen Kultur.
Urk. I	K. Sethe, 1933. *Urkunden des Alten Reichs, I.* Leipzig.
VA	Varia Aegyptiaca.
WA	World Archaeology.
Wb	Erman, A. & Grapow, H., 1926. *Wörterbuch der Ägyptishen Sprache.* Leipzig.
ZÄS	Zeitschrift für Ägyptische Sprache und Altertumskunde.

BIBLIOGRAPHY

Adams, B., 1974a.
Ancient Hierakonpolis. Warminster.

Adams, B., 1974b.
Ancient Hierakonpolis: Supplement. Warminster.

Adams, B., 1987.
The Fort Cemetery at Hierakonpolis. London & New York.

Adams, B., 1995.
Ancient Nekhen. Garstang in the City of Hierakonpolis. Whitstable, Kent.

Adams, B., 1999.
Early temples at Hierakonpolis and Beyond, in *Centenary of Mediterranean Archaeology at the Jagiellonian University 1897-1997*, pp. 15-28, Cracow.

Adams, B., & Cialowicz, K. M., 1997.
Protodynastic Egypt. Buckinghamshire.

Adams, W. Y., 1977.
Nubia: Corridor to Africa. Princeton, New Jersey.

Adams, W. Y., 1985.
Doubts about the "Lost Pharaohs", *JNES* 44 (no. 3): 185-192.

Alexanian, N., 1998.
Die Reliefdekoration des Chasechemui aus dem sogennanten *Fort* in Herakonpolis, in N. Grimal (ed.): *Les Critères de Datation Stylistiques à l'Ancien Empire*, pp. 1-21, Cairo.

Allen, J. P., 1992.
Menes the Menphite, *GM* 126: 19-22.

Allen, J. P., 2000.
Middle Egyptian. An Introduction to the language and Culture of Hieroglyphs. Cambridge.

Altenmüller, H., 1980.
Horus von Letopolis, *LdÄ* III: 41-46.
Amélineau, E., 1899-1905.
Les Nouvelles Fouilles d'Abydos, 3 vols. Paris.
Amiran, R., 1974.
An Egyptian Jar Fragment with the Name of Narmer from Arad, *IEJ* 24: 4-12.
Anthes, R., 1957.
Die Sonnenboote in den Pyramidentexten, *ZÄS* 82: 77-89.
Arkell, A. J., 1950.
Varia Sudanica, *JEA* 36: 24-40.
Arkell, A. J., 1963.
Was King Scorpion Menes?, *Antiquity* 37: 31-35.
Arnett, W. S., 1982.
The Predynastic origin of Egyptian Hieroglyphs. Washington.
Assmann, J., 1989.
Maât, l'Egypte pharaonique et l'idée de justice sociale. Paris.
Ayrton, E. R., Currelly, C. T., & Weigall, A. E. P., 1904.
Abydos. Part III. London.

Baines, J., 1989.
Communication and Display: The Integration of Early Egyptian Art and Writing, *Antiquity* 63: 471-482.
Baines, J., 1990.
Trône et dieu: aspects du symbolisme royal et divin des temps archaïques, *BSFE* 118: 5-37.
Baines, J., 1991.
On the symbolic context of the principal hieroglyph for "god", in U. Verhoeven & E. Graefe (eds.): *Religion und Philosophie im Alten Ägypten*, pp. 29-46, Leuven.
Baines, J., 1995.
Origins of Egyptian Kingship, in D. O'Connor and D. P. Silverman (eds.): *Ancient Egyptian Kingship*, pp. 95-156, Leiden, New York & Köln.
Baines, J., 1997.
Temples as symbols, guarantors, and participants in Egyptian civilization, in S. Quirke (ed.): *The Temple in Ancient Egypt*, pp. 216-241, Dorset.
Baines, J. & Málek, J., 1980.
Atlas of Ancient Egypt. London.
Bard, K. A., 1994.
From farmers to pharaohs. Mortuary Evidence for the Rise of Complex Society in Egypt. Oxford.
Bard, K. A. & Carneiro, R. L., 1989.
Patterns of Predynastic Settlement Location, Social Evolution and the Circumscription Theory, *CRIPEL* 11: 15-23.
Barta, W., 1975.
Untersuchungen zur Göttlichkeit des regierenden Königs. Berlin.
Barta, W., 1981.
Die Chronologie der 1. bis 5. Dynastie nach den Angaben des rekonstruirten Annalensteins, *ZÄS* 108: 23-33.
Barta, W., 1982.
Bemerkunden zur Bedeutung der *mr*-Hacke, *GM* 54: 11-16.
Baumgartel, E. J., 1955.
The Cultures of Prehistoric Egypt, vol. I.Oxford.
Baumgartel, E. J., 1960.
The Cultures of Prehistoric Egypt, vol. II. Oxford.
Belova, G., 1998.
The Egyptians' Ideas of Hostile Encirclement, in C. J. Eyre (ed.): *Proceedings of the Seventh International Congress of Egyptologists*, pp. 143-148, Leuven.
Berlev, O. D., 1971.
Les prétendus „citadins" au Moyen Empire, *RdE* 23: 23-48.
Berry, A. C., Berry, R. J. and Ucko, P. J., 1967.
Genetical change in ancient Egypt, *Man* N. S. 2: 551-568.
Bettles, E., Clarke, J., Dittmer, J., Duhig, C., Ikram, S., Mathieson, I., Smith, H., Tavares, A., 1995.
National Museums of Scotland Saqqara Project Report 1995. Edinburgh.
Blackman, A. M., and Fairman, H. W., 1942.
The Myth of Horus at Edfu – II, *JEA* 28: 32-38.
Blackman, A. M., and Fairman, H. W., 1943.
The Myth of Horus at Edfu – II, *JEA* 29: 2-36.
Blackman, A. M., and Fairman, H. W., 1944.
The Myth of Horus at Edfu – II, *JEA* 30: 26-36.
Bleeker, C. J., 1967.
Egyptian Festivals. Leiden.
Borchardt, L., 1898.
Das Grab des Menes, *ZÄS* 36: 87-105.
Borchardt, L., 1917.
Die Annalen und die zeitliche Festlegung des alten Reiches der ägyptischen Geschichte. Berlin.
Breasted, J. H., 1931.
The Predynastic union of Egypt. *BIFAO* 30: 709-724.
Bresciani, E., 1969.
Letteratura e Poesia dell'Antico Egitto.

Torino (seconda edizione).
Brovarski, E., 1977-78.
Hor-aha and the Nubians, *Serapis* 4: 1-2.
Burgess, E. M. & Arkell, A. J., 1958.
The reconstructions of the Hathor bowl, *JEA* 44: 6-11.

Campagno, M., 1996.
Caos y orden. Acerca de dos paletas del Predinástico Tardío, *Aula Orientalis* 14: 151-162.
Campagno, M., 1998.
God-kings and King-gods in Ancient Egypt, in C. J. Eyre (ed.): *Proceedings of the Seventh International Congress of Egyptologists*, pp. 237-243, Leuven.
Cannadine, D., 1987.
Introduction: divine rites of kings, in D. Cannadine & S. Price (eds.): *Rituals of Royalty. Power and Ceremonial in Traditional Societies*, pp. 1-19, Cambridge.
Case, H., & Payne, J. C., 1962.
Tomb 100: the decorated tomb at Hierakonpolis, *JEA* 48: 5-18.
Cénival, J. L., 1965.
Un nouveau fragment de la pierre de Palerme, *BSFE* 44: 13-17.
Cervelló Autuori, J., 1996.
Egipto y África. Origen de la civilización y la monarquía faraónicas en su contexto africano. Sabadell (Barcelona).
Cervelló Autuori, J., 1997.
A proposito degli stendardi della prima regalità faraonica, in A. Bogioanni & E. Comba (eds.): *Bestie o Dei? L'animale nel simbolismo religioso*, pp. 77-96.
Cervelló Autuori, J., in press.
Narmer, Menes and the Seals from Abydos, in Z. Hawass & M. Jones (eds.): *Eighth International Congress of Egyptologists*, Cairo.
Childe, V. G., 1969.
New Light on the Most Ancient East. New York.
Cialowicz, K. M., 1987.
Les têtes de massues des périodes prédynastique et archaïque dans la Vallée du Nil, *Prace Archeologiczne* 41, Warsawa-Kraków.
Cialowicz, K. M. ,1998.
Once more the Hierakonpolis Wall Painting, C. J. Eyre (ed.): *Proceedings of the Seventh International Congress of Egyptologists*, pp. 274-279, Leuven.
Cialowicz, K. M., 1999.
The Earliest Evidence of Egypt's Expansion into Nubia?, *Gdansk Archaeological Museum African Reports* 1: 17-22.
Clère, J. J., 1938.
Un Graffito du roi Djet dans le Désert Arabique, *ASAE* 38: 85-93.
Costa Llerda, S., Baqué Manzano, L., & García Vilalta, J., 1999.
Voces en el umbral de la muerte. El faraón frente a las divinidades en el Valle de los Reyes: Tumba de Horemheb (KV 57). Barcelona.

Daressy, G., 1916.
La pierre de Palerme et la chronologie de l'Ancien Empire, *BIFAO* 12: 161-214.
Davies, V. & Friedman, R., 1998.
The Narmer Palette: a forgotten member, *Nekhen News* 10: 22.
Davis, W., 1992.
Masking the blow. Berkeley, Los Angeles & Oxford.
De Morgan, J., 1897.
Recherches sur les origines de l'Égypte. Ethnographie préhistorique et tombeau royal de Négadah. Paris.
Derry, D. E., 1956.
The dynastic race in Egypt, *JEA* 42: 80-85.
Dreyer, G., 1986.
Elephantine VIII. Der Tempel der Satet. Mainz & Rhein.
Dreyer, G. 1987.
Ein Siegel der frühzeitlichen Königsnekropole von Abydos, *MDAIK* 43: 33-43.
Dreyer, G., 1990.
Umm el-Qaab. Nachuntersuchungen im frühzeitlichen Königsfriedhof. 3./4. Vorbericht, *MDAIK* 46: 53-89.
Dreyer, G., 1992a.
The royal tombs of Abydos, in S. Kerner (ed.): *The Near East in Antiquity*, pp. 55-69, Amman.
Dreyer, G., 1992b.
Horus Kokodril, ein Gegenkönig der Dynastie 0, in B. Adams & R. Friedman (eds.): *The Followers of Horus*, pp. 259-263,Oxford.
Dreyer, G., 1992c.
Recent Discoveries at Abydos Cemetery U, in E. C. M. van den Brink (ed.): *The Nile Delta in Transition: 4th-3rd millennium B.C.*, pp. 293-299. Tel Aviv.
Dreyer, G., 1993 (with U. Hartung & F. Pumpenmeier).
Umm el-Qaab. Nachuntersuchungen im frühzeitlichen Königsfriedhof. 5./6. Vorbericht, *MDAIK* 49: 23-62.

Dreyer, G., 1998.
Umm el-Qaab I. Das prädynastische Königsgrab U-j und seine frühen Schriftzeugnisse. Mainz.

Dreyer, G., Engel, E.-M., Hartung, U., Hikade, Th., Köhler, E. Chr., & Pumpenmeier, F., 1996.
Umm el-Qaab. Nachuntersuchungen im frühzeitlichen Königfriedhof 7./8. Vorberich, *MDAIK* 52: 11-81.

Dreyer, G. Engel, E.-M., Hartung, U., Hikade, Th., Köhler, E. Chr., Müller, V., & Pumpenmeier, F., 1998.
Umm el-Qaab. Nachuntersuchungen im frühzeitlichen Königfriedhof 9./10. Vorberich, *MDAIK* 54: 77-167.

Drioton, E. & Vandier, J., 1952.
Les Peuples de l'Orient méditerranéen. Vol. II: L'Egypte. Paris.

Eaton-Krauss, M., 1984.
The representations of statuary in private tombs of the Old Kingdom. Wiesbaden.

Edwards, I. E. S., 1971.
The Early Dynastic Period in Egypt, in I. E. S. Edwards, C. J. Gadd and N. G. L. Hammond (eds.): *The Cambridge Ancient History*, vol. I, part 2, pp. 1-70. Cambridge.

El-Sayed, R., 1982.
La Déesse Neith de Saïs I-II. Cairo.

Emery, W. B., 1938.
Excavations at Saqqara: The Tomb of Hemaka. Cairo.

Emery, W. B., 1939.
Excavations at Saqqara (1937-38). Hor-Aha. Cairo.

Emery, W. B., 1949.
Great Tombs of the First Dynasty, I. Cairo.

Emery, W. B., 1952.
Saqqara and the Dynastic Race. London.

Emery, W. B., 1954.
Great Tombs of the First Dynasty, II. London.

Emery, W. B., 1958.
Great Tombs of the First Dynasty, III. London.

Emery, W. B., 1961.
Archaic Egypt. Harmondsworth.

Engelbach, R., 1934.
A foundation scene of the Second Dynasty, *JEA* 20: 183-184.

Engelbach, R., 1943.
An essay on the advent of the dynastic race in Egypt and its consequences, *ASAE* 42: 193-221.

Fairman, H. W., 1935.
The Myth of Horus at Edfu, I: The Legend of the Winged Disk, *JEA* 21: 26-36.

Fairman, H. W., 1958.
The Kingship Rituals of Egypt, in S. H. Hooke (ed.): *Myth, Ritual and Kingship. Essays on the Theory and Practice of Kingship in the Ancient Near East and in Israel*, pp. 74-104, Oxford.

Fairservis, W. A., Jr., 1983a.
The Hierakonpolis Project. Occasional Papers in Anthropology no. Y. Excavation of the Temple Area on the Kom el Gemuwia: Season of 1978. New York.

Fairservis, W. A., Jr., 1983b.
The Hierakonpolis Project. Occasional Papers in Anthropology no. II. Hierakonpolis- The Graffiti and the Origins of Egyptian Hieroglyphic Writing. New York.

Fairservis, W. A., Jr., 1991.
A revised View of the Narmer Palette, *JARCE* 28: 1-20.

Faulkner, R. O., 1962.
A Concise Dictionary of Middle Egyptian. Oxford.

Faulkner, R. O., 1969.
The Ancient Egyptian Pyramid Texts. Oxford.

Finnestad, R. B., 1985.
Image of the World and Symbol of the Creator. Wiesbaden.

Firth, C. M., & Quibell, J. E., 1935.
Excavations at Saqqara. The Step Pyramid, vol. I. Cairo.

Fischer, H. G., 1989.
The Origin of Egyptian Hieroglyphs, in W. M. (ed.): *The Origins of Writing*, 59-76, Nebraska.

Frankfort, H., 1948.
Kingship and the Gods. Chicago.

Friedman, F. D., 1995.
The Underground Relief Panels of King Djoser at the Step Pyramid Complex, *JARCE* 32: 1-42.

Friedman, R., 1996.
The Ceremonial Centre at Hierkonpolis Locality HK29A, in J. Spencer (ed.): *Aspects of Early Egypt*, 16-35, London.

Friedman, R., 1999.
Investigations in the Fort of Khasekhemui, *Nekhen News* 11: 9-12.

Gaballa, G. A. and Kitchen, K. A., 1969.
The Festival of Sokar, *Orientalia* 38: 1-76.

Galán, J. M., 2000.
The Ancient Egyptian *Sed*-Festival and the Exemption from Corvée, *JNES* 59 (no. 4): 255-264.
Gardiner, A. H., 1915.
The Nature and Development of the Egyptian Hieroglyphic Writing, *JEA* II: 61-75.
Gardiner, A. H., 1943.
The God Semseru, *JEA* 29: 75-76.
Gardiner, A. H., 1944.
Horus the Beḥdetite, *JEA* 30: 23-60.
Gardiner, A. H., 1957.
Egyptian Grammar (Third Edition). London.
Gardiner, A. H., 1958.
The personal name of King Serpent, *JEA* 44: 38-39.
Gardiner, A. H., 1961.
Egypt of the Pharaohs. Oxford.
Garstang, J., 1905.
The Tablet of Mena, *ZÄS* 42: 61-64.
Garstang, J., 1907.
Excavations at Hierakonpolis, at Esna, and in Nubia, *ASAE* 8: 132-148.
Gauthier, H., 1925-1929.
Dictionnaire des noms géographiques contenus dans les textes hiéroglyphiques, 6 vols. Cairo.
Gauthier, H., 1931.
Les Fêtes du dieu Min. Cairo.
Gautier, P. & Midant-Reynes, B., 1995.
La tête de massue du roi Scorpion, *Archeo-Nil* 5: 87-127.
Godron, G., 1949.
A propos du nom royal , *ASAE* 49: 217-221, 547.
Godron, G., 1957.
Notes d'épigraphie thinite, *ASAE* 54: 191-206.
Godron, G., 1990.
Études sur l'Horus Den et quelques problèmes de l'Egypte archaïque. Genève.
Goedicke, H., 1985.
zmꜣ-tꜣwy, in P. Posener-Kriéger (ed.): *Mélanges Gamal Eddin Mokhtar*, vol. I, pp. 307-324, Cairo.
Gohary, J., 1992.
Akhenaten's Sed-festival at Karnak. London & New York.
Goldwasser, O., 1992.
The Narmer Paletter and the "Triumph of Metaphor", *Lingua Aegyptiaca* 2: 67-85.
Goneim, M. Z., 1957.
Horus Sekhem-khet. The unfinished step pyramid at Saqqara, vol. I. Le Caire.
Grdseloff, B., 1944.
Notes d'épigraphie archaïque, *ASAE* 44: 279-310.
Griffith, F. Ll., 1898.
A Collection of Hieroglyphs. London.
Griffiths, J. G., 1980.
The Origins of Osiris and his cult. Leiden.

Habachi, L. & Kaiser, W., 1985.
Ein Friedhof der Maadikultur bei es-Saff, *MDAIK* 41: 43-46.
Handleman, D., 1990.
Models and mirrors: towards an anthropology of public events. Cambridge.
Hassan, F. A., 1988.
The Predynastic of Egypt, *JWP* 2 (no. 2): 135-185.
Hassan, F. A., 1992.
Primeval Goddess to Divine King. The Mythogenesis of Power in the Early Egyptian State, in R. Friedman & B. Adams (eds.): *The Followers of Horus*, pp. 307-321. Oxford.
Hassan, F. A., 1993a.
Town and village in ancient Egypt: ecology, society and urbanization, in T. Shaw, P. Sinclair, B. Andah, & A. Okpoko (eds.): *The Archaeology of Africa. Food, metals and towns*, pp. 551-569, London.
Hassan, F. A., 1993b.
Population, Ecology, and Civilization in Ancient Egypt, in C. L. Crumley (ed.): *Historical Ecology. Cultural knowledge and changing landscapes*, pp. 155-181, Santa Fé.
Hassan, F. A., 1998a.
L'Egitto come stato unitario, *KEMET*: 39-46.
Hassan, F. A., 1998b.
Les relations culturelles entre l'Égypte et ses voisins orientaux durant la Préhistorie récente, in D. Valbelle & C. Bonnet (eds.): *Le Sinaï durant l'antiquité et le Moyen Âge*, pp. 12-19, París.
Hassan, F. A., 1998c.
The Earliest Goddesses of Egypt, in L: Goodison & C. Morris (eds.): *Ancient Goddesses*, pp. 98-112, London.
Hassan, F. A. & Matson, R. G., 1984.
Seriation of Predynastic Potsherds from the Naqada Region, in L. Krzyzaniak & M. Kobusiewicz (eds.): *Late Prehistory of the Nile Basin and the Sahara*, Poznan.
Hassan, F. A., & Jiménez Serrano, A., unpublished.

The Chronology of the Late Predynastic period and the First Dynasty.

Helck, W., 1954.
Untersuchungen zu den Beamtentiteln des ägyptischen alten Reiches. Glückstadt.

Helck, W., 1966.
Nilhöhe und Jubiläumsfest, *ZÄS* 93: 74-79.

Helck, W., 1970.
Zwei Einzelprobleme der Thinitischen Chronologie, *MDAIK* 26: 83-85.

Helck, W., 1972.
Zu den "Talbezirken" in Abydos, *MDAIK* 28: 95-99.

Helck, W., 1974.
Bemerkunden zum Annalenstein, *MDAIK* 30: 31-35.

Helck, W., 1986a.
Wer, *LdÄ* VI: 1221.

Helck, W., 1986b.
Tekenu, *LdÄ* VI: 308-309.

Helck, W., 1987.
Untersuchungen zur Thinitenzeit. Wiesbaden.

Hocart, A. M., 1970.
Kings and Councillors. Chicago & London (first published in 1936).

Hoffman, M. A., 1976.
The City of the Hawk: seat of Egypt's Ancient Civilization, *Expedition* 18 (no. 3): 32-41.

Hoffman, M. A., 1979.
Egypt before the Pharaohs. London.

Hoffman, M. A., 1980.
A Rectangular Amratian House from Hierakonpolis and Its Significance for Predynastic Research, *JNES* 39: 119-137.

Hoffman, M. A., Hamroush, H., & Allen, R., 1986.
A model of urban development for the Hierakonpolis region from the Predynastic through Old Kingdom times, *JARCE* 23: 175-187.

Hoffman, M. A., Adams, B., Berger, M., El Hadidi, M. N., Harlan, J. F., Hamroush, H. A., Lupton, C. McArdle, J., McHugh, W., Allen, R. O., & Rogers, M. S., 1982.
The Predynastic of Hierakonpolis. Oxford.

Holmes, D., 1987.
The Predynastic Lithic Industries of Badari, Nagada and Hierakonpolis, Upper Egypt, Ph. D. dissertation, Institute of Archaeology, University College London.

Hornung, E., 1992.
Idea into Image. Essays on Ancient Egyptian Thought. Princeton.

Hornung, E., 1999.
El uno y los múltiples. Valladolid (original edition: *Der Eine und die Vielen*, 1971, Darmstadt).

Hornung, E. & Staehelin, E., 1974.
Studien zum Sedfest, *Aegyptiaca Helvetica* 1: 7-103.

Jiménez Serrano, A., 1996.
Nekhen: la eliminación de las aristocracias de Naqada y Buto durante el Predinástico y el Protodinástico, *BAEDE* 6: 3-8.

Jiménez Serrano, A., 1998a.
Las Rutas del Comercio de Egipto con Mesopotamia a finales del IV Milenio a. C., *III Jornadas de Arqueología Subacuática*, pp. 231-235, Valencia.

Jiménez Serrano, A., 1998b.
La representación de aves y su valor simbólico en la Baja Nubia a finales del IV milenio a. C., *BAEDE* 8: 3-13.

Jiménez Serrano, A. 1999.
¿Fue Horus Pe monarca de Qustul? Discusión e hipótesis acerca de un serekh encontrado en la tumba L2 de Qustul, *BAEDE* 9: 7-17.

Jiménez Serrano, A., 2000a.
La evolución del nombre real en Egipto desde finales del Predinástico hasta principios de la Primera Dinastía. Universidad de Jaén, unpublished.

Jiménez Serrano, A., 2000b.
Los reyes del Predinástico Tardío (Naqada III), *BAEDE* 10: 33-52.

Jiménez Serrano, A., 2001a.
Horus Ka and the Cemetery of Helwan, *GM* 180: 81-87.

Jiménez Serrano, A., 2001b.
The Origin of the Palace-Façade as Representation of Lower Egyptian Élites, *GM* 183: 71-81.

Jiménez Serrano, A., 2002a.
Chronology and Local Traditions: The Representation of Power and the Royal Name in the Late Predynastic Period, *Archéo-Nil* 12: in press.

Jiménez Serrano, A., 2002b.
¿El templo de Dyebaut o de Nejen? Estudio comparativo de cuatro etiquetas procedentes de Umm el-Qaab, in J. Cervelló Autuori: *II Congreso Ibérico de Egiptología*, Barcelona, in press.

Jiménez Serrano, A., 2002c.
La Piedra de Palermo: traducción y contextualización histórica. Madrid.*

Jiménez Serrano, A., in press.
Iconografía de la realeza del Dinástico Temprano. La evolución del dualismo como concepto religioso y político, in M. J. López Grande (ed.): *Culturas del Valle del Nilo II: etapas formativas del Egipto faraónico*, Universidad Autónoma de Madrid.

Jiménez Serrano, A., forthcoming.
Two Proto-kingdoms in Lower Nubia at the end of the fourth millennium?, in Lech Krzyzaniak (ed.): *Cultural Marker in the Later Prehistory of Northeastern Africa and Our Recent Research*, Poznan

Johnson, S. B., 1990.
The Cobra Goddess of Ancient Egypt. London & New York.

Kahl, J., 1994.
Das System der ägyptischen Hieroglyphenschrift in der 0.-3. Dynastie. Wiesbaden.

Kaiser, W., 1961.
Einige Bemerkungen zur ägyptischen Frühzeit. II, *ZÄS* 86: 39-61.

Kaiser, W., 1964.
Einige Bemerkungen zur Ägyptischen Frühzeit. III, *ZÄS* 91:86-125.

Kaiser, W., 1985.
Ein Kultbezirk des Königs Den in Sakkara, *MDAIK* 41: 47-60.

Kaiser, W, 1990.
Zur Entstehung des gesamtägyptischen Staates, *MDAIK* 46: 287-299.

Kaiser, W., 1992.
Zur unterirdischen Anlage der Djoserpyramide und ihrer entwicklungsgeschichtlichen Einordnung, in I. Gamer-Wallert & W. Helck (eds.): *Gegenbage: Festschrift für Emma Brunner-Traut*, pp. 167-190, Tübingen.

Kaiser, W., and Dreyer, G., 1982.
Umm el-Qaab. Nachuntersuchungen im frühzeitlichen Königfriedhof 2. Vorberich, *MDAIK* 38: 211-269.

Kantor, H. J., 1942.
The Early Relations of Egypt with Asia, *JNES* 1: 174-213.

Kantor, H. J., 1965.
The Relative Chronology of Egypt and Its Foreign Correlations before the Late Bronze Age, in R. Ehrich (eds.): *Chronologies in Old World Archaeology*. 1-46. Chicago & London.

Kaplony, P., 1963.
Die Inschriften der Ägyptische Frühzeit (I-III t.). Wiesbaden.

Kaplony, P., 1964.
Die Inschriften der Ägyptische Frühzeit. Supplement. Wiesbaden.

Kaplony, P., 1965.
Bemerkungen zu einigen Steingefäßen mit archaischen Königsnamen, *MDAIK* 20: 1-46.

Kaplony, P., 1966.
Kleine Beiträge zu den Inschriften der Ägyptischen Frühzeit. Wiesbaden.

Keita, S. O. Y., 1992.
Further Studies of Crania from Ancient Northern Africa: An Analysis of Crania from First Dynasty Egyptian Tombs, Using Multiple Discriminant Functions, *American Journal of Physical Anthropology* 87.

Kemp, B. J., 1966.
Abydos and the Royal Tombs of the First Dynasty, *JEA* 52: 13-22.

Kemp, B. J., 1967.
The Egyptian 1st Dynasty Royal Cemetery, *Antiquity* 41: 22-32.

Kemp, B. J., 1989.
Ancient Egypt. Anatomy of a Civilization. London.

Kemp, B. J., 1995.
Unification and Urbanization of Ancient Egypt, in J. M. Sasson (ed.): *Civilizations of the Ancient Near East* vol. II, pp. 679-690, New York.

Kemp, B. J., Boyce, A., & Harrell, J., 2000.
The colossi from the early shrine at Coptos in Egypt, *Cambridge Archaeological Journal* 10: 211-242.

Koenig, Y., 1990.
Les textes d'envoûtement de Mirgissa, *RdÉ* 41: 101-125.

Köhler, E. C., 1995.
The State of Research on Late Predynastic Egypt: New Evidence for the Development of the Pharaonic State?, *GM* 147: 79-92.

Köhler, E. C., 1996.
Evidence for interregional contacts between late prehistoric Lower and Upper Egypt.- A view from Buto, in L. Krzyzaniak *et alii* (eds.): *Interregional Contacts in the Later Prehistory of Northeastern Africa*, pp. 215-226, Poznan.

Köhler, E. C., 1998.
Tell el-Fara`in. Buto III. Mainz.

* Available at *Asociación Española de Egiptología*, Paseo de la Habana 17, 4° A, 28036, Madrid (Spain).

Kroeper, K., 1985.
Decorated Ware from Minshat Abu Omar, *Bulletin de Liaison de Grupe International d'étude de la céramique Égyptienne* 10: 12-17.
Kroeper, K., 1986-1987.
The ceramic of the Pre/Early dynastic cemetery of Minshat Abu Omar, *Bulletin of the Egyptological Seminar* 8: 73-94.
Kroeper, K, 1992.
Tombs of the elite in Minshat Abu Omar, in E. C. M. van dem Brink (eds.): *The Nile Delta in Transition: 4th-3rd Millennium BC*. 127-150. Tel Aviv.
Kroeper, K. & Wildung, D., 1985.
Minshat Abu Omar. Müncher Ostdelta-Expedition Vorbericht 1978-84. Munich.

Lacau, P., & Lauer, J. Ph., 1959.
Fouilles à Saqqarah. La Pyramide à Degrés. Tome IV. Inscriptions Gravées sur les Vases. 1er Fascicule: Planches. Cairo.
Lacau, P., & Lauer, J. Ph., 1961.
Fouilles à Saqqarah. La Pyramide à Degrés. Tome IV. Inscriptions Gravées sur les Vases. 2 Fascicule: Texte. Cairo.
Lane, Ch., 1981.
The rites of rulers. Ritual in industrial society – the Soviet case. Cambridge.
Lansing, A., 1935.
The Museum Excavations at Hierakonpolis, in *The Metropolitan Museum of Art. The Egyptian Expedition. 1934-1935*, pp. 37-45.
Lauer, J. Ph., 1969.
A propos des vestiges des murs à redans encadrés par les «tombs of the courtiers» et des «forts» d'Abydos, *MDAIK* 25: 79-84.
Leclant, J., 1975.
Biene, *LdÄ* I: 786-789.
Legge, F., 1906.
The Tablets of Negadah and Abydos, *PSBA* 27: 252-263.
Legge, F., 1907.
The Tablets of Negadah and Abydos, *PSBA* 28: 18-24, 70-73, 101-106, 150-154, 243-250.
Levy, T., van den Brink, E. C. M., Goren, Y. & Alon, D., 1995.
New Light on King Narmer and the Protodynastic Egyptian Presence in Canaan, *Biblical Archaeologist* 58/1: 26-36.
Lichtheim, M., 1975.
Ancient Egyptian Literature. Volume I: The Old and Middle Kingdoms. Los Angeles.
Logan, T. J., 1990.
The Origins of the Jmy-wt Fetish, *JARCE* 27: 61-69.
Logan, T. J., 1999.
Royal Iconography of Dynasty 0, in E. Teeter & J. A. Larson (eds.): *Gold of Praise. Studies on Ancient Egypt in Honor of E.dward F. Wente*, pp. 261-276, Chicago.

Málek, J., 1984.
Sais, *LdÄ* V: 355-357.
Massoulard, E., 1949.
Préhistoire et Protohistoire d'Égypte. Paris.
Mathieson, I. & Tavares, A., 1993.
Preliminary report of the National Museums of Scotland Saqqara Survey Project, 1990-1991, *JEA* 79: 17-31.
Midant-Reynes, B., 1992.
Préhistoire de l'Égypte. Des premiers hommes aux premiers pharaons. Paris.
Millet, N. B., 1990.
The Narmer Macehead and Related Objects, *JARCE* 27: 53-59.*
Miroschedji, P., 1998.
Les Égyptiens au Sinaï du nord et en Palestine au Bronze ancien, in D. Valbelle & C. Bonnet (eds.): *Le Sinaï durant l'antiquité et le moyen âge*, pp. 20-32, París.
Monnet-Saleh, J., 1969.
Forteresses, ou villes-protégées thinites?, *BIFAO* 67: 173-187.
Montet, P., 1957.
Géographie de L'Égypte Ancienne, 2 vol., Paris.
Montet, P., 1964.
Le rituel de fondation des temples égyptiens, *Kêmi* 17: 74-100.
Moreno García, J. C., 1999.
Hwt et le milieu rural égyptien du IIIe millénaire: Economie, administration et organisation territoriale. Paris.
Munro, P., 1961.
Bemerkungen zu einem Sedfest-Relief in der Stadtmauer von Kairo, *ZÄS* 86: 61-74.
Murnane, W. J., 1981.
The Sed Festival: A problem in Historical Method, *MDAIK* 37: 369-376.
Murnane, W. J., 1987.
The Gebel Sheikh Suleiman Monument:

* In *JARCE* XXVIII: 224-225 are printed correctly the plates, which in the original article were printed reversed.

Epigraphic Remarks, *JNES* 46 (no. 4): 282-285.

Murray, M. A., 1956.
Burial customs and beliefs in the hereafter in Predynastic Egypt, *JEA* 42: 86-96.

Naville, E., 1892.
The Festival Hall of Osorkon II in the Great Temple of Bubastis. London.

Naville, E., 1902.
Les plus anciens monuments égyptiens, *Rec. Trav.* XXIV: 109-120.

Naville, E., 1914.
The Cemeteries of Abydos. Part I. London.

Needler, W., 1956.
A flint knife of king Djer, *JEA* 42: 41-44.

Needler, W., 1967.
A Rock-drawing on Gebel Sheikh Suleiman (near Wadi Halfa) showing a Scorpion and Human Figures, *JARCE* 6: 87-91.

Needler, W., 1984.
Predynastic and Archaic Egypt in The Brooklyn Museum. New York.

Newberry, P. E., 1908.
The Petty-kingdom of the Harpoon and the Egypt's Earliest Mediterranean Port, *LAAA* 1: 17-22.

Newberry, P. E., 1912.
The wooden and ivory labels of the First Dynasty, *PSBA* 34: 279-289.

Newberry, P. E. & Wainwrght, G. A., 1914.
King Udy-mu (Den) and the Palermo Stone, *Anc. Eg.* 1: 148-155.

Nordström, H. A., 1972.
Neolithic and A-Group Sites. Uppsala.

O'Connor, D., 1987.
The Earliest Pharaohs and the University Museum. Old and New Excavations: 1900-1987, *Expedition* 29 (1): 27-39.

O'Connor, 1989.
New Funerary Enclosures (Talbezirke) of the Early Dynastic Period at Abydos, *JARCE* 26: 51-86.

O'Connor, D., 1992.
The Status of Early Egyptian Temples: An Alternative Theory, in R. Friedman & B. Adams (eds.): *The Followers of Horus*. 83-97. Oxford.

O'Connor, D., 1995.
The Earliest Royal Boat Graves, *Egyptian Archaeology* 6: 3-7.

Ogdon, J., 1981.
A note on the meaning of in archaic texts, *GM* 49: 61-64.

Ogdon, J., 1982a.
Studies on archaic epigraphy II. On the nature of *st.w-nṯr.w*, *GM* 57: 41-47.

Ogdon, J., 1982b.
Studies in archaic epigraphy III. On the meaning of , *GM* 60: 81-84.

Ogdon, J., 1983.
Studies on archaic epigraphy IV. On architectural design for names of constructions in Archaic Hieroglyphs, *GM* 62: 55-61.

Ogdon, J., 1984.
Studies on archaic epigraphy VIII. On the reading of the nebty-name of king Semerkhet, *GM* 72: 15-19.

O'Mara, P. F., 1979.
The Palermo Stone and the Archaic kings of Egypt. La Cañada, California.

O'Mara, P. F., 1999.
The Cairo Stone II. The Question of Authenticity, *GM* 170: 69-82.

Oren, E. D., 1973.
The overland route between Egypt and Canaan in the Early Bronze Age. A preliminary report, *IEJ* 23: 198-205.

Oren, E. D., 1989.
Early Bronze Age settlement in northern Sinai: a model for Egypto-Cannanite interconnections, in P. Miroschedji (ed.): *L'urbanisation de la Palestine à l'âge du Bronze ancien*, pp. 389-405, Oxford.

Payne, J. C., 1992.
Predynastic Chronology at Naqada, in R. Friedman & B. Adams (eds.): *The Followers of Horus*, pp. 185-192, Oxford.

Peet, T. E., 1914.
The Cemeteries of Abydos, II. London.

Pérez Largacha, A., 1989.
The Libyan Palette; a New Interpretation, *VA* 5 (no. 4): 217-226.

Pérez Largacha, A., 1993a.
El nacimiento del Estado en Egipto. Alcalá de Henares.

Pérez Largacha, A., 1993b.
Some Reflexions about Maadi culture and Upper Egypt expansion, *GM* 135: 41-52.

Pérez Largacha, A., 1994.
Ejército y Estado en el Antiguo Egipto, *BAEO* 30: 59-71.

Pérez Largacha, A., 1997.
Ejército y relaciones exteriores en el Reino Antiguo egipcio, in L. A. García Moreno & A. Pérez Largacha (eds.): *Egipto y el exterior*, pp. 29-46, Alcalá de Henares.

Petrie, W. M. F., 1900.
The Royal Tombs of the First Dynasty, I.

London.
Petrie, W. M. F., 1901.
The Royal Tombs of the Earliest Dynasties, II. London.
Petrie, W. M. F., 1902.
Abydos, I. London.
Petrie, W. M. F., 1903.
Abydos, II. London.
Petrie, W. M. F., 1914.
Tarkhan II. London.
Petrie, W. M. F., 1916.
New Portions of the Annals, *Anc. Eg.* 3:114-120.
Petrie, W. M. F., 1920.
Prehistoric Egypt. London.
Petrie, W. M. F, 1921.
Corpus of Prehistoric Pottery and Palettes. London.
Petrie, W. M. F, 1925.
Tombs of the Courtiers and Oxyrhynkhos. London.
Petrie, W. M. F., 1939.
The making of Egypt. London,
Petrie, W. M. F. & Quibell, 1896.
Naqada and Ballas. London.
Petrie, W. M. F., Wainbright, G. A. & Gardiner, A. H., 1913.
Tarkhan I & Memphis V. London.
Porat, N. & Adams B., 1996.
Imported pottery with potmarks from Abydos, in J. Spencer (ed.): *Aspects of Early Egypt*, pp. 98-107, London.
Posener, G., 1960.
De la divinité du pharaon. Paris.
Posener, G., 1965.
Le nom de l'enseigne appelée "Khons", *RdE* 17: 193-195.

Quibell, J. E., 1900.
Hierakonpolis. Part I. London (1989 edition).
Quibell, J. E., 1923.
Excavations at Saqqara (1912-1914). Archaic Mastabas. Cairo.
Quibell, J. E. & F. W. Green, 1902.
Hierakonpolis. Part II. London (1989 edition).
Quirke, S., 1992.
Ancient Egyptian Religion. New York.

Rappaport, R. A., 1999.
Ritual and Religion in the Making of Humanity. Cambridge.
Redford, D. B., 1986.
Pharaonic King-lists, annals and day-books. Mississauga.
Reymond, E. A. E., 1969.
The Mythical Origin of the Egyptian Temple. New York.
Ricci, S., 1917.
La table de Palerme, *CRAIBL* 1917: 107-115.
Rizkana, I. & Seeher, J, 1987.
Maadi I. The pottery of the Predynastic settlement. Mainz and Rhein.
Rizkana, I. & Seeher, J., 1988.
Maadi II. The lithic industries of the Predynastic settlement. Mainz and Rhein.
Rizkan, I. & Seeher, J., 1989.
Maadi III. The non-lithic small finds and the structural remains of the Predynastic settlement. Mainz and Rhein.
Rizkana, I. & Seeher, J., 1990.
Maadi IV. The Predynastic Cemeteries of Maadi and Wadi Digla. Mainz and Rhein.
Roth, A. M., 1991.
Egyptian Phyles in the Old Kingdom. The evolution of a system of social organization. Chicago.
Roth, A. M., 1993.
Social Change in the Fourth Dynasty: The Spatial Organization of Pyramids, Tombs, and Cemeteries, *JARCE* 30: 33-55.
Rowe, A., 1941.
Some remarks on *A Collection of Hieroglyphs from the Monuments of Hor-Aha*, forming Appendix IV of the volume Hor-Aha, 1939, by W. B. Emery, *ASAE* 41: 342-345.

Saad, Z. Y., 1969.
The Excavations at Helwan: Art and Civilization in the First and Second Egyptian Dynasties. Oklahoma.
Sainte Fare Garnot, J., 1958.
Sur le nom de "l'Horus cobra", *MDAIK* 16: 138-146.
Sauneron, S., 1962.
Les Fêtes Religieuses d'Esna aux derniers siècles du paganisme. Cairo.
Säve-Söderbergh, T., 1953.
On Egyptian representations of hippopotamus hunting as a religious motive. Uppsala.
Schäfer, H., 1902.
Ein Bruchstück Altägyptischer Annalen. Berlin.
Schott, E., 1972.
Das Goldhaus unter König Snofru, *GM* 3: 31-36.
Schott, S., 1950.
Altägyptische Festdaten. Wiesbaden.
Schulman, A. R., 1976.
The Egyptian Seal Impressions from 'En Besor, *'Atiqot* XI: 16-26.

Schulman, A. R., 1980.
More Egyptian seal impressions from 'En Besor, *'Atiqot* 14: 17-33.

Schulman, A. R., 1991/1992.
Narmer and the Unification: a Revisionist View, *BES* 11: 79-105.

Schulman, A. R., 1992.
Still More Seal Impressions from 'En Besor, in E. C. M. van den Brink (de.): *The Nile Delta in Transition: 4th-3rd Millennium B. C.* pp. 395-417. Tel Aviv.

Seidlmayer, S. J., 1996.
Town and State in the early Old Kingdom. A view from Elephantine, in J. Spencer (ed.): *Aspects of Early Egypt*, pp. 108-127. London

Senk, H., 1952.
Remarques sur la palette de Narmer, *CdE* 53: 23-30.

Serpico, M., & White, R., 1996.
A report on the analysis of the contents of a cache of jars from the tomb of Djer, in J. Spencer (ed.): *Aspects of Early Egypt*, pp. 128-139. London.

Sethe, K., 1905.
Beiträge zur ältesten Geschichte Aegyptens. Leipzig.

Sethe, K., 1914.
Hitherto unnoticed evidence regarding copper works of art of the oldest period of Egyptian History, *JEA* 1: 233-236.

Sethe, K., 1930.
Urgeschichte und alteste Religion der Ägypter. Leipzig.

Shinnie, P. L., 1996.
Ancient Nubia. London & New York.

Simpson, W. K., 1956.
A statuette of king Nyneter, *JEA* 42: 45-49.

Smith, W. E., 1946.
A History of Egyptian Sculpture and Painting in the Old Kingdom. London.

Spalinger, A. J., 1996.
The Private Feast Lists of Ancient Egypt. Wiesbaden.

Spencer, A. J., 1978.
Two enigmatic hieroglyphs and their relation to the Sed-Festival, *JEA* 64: 52-55.

Spencer, A. J., 1980.
Catalogue of Egyptian Antiquities in the British Museum V: Early Dynastic Objects. Oxford.

Spencer, A. J., 1993.
Early Egypt. The Rise of Civilisation in the Nile Valley. London.

Spencer, P., 1984.
The Egyptian Temple. A Lexicographical Study. London, Boston Melburne and Henley.

Stadelmann, R., 1985.
Die Oberbauten der Königsgräber der 2. Dynastie in Sakkara, in P. Posener-Kriéger (ed.): *Mélanges Gamal Eddin Mokhtar (*volume II), pp. 295-307.

Swelim, N. M. A., 1983.
Some Problems on the History of the Third Dynasty. Alexandria.

Swelim, N. M. A., 1991.
Some Remarks on the Great Rectangular Monuments of Middle Saqqara, *MDAIK* 47: 389-402.

Trigger, B. G., 1984.
The mainlines of socio-economic development in dynastic Egypt to the end of the Old Kingdom, in L. Krzyzaniak & M. Kobusiewicz (eds.): *Origin and Early Development of Food-producing Cultures in North-Eastern Africa*, pp. 101-108, Poznan.

Trigger, B. G., Kemp, B. J., O'Connor, D., & Lloyd, A. B., 1983.
Ancient Egypt. A Social History. Cambridge.

Van den Brink, E. C. M., (eds.), 1988.
The Amsterdam University survey expedition to the Northeastern Delta (1984-1986), en E. C. M. van den Brink (ed.): *The Nile Delta: problems and priorities*, pp. 65-110, Tel Aviv.

Van den Brink, E. C. M. (ed.), 1992.
The Nile Delta in Transition: 4th-3rd Millennium BC. Tel Aviv.

Van den Brink, E. C. M., 1996.
The incised serekh-signs of the Dynasties 0-1. Part I: complete vessels, in J. Spencer (eds.): *Aspects of Early Egypt*, pp.140-158. London.

Vandier, J., 1952.
Manuel d'archéologie égyptienne. Paris.

Vikentiev, V., 1931.
Nâr-Ba-Thai, *JEA* 17: 67-80.

Vikentiev, V., 1933.
Les monuments archaïques. I.- La tablette en ivoire de Naqâda, *ASAE* 33: 208-234.

Vikentiev, V., 1948.
Les monuments archaïques. III.- A propos du soi-disant nom de Ménès dans la tablette de Naqâda, *ASAE* 48: 665-685.

Vikentiev, V., 1949-1950.
Les monumentes archaïques. IV-V.- Deux rites du jubilé royal à l'époque protodynastique, *BIE* 32: 171-228.

Vikentiev, V., 1959.
Études d'Épigraphie Protodynastique. II. -Deux tablettes en Ivoire (I dyn.) et les Linteaux de Médamoud (XII-XIIIe dyn.), *ASAE* 56: 1-30.
Von Bissing, F. W. F., & Kess, H., 1923.
Das Re-Heiligtum des Königs Ne-Woser-Re (Rathures). Band II. Die Kleine Festdarstellung. Leipzig.
Von der Way, T., 1992a.
Excavations at Tell el-Fara`in/Buto in 1987-1989, in E. C. M. van den Brink (eds.): *The Nile Delta in Transition: 4th-3rd Millennium B.C.*, pp. 1-10, Tel Aviv.
Von der Way, T., 1992b.
Indications of Architecture with Niches at Buto, in R. Friedman & B. Adams (eds.): *The Followers of Horus*, pp. 217-226, Oxford.
Von der Way, T., 1997a.
Palestinian Features on Pottery from Buto, Lower Egypt, in L. A. García Moreno & A. Pérez Largacha (eds.): *Egipto y el exterior. Contactos e influencias*. Aegyptiaca Complutensia III, pp. 7-27, Alcalá de Henares.
Von der Way, T., 1997b.
Tell el-Fa`în Buto I. Mainz.

Weeks, K., 1971-1972.
The Niched Gateway at Hierakonpolis, *JARCE* 9: 29-33.
Weill, R., 1907.
Notes sur les monuments de la Période Thinite, *Rec. Trav*. XXIX: 26-53.
Weill, R., 1908.
Des Monuments et de l' Histoire des IIe et IIIe Dynasties Égyptiennes. Paris.
Weill, R., 1961.
Recherches sur la Ire Dynastie et les temps prépharaoniques (2 parts). Le Caire.
Wignall, S. J., 1998.
The identification of the Late Prehistoric serekh, *GM* 162: 93-105.
Wilkinson, R. H., 1992.
Reading Egyptian Art. A Hieroglyphic Guide to Ancient Egyptian Painting and Sculpture. London
Wilkinson, T. A. H., 1996a.
State Formation in Egypt. Chronology and Society. Oxford.
Wilkinson, T. A. H., 1996b.
A Re-examination of the Early Dynastic Necropolis at Helwan, *MDAIK* 52: 337-354.
Wilkinson, T. A. H., 1999.
Early Dynastic Egypt. London and New York.
Wilkinson, T. A. H., 2000a.
Political Unification: towards a reconstruction, *MDAIK* 56: 377-395.
Wilkinson, T. A. H., 2000b.
Royal Annals of Ancient Egypt. The Palermo Stone and its associated fragments. London & New York.
Wilkinson, T. A. H., 2000c. What a king is this: Narmer and the concept of the ruler, *JEA* 86: 23-32.
Williams, B. B., 1980.
The Lost Pharaohs of Nubia, *Archaeology* 33: 12-21.
Williams, B. B., 1986.
The University of Chicago Oriental Institute Nubian Expedition, vol. III. Excavations Between Abu Simbel and the Sudan Frontier. Keith C. Seele, Director. Part 1: The A-Group Royal Cemetery at Qustul: Cemetery L. Chicago.
Williams, B. B., 1987.
Forebears of Menes in Nubia: Myth or Reality?, *JNES* 46 (no.1): 15-26.
Williams, B. B., 1988.
Narmer and the Coptos Colossi, *JARCE* XXV: 35-59.
Williams, B. B. & Logan, T. J.,1987.
The Metropolitan Museum Knife Handle and Aspects of Pharaonic Imagery before Narmer, *JNES* 46 (no. 4): 245-285.
Winkler, H. A., 1938.
Rock-drawings of Southern Upper Egypt, vol. 1. Oxford.

Yeivin, S., 1960.
Early Contacts between Canaan and Egypt, *IEJ* 10: 193-203.

EGYPTIAN TERMS (IN TRANSLITERATION)

ꜣḫt "The Horizon", 26.

jꜣbt "East", 86, 91.

jʿb-nṯrw (type of bark), n. 817.
jʿb-sḫmw (type of bark), n. 817.
jwnwt "foreigners", 67.
jwntjw "foreigners", 14.
jb "heart", 80.
jmt-pr, 49; see also *mks*.
jmj-wt (fetish), 60, 61.
jmnt "West", 87.
jn (participle), n. 599.
jnw-šmʿw "tax from Upper Egypt", 89.
Jnpw (god), 87.
jr-jḫt "maker of substances", 27.
Jry-nṯr (Semerkhet's *nebti* name), n. 142, 96.
jtrw "river", n. 811.
jtrtj (two opposite lines of shrines), 65, n. 585.

ʿꜣ-wr "The Great Door", 85.
ʿꜣ-ʿn "The beatiful door", 67.
ʿnḫ, 49.
(ʿḥ)-ḥḏ (small shrine), 97, n. 835.
ʿḥꜣ (verb), 87.
ʿḥꜣ (king), n. 811.
ʿḥʿ wrt (place), 63.
ʿš (a type of wood), 59.
ʿḏ-mr "administrator", n. 148.

wꜣs, 49.
Wꜣḏt (goddess), n. 88, n. 815.
wʿ "one", 84.
Wʿšj (personal name), 82.
wbꜣ "state temple", 26.
wnt, n. 811.
wpt-š "opening the lake", 28.
wrw "ancestral fathers/Great Ones", 49, n. 468, 64, 70, Table 2, 98.
wsḫ "to be broad", 47.
wsḫt "festival hall", 47, n. 452, 48, 96.
wṯtw "offpring", 83.
wdpw "butler", n. 722.
wḏ-nṯr (the name of a fortress), 89.

bꜣ (verb), n. 811.
bꜣ, "soul", 35.
bʿḥ, 35.
bjꜣ mḥ "mineral", 96, n. 819.
bjt(j), 39, 40, n. 589; see also *nzwt bitj*.
bw "place", 27, n. 276.
bw tpj "The First Place", 27.

P (place), 63; see also *Dp*.
pʿy "shore", 27-28.
pr, 26.
pr-wr "temple at Hierakonpolis", 27, 29, 35, 48, 54, n. 509, 79.
pr-nw "temple of Dep (Buto)", 29, n. 304, 35, 65, 78.
pr-nsr "temple of Pe (Buto), 29, n. 304.
pr.w nṯr "temple", 12.
pr kꜣ Nt "the temple of Neith", n. 535.
pr-ḏbʿwt "shrine at Buto", 36; see also *ḏbʿwt*.
r-pr "temple", 26.
pḫrr (verb), 69.
pḫr-ḥꜣ-jnb(w) (ceremony), 38, 46, n. 442, 49, 94, 99.
pḫr ḥr ḥsꜣt (the name of a fortress?), 87.
Pš (place), 59.
pḏ (verb), n. 791.

mꜣʿt, 70.
mꜣʿtj (sacred bark), 93.
mwt nzwt "queen mother", 10.
mn (name?), 11, 63, 64, 94, 95.

mn-nbtj "the Two Ladies shall abide", n. 815.
mr, 59.
Mr-pj-bjꜣ (Anedjib's *nzwt bjtj* name), 15, n. 633.
mr nṯrwj (edifice), 89.
mry n nṯr "beloved of god", 70.
mry-rʿ mn-nfr (the pyramid of Pepi), n. 397.
mrw (type of wood), 63, 64, 97.
Mḥw "Lower Egypt", 64; see also *tꜣ mḥw*.
ms.(t), 60, 65, 87.
msw nsw "the royal children", 44.
mks, 49, 64, Table 2; see also *jmt-pr*.
Mtwn (place), n. 539.
mḏḥ-mḏḥ(w) nsw "carptenter", n. 601.
mḏḥtj-nsw "carpenter", 66, 96.
mḏḥ pr nsw "carpenter in the royal palace", 97.

njwt, 64.
Nʿrmr (king), 11. Different readings of this name, 11, n. 75.
nb "Lord", 80.
nbwj "The Two Lords", 15.
nbtj "The Two Ladies", 32, 38, 64, 65, 80, 95, 97.
nbw "gold", 80.
Nḫbt (goddess), n. 88.
nḫn (shrine), 59.
nḫn.j (Horus' epithet), n. 513.
Nzwt/nsw, 39, 40.
nzwt bjtj "He who belongs to the sedge and the bee" (King of Upper and Lower Egypt), 14, 15, 39, 40, n. 633, 97.

nsw [n] ḏt.f "the king himself", 96.
nṯr, 70, n. 722.
nṯry.t (festival), 93.

r (preposition), 87.
rnpt, 21, 65, 66, n. 703, 97.
rḫyt, 63.

ḥꜣ (preposition), 93; see also *pḫr ḥꜣ jnbw*.
ḥꜣ (god), n. 717
ḥꜣtj-ꜥ "The finest", n. 609, 97.
ḥw see *ḥꜣ*.
ḥwt, 26, 31, 32.
ḥwt-nṯr "temple", 26, 28.
ḥwt ḥb sd "jubilee mansion", 43.
ḥwt-kꜣ "funerary temple", 32.
ḥwt mr(y) Jnpw "House of the beloved Anubis", 12.
ḥb sd (festival), 43, 69; see also *sd*.
ḥp (god), 69.
ḥm "priest", 85.
ḥnw "jar", 64, 67.
ḥnw "boat of Sokar", 92.
ḥnwkꜣ (personal name), 97.
ḥr/ḥrw (god), 80, n. 722; see also *ḫntj ḫm*.
ḥr ꜥrt ḏr (Djer's state), 64.
ḥr-pḫr-jḫw (name of a fortress), 87.
ḥrj wḏb (title), n. 455.
ḥsꜣt (goddess), 87, n. 751.
ḥqꜣ (sceptre), 51, n. 478.
ḥts (sceptre), 70.
ḥḏ (sanctuary), 48.
ḥḏ-wrw, see *wrw*.

ḫꜣ, 82.
ḫꜣstj (Den's name), 14, 67.
ḫꜥ.t (infinitive), n. 825.
ḫꜥ.t bjtj "Appearance of the King of Lower Egypt", 52, 94.
ḫwsj (verb), 96, n. 820.
ḫnt (place), n. 599.
ḫntj-box, 67.
ḫntj ḫm (a form of Horus in Letopolis), 49.
ḫntj.t "the foremost (wife)", 12.
ḫtjw "administrative building", n. 833.
ḫntj "statue", 96.

swt.-nṯr.w (Den's construction), 28.
sbtj "enclosure", 27.
zp tpj "the first time/occasion", 42, 69, 91.
zp tpj sd "First occasion of the Jubilee", n. 467, 69.
sm, 59, n. 616, 66.
sm "*sem*-priest", 32.
smꜣ.t, 59.
smꜣ.(t) nbwj "the union of the Two Lords" 12.
smꜣ/zmꜣ tꜣwj "the union of the Two Lands", n. 61, 38, 40.
zmjtj (Den's name), 14.
smw, n. 599.
smr nṯrw "name of Djer's construction", 13; 63.
smsw (Semerkhet's *nebti* name), 15, 97.
zḫ-nṯr (shrine), 47, 64, n. 811.
sḥtp(-nbtj) (Qaa's *nebti* name), 16.
sḫm-ḥr-jb (title), 16.
sḫmtj "the Two Powerful Ones", 14.
Sḫm-kꜣ.j (personal name), 65.
sqr (verb), n. 703, 91.
Zkr (god), 97.
stj-ḥrw (a type of oil), 59, 60, n. 600.
sttjw "the castle of the Asiatics", n. 728.
sd (festival/god), 42, 63; see also *ḥb sd*.
sḏꜣwty bjtj "seal bearer of Lower Egypt", 65, 69.

šwbtjw "the Creators of the Earth", 27, n. 279.
šmꜥw "Upper Egypt", 63.
šmsw ḥr "Following of Horus", 12, 96, 97.
šnj.t "Circular procession", n. 751.
šzp šmꜥw mḥw "receive Upper and Lower Egypt", 61, 65.

kꜣ n ḏt.j "my own ka", n. 822.
kꜣ nḫt (title), n. 736.

tꜣ "land", 82.
tꜣ mḥw "Lower Egypt", n. 703.
tꜣ-stj (region), 75, 87.
tꜣwj "the Two Lands", 26.
tj-tjwntj (personal name?), 67.
tpj jdt "the best fragrance", 97.

ṯꜣtj "vizier", 83.
ṯḥnw (region), n. 609, 89, Fig. 49.
ṯḥnw (type of oil), 89.
ṯt (personal name?), 83, 86.

dꜣj, n. 603.
Dp (place), 63-64; see also *P*.
dn/dwn (king), n.123.
dšr (?), 13.
dšrt (the red crown), n. 668.

ḏbꜥwt (shrine at Buto), 52, 57, 59; see also *pr-ḏbꜥwt*.
ḏnb "to turn away/around", n. 452.
ḏnbw (stone markers), 47, n. 452, 48, Table 2, 75.
ḏḥwtj (god), 65.
ḏd "pillar", 27, 93, 98, n. 842.

www.ingramcontent.com/pod-product-compliance
Lightning Source LLC
Chambersburg PA
CBHW041704290426
44108CB00027B/2852
* 9 7 8 1 8 4 1 7 1 4 5 5 4 *